THE **APPETITE AWARENESS WORKBOOK**

how to listen to your body &
overcome bingeing, overeating
& obsession with food

LINDA W. CRAIGHEAD, PH.D.

New Harbinger Publications, Inc.

Distributed in Canada by Raincoast Books

Copyright © 2006 by Linda Craighead
New Harbinger Publications, Inc.
5674 Shattuck Avenue
Oakland, CA 94609

Cover design by Amy Shoup; Cover image: John Dowland /PhotoAlto /Getty Images; Acquired by Spencer Smith; Edited by Spencer Smith; Text design by Tracy Carlson

Library of Congress Cataloging-in-Publication Data

Craighead, Linda W.
   The appetite awareness workbook : how to listen to your body and overcome binging, overeating, and obsession with food / Linda W. Craighead.
      p. cm.
   Includes bibliographical references.
   ISBN 1-57224-398-8
   1. Compulsive eating—Popular works. 2. Appetite disorders—Popular works. I. Title.
   RC552.C65C69 2005
   616.85'26—dc22
                              2005029562

New Harbinger Publications' Web site address: www.newharbinger.com

08   07   06

10   9   8   7   6   5   4   3   2   1

First printing

Contents

Acknowledgments   v

Introduction   1

1   Today's Food and Weight Dilemma   5

2   The Appetite Awareness Training Solution   15

3   Disordered Eating or Eating Disorder?   31

4   Discover Your Stomach Signals   49

5   Take Back Your Power   63

6   Reduce Binges to Mere Overeating   75

7   Effective Emotional Eating   93

8   Food Awareness Training   111

9   Self-Coaching for Life   125

10   Leaving the Maze of Disordered Eating   141

Appendix A
The Purging Trap   147

Appendix B
The Fear of Weight Gain Trap   159

Appendix C
The Weight Loss Window   171

References   187

Acknowledgments

I would like to acknowledge my first mentors whose personal enthusiasm and dedication to understanding problems with eating and weight set me on the path I have followed, which has culminated in this book: Dr. Martin Katahn and Dr. Albert Stunkard. I would also like to express my appreciation to two of my colleagues who have served as my models for clinically relevant research, and whose work has strongly influenced my thinking about mindfulness and the role of internal cues: Dr. Marsha Linehan and Dr. David Barlow. Dr. James Blumenthal, Dr. Kelly Brownell, and Dr. Charles Nermeroff have provided invaluable professional as well as personal support for my work over many years. The National Institute of Mental Health has provided funding for several studies on Appetite Awareness Training (AAT). Most importantly, I want to acknowledge the many contributions that my students, former students, and colleagues have made. They have contributed in so many ways that I cannot specify them all, but their ideas and their feedback made AAT what it is today: Dr. Heather Allen, Dr. Carolyn Aibel, Dr. Kathy Elder, Dr. Stacy Dicker Hartman, Dr. Heather Niemeier, Dr. Meredith Pung, Dr. Nancy Zucker, Dr. Debra Safer, Dr. Alisha Shanks, Dr. Malia Sperry, Dr. Heather Nations, Dr. Elizabeth Olsen, Dr. Lara LaCaille, and current students Arnika Buckner, Diana Hill, and Lucy Trenary Smith. Thanks for your enthusiastic and unwavering support, which has allowed me to get the message of AAT out to all of you reading this book. Thanks to all of their clients and mine. Your willingness to try out new ideas and to give us feedback about how these strategies worked for you was an essential part of the process of refining AAT so it would be more understandable and more effective for others. A special thank you for the young woman who wrote the essay included in this book.

I would like to thank my children for showing me firsthand how babies learn to eat, and how soon and how strongly the food environment starts to influence the biological appetite regulation system we are born with. My husband, Ed, has been my strongest support both personally and professionally. He has always believed in me even more than I was able to believe in myself and has pushed me to achieve my own goals. I thank all my family for encouraging me to work on this book even when it took away some of their time with me.

Introduction

Appetite awareness training (AAT) emerged from my years of research and clinical work helping people figure out how to feel better about the way that they eat and how they look. As I look back on my very first effort (I was a college senior leading a group for college women who wanted to lose weight for my honors project in psychology), I realize how radically I have changed the way I think about eating and weight. As I worked with (mostly) women, I came to the conclusion that the fundamental basis for the way I learned to treat disordered eating left much to be desired. The basis for cognitive and behavioral interventions for eating problems is to have the client self-monitor in a way that requires her to write down everything she eats each day. The purpose of this self-monitoring is to draw your attention to how you are eating so that you (with the help of your therapist) can figure out what is not working for you and can develop a way to eat that works better. There is nothing inherently problematic about self-monitoring. It is in fact the most powerful tool that anyone can use to change their own behavior. However, I came to believe that recording what one ate put way too much emphasis on the kind of food eaten and not enough emphasis on a person's eating decisions, which were, ultimately, what had to change.

Most clients who came to see me had already tried food monitoring in one form or another. Recording your food intake is regularly touted in current diet magazine articles as the most effective way to limit what you eat. Clients who were overweight and might have benefited from paying attention to the differential calorie content of different foods were often the most turned off by my request that they monitor their food intake; some refused to do it at all. Some loved food records but became too dependent on this external source of control; they gained weight whenever they weren't monitoring very carefully. For my clients who were not objectively overweight, the food part of the monitoring often seemed irrelevant or it increased their distress and compulsivity around eating.

In the process of experimenting with alternative ways to help my clients pay more attention to what seemed important, I developed the intervention I call *appetite awareness training*. My clients' responses have been overwhelmingly positive. Almost all of them report that they are more willing to do appetite monitoring and that it focuses more on what seems important to them. I have trained many other professional therapists to use this technique, and they have reported similar positive results. Therapists often tell me how much better they feel about asking their clients to monitor appetite rather than food.

To provide scientific support for AAT, my research team reported several initial studies (Allen and Craighead 1999; Craighead and Allen 1995). Our current work suggests that treatment for eating problems that is based on the principles of AAT is at least as effective as any other treatment that has been evaluated at this time, and is preferred by many of those we have treated. Craighead et al. 2002 evaluated AAT-based individual treatment for women diagnosed with binge eating disorder and found that over 80 percent had stopped binge eating by the end of treatment. None of these women reported that they would have preferred to monitor food only. A few indicated they were only willing to monitor appetite, because they had very negative reactions to monitoring food, but most indicated they were willing to include some limited food monitoring with the appetite monitoring the strategy you will see described in chapter 8 and appendix C in this workbook. A subsequent study (Elder et al. 2002) evaluated group treatment for college women with binge-eating problems and found a similar, very positive response to this model of treatment and type of self-monitoring.

Most recently, we have evaluated an AAT-based twelve-session individual treatment for women diagnosed with bulimia (Dicker and Craighead 2003; 2004). In this study, clients were not allowed to monitor food, only appetite. Since none of these women were significantly overweight (most were quite normal weight), we did not believe food monitoring was necessary and we wanted to test the effect of appetite monitoring by itself. Most of these women (80 percent) fully recovered; they had completely stopped bingeing and purging as assessed one year following the end of treatment. A few, all of whom were substantially improved, had been particularly severe at the beginning of treatment (purging at least once a day) and needed longer or more intensive intervention. All but one of the participants had tried some form of food monitoring in the past, and almost all reported they did not like doing it or did not find it helpful. All who had ever tried food monitoring reported that they found the appetite monitoring more helpful than their past experiences with food monitoring, and they highly recommended AAT treatment for other women having problems with binge eating. Currently, my colleagues James Blumenthal, Ph.D., and Frank Keefe, Ph.D., are evaluating appetite monitoring at Duke University as a component of comprehensive weight management programs for individuals with significant medical concerns.

I encourage you to give AAT a chance to help you with your eating concerns. I realize this approach will feel quite different from many of the strategies you have already tried or are currently using, but I believe that you will find this approach a better alternative. Give it a try.

You are obviously not happy with the strategies you are currently using. One of my clients who recovered described her response to AAT as follows:

> When I first started the appetite monitoring I was pretty skeptical of it, but I was open to any kind of help I could get. So I followed through with it and stayed dedicated, and it turned out to be very, very helpful. It puts you back in touch with your body and helps you realize when you're hungry and when you're not. I would tell other women to be open-minded and willing to try it, because it could turn out to be more helpful than they realize. The appetite monitoring was definitely one of the most important things that helped me get on the road to recovery.

Today's Food and Weight Dilemma

If you picked up this book, you are probably concerned about the way you eat, how much you weigh, and how you look. In today's world, most women are dissatisfied with some part of their body. You may even blame a lot of your life's other problems on your weight or shape. You may think, "If I were thinner or had a better shape, I would be happier." Learning to eat in a way that feels natural and comfortable is very valuable; it is the goal of this book and it may allow you to change your weight or shape to a degree. But you are not likely to ever be completely satisfied with how you look, and solving your eating problems is not going to make all your other problems go away. The reality is that changing your weight may make less of a difference than you antici-pate. Fortunately, once you start feeling better about the way you eat, you will have more time and energy to focus on changing those aspects of your life that have greater potential to make you a happier and more fulfilled human being.

THE DEVELOPMENT OF EATING PROBLEMS

Babies are the ideal eaters. Adults obviously cannot eat exactly like babies because we must eat a wider variety of foods to meet our nutritional needs. However, observing how babies learn to eat is very informative. Babies learn to regulate the amount of food they eat before they have to face choices between different types of food. When a baby feels hungry, she cries until someone responds to her demands. If the baby is allowed to eat as much as she pleases, she will nurse until she is full and stop on her own. Eating is such a positive, soothing experience for babies that they often nurse themselves to sleep. If a baby gets a little too full, she may naturally regurgitate as she is burped. For babies, being too full does not feel comfortable. If a baby is interrupted during a feeding before she feels even moderately full, she will resume nursing if allowed to do so. If she is not allowed to do so, she is likely to cry and demand more. However, if she is interrupted just a little before she would have stopped on her own, she is not likely to be upset. She can be easily distracted with a toy or game. A baby whose intake is overly restricted is likely to be irritable much of the time. Feeling hungry is not a pleasant state.

Unless a baby has a problem such as colic, food allergies, or swallowing difficulties, she will naturally regulate her eating to maintain healthy weight gain. Observing this natural process is very instructive. Nursing mothers do not know exactly how much a baby eats, so they can interfere only minimally with the baby's natural regulation process. As you can see, we are all born with a biologically based appetite regulation system that is designed to regulate the amount of food eaten, which in turn regulates our weight.

As babies transition to table foods, they are exposed to the negative influences of our current food environment (like heavily promoted and highly sugared cereals, sugar-enhanced juices, and fruit roll-ups). However, even in this environment, young children typically regulate their intake to obtain appropriate, but not excessive, calories as long as they are given access to a variety of healthy foods. Overeating becomes more of a problem as children get older and they have access to many nonnutritious, high-calorie snacks, or they are pressured to clean their plate even when they aren't hungry. Caretakers may also cause problems by restricting a child's or adolescent's food too severely. When a child feels deprived, she is likely to start sneaking food or overeating whenever food is available.

Over time, children experience an increasing number of social and emotional situations that teach them what, when, and how much it is appropriate to eat within their culture and within their family. They learn how they should feel about what and how much they eat, how they should look, and how important (or unimportant) appearance is to those around them. In addition to their own experiences with food, they learn by watching others eat and listening to others talk about food, weight, and appearance. Some children learn effective strategies to manage their eating. Others develop eating patterns that are distressing and interfere with their lives, or they become overweight, which compromises their health and well-being. The eating preferences we develop as children tend to stay with us our entire lives.

The Adult's Food and Weight Dilemma

Most adults have learned to overeat. The majority become overweight by middle age (Brownell and Horgen, 2004). However, most people, especially women, want to be quite thin. Many people simply do not know how to live in today's food environment without gaining weight, nor do they know how to lose weight if they become overweight. Many popular diets ignore the most important reality of our biological systems: Excessive restriction or feeling deprived triggers binges or overeating. Of course, dieting is not the only reason that women develop problems with eating. Many women learn, early in life, to rely on eating as a way to cope with uncomfortable feelings. Other women, as alluded to before, develop poor eating habits as children. Many women learn to associate eating with feeling "fat." Skipping meals or eating tiny amounts become ways to cope with those bad feelings.

Most women believe that dieting (in conjunction with exercise) is the most effective way to achieve the figure they desire. However, when you become overfocused on achieving an ideal figure, you spend excessive amounts of time, energy, and money on dieting and/or exercise. Often these efforts end up interfering with more important aspects of your life. Obsessing about food and eating is a manifestation of disordered eating. Many women never meet the criteria for a diagnosable "eating disorder," but they become anxious and depressed, and they upset their family and friends by dwelling on how badly they feel about their weight. Some of these women become isolated because they avoid social situations in which they are expected to eat. Some neglect their friends or their work in their pursuit of thinness. Excessive concern about weight and appearance can make you far more miserable than your actual weight.

Aren't Men Worried About Eating and Weight?

Many men are dissatisfied with their bodies, but they tend to be concerned more about shape (muscularity) than weight. They typically put more of their energy into exercise than dieting. However, men may become obsessed with the type of food they eat as they attempt to attain the ideal (highly muscular) masculine shape.

Men are just as likely as women to develop binge eating. However, men are less likely to find binge eating distressing. Men who seek treatment for weight loss do not usually identify binge eating as a specific problem; they just want to lose weight. Men find the AAT approach to weight loss particularly appealing because it does not require them to write down what they eat. However, since it is awkward to say he/she every time and because the vast majority of readers will be women, I have chosen to refer to all individuals in this book as women.

APPETITE AWARENESS TRAINING

The goal of this book is to introduce you to a program designed to help you regulate your eating. It is called *appetite awareness training* (AAT). The fundamental principle of AAT is to eat as much like a baby as possible. Using your body's internal signals, you decide when you are hungry and when to stop eating. Eating is an important pleasure in your life, yet you don't want to be thinking about food and eating all the time. There are far too many other exciting and interesting things to do and to experience in this wonderful, stimulating world to spend all your time worrying about what you are going to eat and how you look. I developed this program over the past ten years with input from many colleagues, graduate students, and clients. We all practice what we preach. We have adopted the techniques presented in this book in order to feel better about how we eat in today's difficult food environment. We have taught these principles to our family members and friends as well as to our clients. I share this program with you in the hope that appetite awareness training will change the way you relate to food.

OUR TOXIC CULTURE: AN ULTRATHIN IDEAL IN THE LAND OF PLENTY

Obesity, binge eating, and obsessing about eating and weight have become common problems within the last twenty years, at least in Western culture. Two very strong cultural shifts have led more people, particularly women, to focus on their weight and eating than at any point in the past. Our eating environment has become highly *obesegenic*. At the same time, the ideal female shape has become *ultrathin*.

By obesegenic, I mean the culture promotes and encourages the development of obesity and does little to promote or encourage healthy eating and exercise. In today's world, tasty, high-fat and high-calorie foods are easily available, are often less expensive than healthier options, and are heavily promoted through advertising. At the same time, the need for physical activity has decreased significantly. For many people, opportunities for leisure or health-promoting exercise are limited. Both the food and dieting industries are very profitable. These industries have clear financial incentives to maintain the status quo. Profits can be made in industries providing tasty, high-calorie, convenient foods that promote weight gain, as well as in businesses providing diet-related products and services (such as low-fat or reduced-calorie foods, weight-loss programs, exercise equipment, trainers, and athletic facilities). There are few incentives for either the food or the diet industry to correct the current situation, as Dr. Kelly Brownell clearly documents in his book *Food Fight* (Brownell and Horgen 2004).

The Cultural Basis for "Ideal" Weight

A culture's "ideal" appearance involves both facial features and body shape (the relative proportion of chest, waist, and hips), but weight is one of its most obvious characteristics. A culture's most popular models, actors, and actresses represent that culture's "ideal" weight/shape. A culturally ideal weight is not necessarily the healthiest weight, which is determined by actual mortality rates.

For the past fifty years, Western media (movies, television, and fashion magazines) have promoted a relatively thin ideal weight for women. That thin ideal has reflected weights ranging from the center to the low end of the healthy weight range. Recently, the Western ideal is more accurately described as ultrathin. The majority of women who represent today's ideal female figure are at (or below) the lowest end of the healthy range.

Body Mass Index and Ideal Weight

A useful way to understand the significance of recent changes in our culture's ideal figure is to look at the entire range of healthy to unhealthy weights. The body mass index (BMI) is a measurement that takes both height and weight into account, so it is easier to compare the relative thinness of individuals of different heights.

Figure 1.1 shows the relationship between height, weight, and BMI. The white area is the healthiest weight range, with medical risk increasing both above and below that range. A BMI below 17.5 is commonly used as the weight criteria for a diagnosis of anorexia, but many experts consider a BMI of 18.5 necessary to consider a person recovered from anorexia. Thus, weights below the white range increase psychological risk for disordered eating even when physical health is not yet compromised.

What Is the Healthiest Weight Range?

As shown in figure 1.1, the healthiest weight range (white area) is fairly large; it goes from a BMI of 19 to 26. This range needs to be large because individuals vary considerably in terms of build and genetic tendencies. I refer to this entire range as *normal weight*, because the average BMI of American college women (21–22) and of American women of all ages (24–26) is within this range. Some people have additional risk factors, such as high blood pressure, that can be improved by staying on the thin side of normal, but otherwise all weights within this range are healthy weights. Unfortunately, the current cultural ideal for women in Westernized countries is so low that most women cannot realistically achieve it, much less maintain it as they age.

Although cultural ideals for weight have varied over time, they have never been this low. Statues of gods and goddesses in various cultures (like ancient Greece and Rome) suggest what was likely perceived as the ideal figure during those times. The majority of these representations depict women whose weight would be in the middle to upper end of the healthy weight range. At other times, the ideal in a culture has been mildly overweight (for example, during the Renaissance), probably because being mildly overweight was a sign of health and prosperity. Historically, extreme thinness has been associated with sickness or poverty, and has not been seen as desirable.

In modern times, the negative, long-term health consequences of maintaining an extremely low weight have been well documented among women with anorexia. It is interesting that the weight criterion for a diagnosis of anorexia only requires that one's BMI be less than 17.5, while high fashion models are required to be below that level. Of course, BMI is not the only criterion for making such a diagnosis, but the likelihood that a woman does meet all the criteria for a clinically significant eating disorder clearly increases as her weight goes below a BMI of 18. Since such extreme thinness has never before been popular, or very common, I conclude that very few women are naturally that thin. Thus, for most women it is quite unreasonable to maintain a weight that fits current ideals.

The Problem with Models Setting Cultural Ideals

As noted on figure 1.1, the typical high-fashion model is much taller and thinner than typical women. Unfortunately this model-thin standard is now being adopted by the entertainment industry more generally. Many popular actresses who were in the normal range when they began their careers have lost weight in order to approach the model-thin range (see the changes

Figure 1.1: The Healthiest Weight Range

HT＼WT	90	95	100	105	110	115	120	125	130	135	140	145	150	155	160	165	170	175	180	185	190	195	200	205	210	215	220	225	230	235	240	245	250
5'0"	18	19	20	21	21	22	23	24	25	26	27	28	29	30	31	32	33	34	35	36	37	38	39	40	41	42	43	44	45	46	47	48	49
5'1"	17	18	19	20	21	22	23	24	25	26	26	27	28	29	30	31	32	33	34	35	36	37	38	39	40	41	42	43	43	44	45	46	47
5'2"	16	17	18	19	20	21	22	23	24	25	26	27	27	28	29	30	31	32	33	34	35	36	37	37	38	39	40	41	42	43	44	45	46
5'3"	16	17	18	19	19	20	21	22	23	24	25	26	27	27	28	29	30	31	32	33	34	35	35	36	37	38	39	40	41	42	43	43	44
5'4"	15	16	17	18	19	20	21	21	22	23	24	25	26	27	27	28	29	30	31	32	33	33	34	35	36	37	38	39	39	40	41	42	43
5'5"	15	16	17	17	18	19	20	21	22	22	23	24	25	26	27	27	28	29	30	31	32	32	33	34	35	36	37	37	38	39	40	41	42
5'6"	15	15	16	17	18	19	19	20	21	22	23	23	24	25	26	27	27	28	29	30	31	31	32	33	34	35	36	36	37	38	39	40	40
5'7"		15	16	16	17	18	19	20	20	21	22	23	23	24	25	26	27	27	28	29	30	31	31	32	33	34	34	35	36	37	38	38	39
5'8"			15	16	17	17	18	19	20	21	21	22	23	24	24	25	26	27	27	28	29	30	30	31	32	33	33	34	35	36	36	37	38
5'9"			15	16	16	17	18	18	19	20	21	21	22	23	24	24	25	26	27	27	28	29	30	30	31	32	32	33	34	35	35	36	37
5'10"				15	16	16	17	18	19	19	20	21	22	22	23	24	24	25	26	27	27	28	29	29	30	31	32	32	33	34	34	35	36
5'11"				15	15	16	17	17	18	19	20	20	21	22	22	23	24	24	25	26	26	27	28	29	29	30	31	31	32	33	33	34	35
6'0"					15	16	16	17	18	18	19	20	20	21	22	22	23	24	24	25	26	26	27	28	28	29	30	31	31	32	33	33	34
6'1"					15	15	16	16	17	18	18	19	20	20	21	22	22	23	24	24	25	26	26	27	28	28	29	30	30	31	32	32	33
6'2"						15	15	16	17	17	18	19	19	20	21	21	22	22	23	24	24	25	26	26	27	28	28	29	30	30	31	31	32
6'3"							15	16	16	17	17	18	19	19	20	21	21	22	22	23	24	24	25	26	26	27	27	28	29	29	30	31	31
6'4"							15	15	16	16	17	18	18	19	19	20	21	21	22	23	23	24	24	25	26	26	27	27	28	29	29	30	30

Notes:

- ⬭ Thin-ideal (typical actress 19–20)
- ⬭ Typical American college woman (21–22)
- ⬭ Typical American woman over 30 (24–26)
- ◇ Typical high fashion model (16)
- ◇ Typical plus size fashion model (27)
- ┄ Typical weight losses of current actresses now considered ultrathin (17–18)
- ↓/↑ Examples of actresses who have lost then regained to achieve a healthier weight

depicted in figure 1.1). Fashion models are known to be selected because they are unusually tall and thin. Models represent the thin end of the genetic continuum. Thus, even if they are idealized, ordinary women do not always feel extreme pressure to be quite that thin. However, actresses and singers are viewed more as real-life women who could and "should" be imitated. They are often average height, so direct weight comparisons can be made more easily. Adolescents and young women are far more likely to identify with entertainers than with models. When a young woman sees that many well-known entertainers have achieved below-normal weights, she views this as realistically achievable.

Some of the "ideal" women in the entertainment industry have gone public with their struggles with weight and have described how they developed eating disorders. However, in spite of this negative publicity, the media ideal clearly remains at the thinnest end of normal. A few actresses and singers have refused to buy into the model-thin ideal. Several have been quoted as being proud of their more rounded, feminine shapes. However, these women are just in the middle of the normal range. Thus, society's perception of the range of desirable weight has become severely restricted, and the stigma of being overweight has never been higher.

The Thin-Fit Ideal

Recent trends suggest some movement toward a slightly less thin ideal, but there is little indication that the thin ideal is seriously being reconsidered. Rather, this trend reflects an evolution in our cultural conception of the ideal body shape to what I call the thin-fit ideal. The thin-fit ideal is a low normal weight, but it requires well-toned muscles as well. This focus on fitness would appear to be a step in the right direction on the surface of things, but it is clearly falling short in terms of increasing acceptance of the middle to high ranges of normal weight. In fact, adding fitness to the thin ideal has, in some ways, increased the importance of appearance more generally. Now women believe they must not only be thin but also fit, making today's ideal even more difficult to attain. In fact, for many women excessive exercise is now as problematic as excessive dieting. Ideally, our culture would endorse a fit ideal and leave out the thin part. Jonas and Konner (1997) describe this helpful approach in which the goal is to become healthy and fit.

AN EPIDEMIC OF BODY DISSATISFACTION

The clashing trends of increased actual weight and lower ideal weights have created a society in which most girls and women are at least moderately dissatisfied with their weight or shape. Dissatisfaction with one's body is the norm. Surveys of many different groups of females indicate that the majority, perhaps as many as 75 percent, are somewhat dissatisfied with their bodies. Thus, most women spend a lot of time thinking about weight. Very few women over eighteen are naturally so thin that they can maintain a weight below the normal range without enduring chronic restriction or excessive exercise.

Women who are naturally thin differ from women who maintain a thin weight through effortful dieting and exercise. A woman who is naturally thin does not worry much about what she eats. Even if she usually chooses to eat healthy foods, she does not make a big deal out of her diet. Naturally thin women do not count calories or fat grams, and they enjoy what they eat. They eat at least three times a day, and they are not picky. They eat whatever type of food is served or is easily available. A woman who avoids a wide range of foods, especially high-fat foods, is, in fact, dieting even if she claims to be engaging in such restrictive behaviors more for health than for appearance. For our purposes, *dieting* means the voluntary restriction of any type or amount of food for the purpose of losing weight or preventing weight gain. Dieting implies that you would prefer to eat differently if your weight would not be affected.

Significant numbers of girls start dieting as early as junior high school. Many young women remain dissatisfied with their weight and become chronic dieters. Many of these women are not overweight, or are so mildly overweight that other people do not see their weight as a significant issue. Such women are at high risk for the development of disordered eating. Body dissatisfaction (not health concerns) is the main reason women diet. Severe and chronic dieting is a problem because dieting is the most common reason why women begin binge eating.

THE PARADOX OF THE THIN IDEAL

There is a fine line between working hard to achieve a goal and becoming overinvested in a specific method for reaching that goal. When you are overinvested in one method, you are unable to recognize or accept the reality that this method isn't working, so you fail to consider alternatives that might work better.

The ultrathin and thin-fit ideals are harmful because women become overinvested in achieving those ideals. They lose sight of the real reasons they want to be attractive. In most cases, the harder a woman tries to be that thin, the more it eludes her. In many cases, the most obvious of which is anorexia, if a woman actually achieves her goal, it is at a high cost to her physical and mental health. She fails to realize that she isn't getting the desired benefits of achieving a very low weight. Usually, she does not recognize the health risks that she is incurring.

For example, a young woman thinks she will become more popular, find a boyfriend, and be happier or more self-confident if she is thinner. However, getting and staying thin takes up so much of her time and attention that she ends up alienating her friends and cannot find or maintain a satisfactory romantic relationship. Men may find her attractive initially, but they are turned off when they discover that she is so insecure about her appearance (and herself).

OVERCONCERN WITH WEIGHT OR SHAPE

The consequences of body dissatisfaction are relatively mild for many women. They go through occasional bouts of dieting and excessive worry about their weight, typically triggered by shopping for clothes, anticipation of special occasions, or the onset of the swimsuit season. Severe body dissatisfaction, however, leads to chronic unhappiness, insecurity, low self-esteem, and social isolation. The degree of dissatisfaction a person experiences is not necessarily related to the degree to which they are truly (objectively) overweight. Many women in the normal weight range report very high levels of body dissatisfaction, while some women who are overweight are not overly concerned about how much they weigh. Body dissatisfaction is related to the importance a person puts on their physical appearance, and the degree to which weight determines their perceived self-worth.

Women who are overconcerned with weight and shape often don't feel significantly better even if they are thin or have succeeded in losing a substantial number of pounds. The overconcerned woman never believes she is quite thin enough and she remains dissatisfied with some aspect of her shape, even if she feels all right about the number that comes up on the bathroom scale.

Challenging Overconcern with Weight and Shape

If you are overly concerned about your weight and shape, this problem may need to be addressed separately from your problems with binge eating. I encourage you to first work on putting a stop to your binge eating. If you are able to successfully stop binge eating but still feel extremely negative about your weight or shape, you may benefit from seeing a professional to help you challenge your beliefs about the importance of thinness. You might also consider a self-help book that is specifically focused on the acceptance of body shape, such as *The Body Image Workbook* (Cash 1997).

ACCEPTING YOUR WEIGHT AND SHAPE

In appendix C, I discuss further the concept of accepting your current weight and shape. Accepting does not necessarily mean that you have arrived at your desired weight; you may still prefer to be thinner. Accepting simply means that your weight does not make you so unhappy that your quality of life is diminished. It also means you do not avoid or put off activities because of your weight. I encourage you to accept your current weight unconditionally if it is within the normal range. You may gradually lose weight as you continue to eat normally, but an individual's natural weight depends to some extent on genetics and the person's ability or willingness to exercise. You will only be able to recognize what is a reasonable weight for your particular body after you have been eating normally for a substantial period of time. I define a "reasonable weight" as one that you can maintain while eating normally. I will define what I mean by "normal eating" in the next chapter.

If you are objectively overweight, accepting your current weight and shape is still a better option than remaining distressed about it. Accepting where you are right now is the most effective way to work toward where you want to be. You will be better able to work toward your goal if negative emotions (blame and shame) do not interfere with your efforts. Depending on how overweight you are, you may find that it is difficult and takes a long time to reach the normal weight range. However, you may be surprised to find that you can be happy at a higher than normal weight, or that you are not willing to restrict your diet further or exercise more. Weight loss experts (Cooper, Fairburn, and Hawker 2004) report that, on average, people only lose 10 to 15 percent of their body weight during any particular weight-loss effort. Weight loss tends to reach a plateau after about four to six months of dieting. These experts recommend that you make sure you can then maintain your initial loss for at least a few months before you attempt to lose additional weight. Thus, if you are substantially overweight, you will likely need a great deal of social support (from professionals or friends) so that you do not become discouraged about how long it takes to reach a weight that is satisfactory. Accepting your current weight will make this process less painful and help you maintain the motivation you need to be successful.

THE BIOLOGY OF WEIGHT LOSS

The dilemma you face is that you want to be very thin, or at least be in the normal weight range, but today's culinary environment encourages obesity. Biology provides very little help in the fight against obesity; our bodies are set up to protect us from possible starvation, not from an excess of food. Your body responds the same way whether you restrict your intake voluntarily (diet), or whether your food intake is limited by an inadequate food supply (famine). In either case, your body becomes more efficient in order to survive with less food. This response is an advantage when food is actually scarce, but makes it very difficult to lose weight on purpose or to stay significantly underweight.

People don't instinctively know how to eat to avoid becoming overweight in an obesegenic environment. We weren't designed to live in such an environment, and the changes have occurred so quickly that our biology hasn't had time to adapt. When food is tasty and plentiful, limiting intake sufficiently to lose weight is an unpleasant experience and feels punitive. When others are enjoying good food, you feel deprived when you have to restrict. It is important to understand your biological appetite regulation system so that you can work with it instead of fighting against your own physiology. The AAT approach will help you respect your biological limits and find ways to minimize the degree to which your appetite regulation system makes it difficult to maintain a reasonable weight in an environment filled with tempting foods.

2 The Appetite Awareness Training Solution

It is difficult to enjoy eating in today's "toxic" food and weight environment. You are encouraged to enjoy the rich and bountiful food that is easily available, yet the ultrathin ideal demands that you keep your weight low. In this environment, most of us want to eat more often and to eat larger amounts than are necessary to just avoid feeling hungry. However, we aren't happy with the results when we eat as often and as much as we want. And, we are displeased when we have to watch what we eat all the time, refusing ourselves many foods that we enjoy.

Appetite awareness training offers a positive alternative that feels fairly satisfying and natural and does not require excessive effort. This approach is a compromise many people find quite acceptable. It is not truly "natural" in the strictest sense: You can't eat whatever and whenever you want. However, eating the AAT way is likely to feel more natural than whatever distressing eating pattern you have developed. AAT can be the solution for almost any kind of disordered eating pattern.

The basic principles of AAT are simple. First, you take charge of your eating decisions so that you are not as vulnerable to environmental signals to eat or to diet (restrict your eating). Second, you work with your internal appetite signals instead of attempting to fight your biological weight regulation system. My motto is "Don't fight Mother Nature. She has the advantage. She will eventually wear you out. She will win!" However, you can negotiate with Mother Nature. You may be pleasantly surprised to find that you can make peace with your appetite and your body. AAT will help you do this.

AAT establishes reasonable, easy-to-follow eating guidelines so you do not have to rely as heavily on willpower to ignore or override urges to eat. Willpower requires constant effort and attention; consequently, it is extremely difficult to maintain. People who rely on willpower usually become overly preoccupied with maintaining a high level of control over their eating.

This limits the attention they can give to other important parts of their lives. This is ultimately not very satisfying. Most people can successfully put their full attention on dieting for a certain period of time but most find it difficult to maintain that level of effort indefinitely.

You need a moderate amount of so-called willpower to commit to learning AAT. Initially, you will need to practice diligently to shift away from your current eating patterns. However, AAT helps you tune back into your body, so you rely more on automatically generated body signals and less on willpower. Relying on body signals means that less attention will be required to maintain your new eating pattern. Nonetheless, it still takes some effort to stay attentive and respond to your signals. However, unlike willpower strategies, AAT seems to get easier and easier the longer you do it. Most people report that eating the AAT way feels quite different from other methods they have tried. And they like how it feels.

AAT is designed to help anyone who does not feel good about the way she eats. It doesn't matter if you are underweight, normal weight, or overweight. It doesn't matter if you have an eating disorder or are simply tired of spending so much of your life worried about eating and weight. This program is particularly effective in helping people stop binge eating and reduce preoccupation with food. It can also help you reduce overeating if that is a problem for you, and feel generally more comfortable with eating. Once you have mastered the AAT principles, you will understand how your body works, and you will be able to make effective choices about your eating and your weight.

In AAT, you learn to eat when you are hungry and avoid eating when you are not hungry. Most importantly, you learn to stop eating before your stomach becomes uncomfortably full. Your goal is to maintain this limit on fullness while then choosing to eat foods that feel good in your stomach. AAT calls this pattern *normal eating,* though, of course, many people do not actually eat this way.

You may or may not lose weight when you start eating normally. Weight loss depends on many factors, including individual physiology and your prior level of food intake. However, normal eating virtually guarantees that you will not gain weight. Once you know how to maintain a stable weight, you can work toward weight loss or toward acceptance of a weight that you can successfully maintain.

Acceptance doesn't mean you give up on your appearance. You are encouraged to highlight your most positive physical features, as well as your unique personal qualities. When you honor all the best aspects of yourself and make peace with what you cannot change, you will be ready to experience life as a more fully integrated person. You can live richly, making the most out of all life's possibilities. So, let's get started!

HOW THE AAT MODEL WORKS

Appetite awareness training begins with a model that describes the various reasons an individual starts, continues, and ultimately stops eating. The model illustrates how the three most common problem-eating paths differ from normal eating and identifies seven specific intervention points where you can start making different decisions about eating. This model does not explain *why* you developed your current eating patterns; it just helps you figure out why you eat (or don't eat) and why you stop (or don't stop). AAT teaches you to analyze what happens each time you eat, which I refer to as an *eating episode*. You figure out what led you to eat and what led you to stop eating. This is a much easier task than trying to come up with the "real" reason you have an eating problem, or trying to find a simple "solution" to your eating problems. In AAT, you tackle one eating decision at a time, and you get better and better at making more effective eating decisions.

First you break down your eating problem into specific problem-eating episodes. Each time you eat, you make a decision to start eating and a decision to stop eating. If you don't understand why you start eating, you become more aware of what makes you want to start eating. If you don't feel able to stop eating when you want to stop, you become more aware of what it is that eventually makes you stop. You may think, "I just eat because I feel like eating; I don't make eating decisions." However, deciding that you will let your "feelings" determine when and how much you eat is a decision. You make eating decisions all the time.

On the other hand, you may be all too aware of your decisions to start and stop eating. In fact, your problem may be that you obsess about every eating decision, yet you rarely feel good about whatever decision you make. Do you eat mindlessly, with little awareness of your decisions or do you obsess about every bite you take? In this program, you are going to change the way you make decisions to start and stop eating no matter which end of the spectrum you lie on.

You also have to make decisions about the types of food you will eat, but AAT focuses first on learning to make better decisions to start and stop eating. Once you are able to regulate the amount of food you eat, you can decide whether or not you want to alter the type of food you choose to eat. There are many reasons to start with regulating the amount you eat. First, changing preferences for how full you feel is much easier than changing preferences for the types of food you eat. Second, learning how to stop eating effectively is going to do more to reestablish your sense of control over eating. Third, when people try to change the types of foods they eat to low-fat or low-calorie food they tend to compensate by eating more. When you eat more "diet foods," you may or may not end up eating significantly fewer calories. Hence, an exclusive focus on food type is not an effective way to control your weight. AAT can help you alter preferences for types of food (see chapter 8), but only after you can regulate amount.

As you analyze your eating episodes, you will identify the places where you are currently having problems with the process of eating. The severity and types of eating problems you have experienced may have changed over time. You may understand the reason you initially started having eating problems, or your problems may have started so long ago that you don't really know why they started. What is critical is that you understand why you are having problems *now* and what you need to do to change your current patterns.

When a problematic eating pattern becomes well established, that pattern does not always correct itself even if the psychological issues that initially created the problem get resolved. Conversely, you may improve your eating pattern, but that does not necessarily mean you have resolved your other life problems. Once you learn the AAT guidelines and feel more in control of your eating, you will be able to determine if you have other psychological issues that must be addressed. Then you can work on resolving those issues while you continue to practice your new eating pattern. But, never take a vacation from dealing with your eating problems while you resolve those other life difficulties. Chapter 7 will help you identify personal issues that interfere with your ability to make further progress in establishing an AAT eating pattern.

LET YOUR STOMACH BE YOUR GUIDE

The most fundamental concept of AAT is that you learn to use internal, stomach-based signals to make decisions about eating. Obviously, you have to first notice your stomach signals. Thus, the first step is to identify the two critical stomach signals: *moderate hunger* and *moderate fullness*. Since you have a history of restricting or overeating (or both), you have learned to ignore or override these signals that can be your best allies. When you wait as long as possible to eat, you are tuning out the moderate hunger signal. When you binge or overeat, you are tuning out the moderate fullness signal. You must now tune back into these signals. Once you can easily identify the signals, you can start using them to make eating decisions that feel better and work better. You can then commit to using stomach signals instead of debating about what you want or don't want to eat, or about what effect eating some specific food will or will not have on your weight. Once you have established this new strategy for making eating decisions, the process of eating normally can be maintained with a moderate degree of attention and effort.

THE FOUR EATING PATHS

The *normal eating path* is the goal of AAT. Three other paths represent the most common types of problematic eating: *normalized overeating, binge eating,* and *restricted eating*. You may have difficulty with only one of these problem paths, or you may alternate between restricting, overeating, and bingeing. The more often you travel a path, the more likely you are to choose that path the next time you decide to eat. Each problem path has links to the other problem paths. The many connections between these paths explain why your eating problems may change over time. For example, excessive restriction often leads to bingeing. Seven intervention points are identified to show you where you can make different decisions that will lead you out of the maze of disordered eating.

The Normal Eating Path

The *normal eating path* illustrates the ideal way to eat when you are concerned about your weight. This pattern is not normal in the sense of being "typical." It is normal in the sense that it feels right. You take advantage of all the help you can get from your biological appetite regulation system. You focus primarily on regulating amount (not type) of food, just like a nursing baby. Your goal is to avoid getting too hungry before you eat because it is too easy to overeat when you start out very hungry, and to pay close attention as you eat so you can stop at the critical moderate fullness signal.

Benefits of Normal Eating

The normal eating path is associated with many positive consequences. You feel normal and in control. You feel adequately satisfied. You can maintain a stable weight because eating this way protects you from many of the tempting foods in your environment. You have time and energy for valued activities and relationships because you are not preoccupied with food. The best thing about the normal eating path is that it is easier than you might think to learn to eat this way, and it is easier to maintain this way of eating than to adhere to diet plans or food rules.

On the normal path, you are strongly encouraged to enjoy whatever food you decide to eat. Food serves two functions in your life. First, it provides the necessary nutrition to keep you healthy, thus preventing you from feeling aversive hunger sensations. Second, food gives you pleasure. Eating, like sex, is one of the most basic human needs. You wouldn't think of trying to take the pleasure out of sex, would you? So why do that with eating? Having a positive mind-set about the role of food is an essential element of the normal eating path.

The Normalized Overeating Path

The *normalized overeating path* is when you continue to eat past your moderate fullness signal. It is very easy to start eating for reasons besides scheduled meals and moderate hunger. Our biological system is set up to respond to the sight and smell of food, not just to sensations of hunger. It is quite natural for a person to eat just because food is present. It is also perfectly normal to start eating in order to feel better or to celebrate. Our biological system is set up to respond positively to food. Unless you have learned to have negative reactions to eating, food reduces tension, fatigue, and a number of other unpleasant feelings. Food can also enhance positive feelings. If you do not have significant weight concerns, eating for reasons other than hunger will not bother you. Those episodes will end, and you will go back to the normal eating path the next time you eat. However, when you are worried about your weight, you often feel bad when you eat for those reasons. If you try to restrict your eating to make up for indulging, you get on that problem path.

AAT helps you figure out alternative ways to respond to urges to eat when you are not even moderately hungry. You don't need to eliminate all eating for pleasure. Having food available can be a very strong cue to eat. For example, you are full from a substantial dinner and your favorite dessert is served. Emotional cues can also be quite strong. For example, when you are feeling lonely, bored, and depressed you treat yourself to a sundae. The goal of AAT is to stop at moderate fullness no matter why you start eating. When you can maintain this boundary on amount, you will stay on the normal eating path instead of ending up overeating or perhaps triggering a binge.

Our social environment makes overeating the most difficult path to eliminate. Food is an important aspect of most social occasions. Indulgence in rich foods and nutritionally empty, high-calorie drinks is promoted, particularly on celebratory occasions. Overeating is often viewed positively—a sign that you are actively participating in a celebration or appreciating the culinary skills of your host. Providing wonderful, rich food and drink has long been a sign of hospitality, power, affluence, love, and much more. Our appetite regulation system allows and even encourages moderate overeating in times of plentiful food—primarily in order to protect against less plentiful times. However, in the culture we live in, less plentiful times do not occur. This throws the whole system out of balance, and few people today support each other in eating in a healthy, moderate fashion. In fact, failure to appreciate food that is offered may be interpreted quite negatively by those who offer the food.

Normalized overeating does not appear excessive or noticeable to others. Often, you don't even recognize that you are eating more than you need to feel satisfied. When you decide how much to eat based on portions that are served or what you see others eating, you will be "overeating" to a modest degree much of the time. It is for these reasons that I refer to this as the "normalized" overeating path.

Consequences of Normalized Overeating

Occasional overeating is not a serious problem, but overeating on a regular basis will lead to a weight problem unless you are compensating with adequate physical activity. When you are worried about your weight, you often end up feeling fat or feeling bad about yourself after you overeat, even though you enjoyed the food or felt comforted in the short run. From the AAT perspective, the most serious consequence of normalized overeating is that it maintains your lack of awareness of moderate fullness. Every time you overeat it is harder to notice and stop at the moderate fullness level the next time. Choosing to ignore fullness is one of the seven points where you make critical decisions. You make a decision that either puts you on the overeating path or keeps you on the normal eating path.

The Restricted Eating Path

The *restricted eating path* is the trickiest path. If you enjoy food and tend to overeat, you probably don't *want* to restrict, but you probably believe that restriction is the only viable way to achieve or maintain your weight. In AAT, *restriction* means you are deliberately refusing to eat when you are hungry or when you really want a particular food. Everyone has to use willpower to restrict, because restriction is not biologically normal. You may be capable of tolerating hunger, but it is inevitable that you will end up feeling deprived to some degree. Deprivation can lead to *restriction backlash*. Restriction backlash is what I call the "what the heck" response. You temporarily give up restriction, but you know it is only for the moment. This response is discussed further in chapter 6. Because of this response, deprivation is highly likely to undermine your weight goals. AAT views restriction as a seriously problematic path. In AAT, you do not attempt to manage your weight through restriction; you manage your weight by minimizing overeating. Deciding to stop based on moderate fullness means that you often choose to eat less than you prefer to eat, but you don't feel hungry or significantly deprived.

Some women are able to restrict apparently successfully and maintain a thin weight. If you are such an individual, you have probably learned to ignore hunger. However, few women escape the most problematic consequence of severe restriction—preoccupation with food. Many women get stuck on the restricted eating path. When you are stuck there, you may find you dislike the sensation of food in your stomach. You may even like to feel hungry. Feeling hungry may make you feel successful and in control. If you restrict but do not get too thin, preoccupation with food may be the only negative consequence you experience. However, most women who start off restricting eventually develop problems with binge eating. They feel a loss of control when they break one of their strict food rules or eat just a little more than they intended to eat. You must give up the restriction path in order to eat normally.

Consequences of Restricting Your Eating

The restricted eating path beckons you with the promise of quick weight loss or achieving the ultrathin ideal. When you are successful in restricting, you immediately feel very good. You feel thin (or at least that you have a chance of getting thin) and in control. You may even feel smugly proud when you are able to restrict in situations where others are not so successful. However, restriction turns out to be the "devil in disguise." Excessive restriction, either of calories or of types of food, is the most common reason that women develop binge eating (Fairburn 1995). Thus, severe restriction ultimately sabotages your "dream." Excessive restriction robs you of feeling in control of your eating, and robs you of precious time and energy you could devote to valued activities and important relationships.

Most of us wish that restriction was a viable solution for weight problems. Since it is not, AAT teaches you to travel the middle path, to avoid excessive restriction while also maintaining boundaries to prevent overeating.

The Binge Eating/Getting Stuffed Path

The *binge eating/getting stuffed* path is the third problematic eating path. This pattern of eating feels the most distressing while it is occurring, and it is probably the reason most of you are reading this book. However, it is important to recognize that some people do eat large amounts, colloquially referred to as "pigging out," and enjoy doing so. Thus, eating large amounts is not necessarily distressing to everyone. Within the AAT program, this problematic path refers to eating that feels different, not normal, and very distressing. Binge eating refers specifically to the subjective experience of feeling out of control at some point during the process of eating. Binge eating may involve truly large amounts of food or it may involve lesser amounts of "forbidden" foods. When someone eats an objectively large amount of food but does not feel loss of control, I call the episode *getting stuffed.* The first goal of AAT is to eliminate eating large amounts and getting stuffed, regardless of whether or not you feel loss of control.

As you can see in figure 2.1, there are three different ways to end up on this problem path. You can plan to binge; you can break a food rule; or overeating can turn into a binge through the "what the heck" response. When you are on this path, you may eat foods that you

Figure 2.1: The AAT Model for Bingeing and Overeating

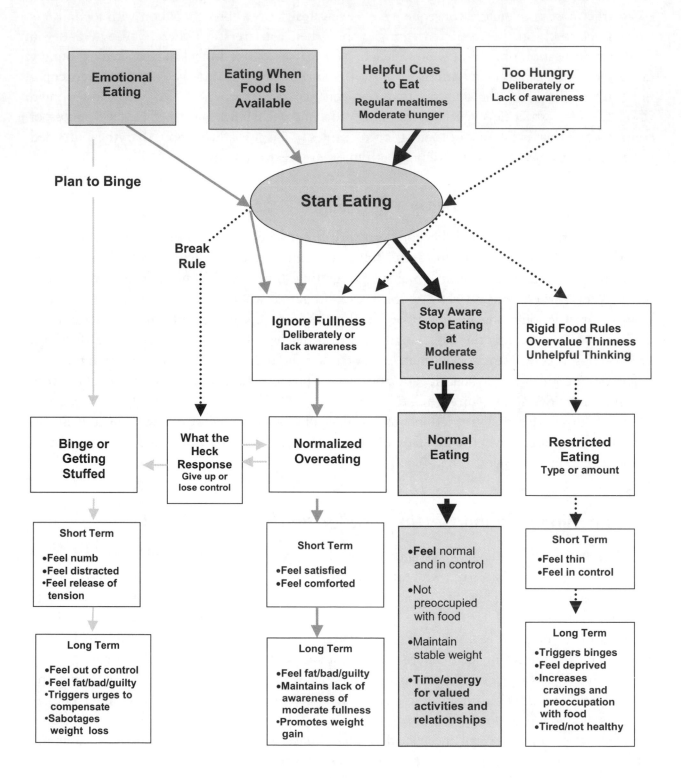

aren't even enjoying, and you may not be able to stop eating until you are painfully stuffed or some external force intervenes (the food is gone, someone interrupts you, or you are able to fall asleep).

The Consequences of Binge Eating/Getting Stuffed

While binges always end up feeling distressing, it is important to acknowledge what these episodes do for you in the short run. Some people enjoy the process of eating large amounts of food even though they feel uncomfortable, upset, or even sick afterward. Other people do not describe the experience of bingeing as positive in any way; to them it feels more like a compulsion—something they must do even though they don't enjoy it.

Binge eating is associated with a unique form of distress: loss of control. This feeling is particularly distressing because it suggests that if you cannot control what you eat, you may not be able to control other aspects of your life. Thus, loss of control over eating can sabotage your self-esteem and your overall sense of self-efficacy. Many people report feeling numb or tuned out during the binge process, so we infer that their binges help them avoid experiencing negative emotions. Avoidance of negative feelings is often the "positive" consequence that maintains binge eating. Because this reason isn't usually obvious, many people have a difficult time explaining (to themselves and to others) why they binge.

From the AAT perspective, the most negative consequence of binge eating is that it maintains your lack of awareness of the critical moderate fullness point. You frequently override your moderate stomach signals, and, consequently, you lack awareness of these signals. This lack of awareness leaves you quite vulnerable to overeating. You cannot learn to use moderate stomach signals until you are aware of them. As long as you binge, you continue to mask the very signals you need to be using. This is why giving up this path needs to take priority over losing weight.

Binge eating can override or drown out painful emotions by creating strong bodily sensations. This is most likely the reason that binge eating feels like an addiction, although it is clear that there are very important differences between eating problems and other addictions. The similarity is that people who binge develop a very strong expectation that binge eating will temporarily relieve their emotional pain, just as addicts expect a chemical substance to relieve their pain. When you have an urge to binge, you may fight the urge for some time, but the pressure to binge builds up until you give in to it. As you binge, you experience a brief period of relief from the pressure of maintaining control over your eating. In some cases, an individual then has a few days of relief, when the urge to binge is weak. In other cases, the first binge triggers several days of uncontrolled eating.

Many people are not clear about the point at which normalized overeating turns into getting stuffed, but the exact point isn't important. What is important is that neither binge eating nor getting stuffed feels quite normal. The feeling associated with eating on this path is forced, hurried, or driven. In comparison, normalized overeating feels all right while you are doing it. It's only afterward that you may regret what or how much you ate.

THE SEVEN POINTS OF INTERVENTION

Now that I've described the four eating paths, let's turn to what I call "helpful cues to start eating." You can't avoid eating altogether. Choosing to use these cues (scheduled meals/snacks and moderate hunger) will make it easier for you to stay aware as you eat and to stop at the moderate fullness point.

I will also identify seven specific points that are targeted as places where you can make different decisions, decisions that put you back on the normal eating path: *getting too hungry, breaking food rules, ignoring fullness, eating when food is available, emotional eating,* the *"what the heck" response,* and *planning to binge.* In the following chapters, you will learn specific strategies for intervening at each of these points.

Point One: Getting Too Hungry

When you allow yourself to get too hungry before you eat, you are restricting. You may restrict the overall amount of food you eat (calorie intake), or certain types of food (usually high fat, sugar, or carbohydrate content). You may be quite aware of when you are too hungry but deliberately ignore your hunger because you are dieting. Or, you may lack awareness of moderate hunger due to prior dieting. AAT is first concerned about the problem created when you are biologically hungry. However, feeling hungry can also reflect psychological deprivation created when you crave certain types of food but do not allow yourself to eat them.

Regardless of the reason, if you are too hungry when you start eating, it is difficult to stay aware and stop at moderate fullness. Thus, the easiest place to intervene and make a difference in your eating is to avoid getting too hungry. To do this you must eat regularly scheduled meals (at least three times a day). In addition, you need to schedule two or three snacks, or at least make sure you eat at any point in the day when you become moderately hungry.

Hunger Gone Underground

Some people have learned to distract or dissociate from their hunger signals. It is easier for these individuals to restrict than for those who experience hunger more intensely. When you don't feel hungry even though you haven't eaten in a long time, your hunger has "gone underground." Though you may have successfully pushed hunger out of your awareness, the signal is still there; when your attention is drawn back to it, you may feel very hungry. It is for this reason that some people don't feel hungry at all for long periods and then suddenly realize they feel very hungry. This may also explain why some individuals experience "loss of control" once they start eating, even though they were not aware of feeling particularly hungry before they started eating.

Is It Hunger or Deprivation?

Many diets claim that you can eat as much as you want. This isn't really true unless the types of food you are allowed (like rice or bananas) are so limited that you wouldn't want to eat that much of them. You can stay on a limited food diet, at least for a while. However, when you limit types of food too severely, feelings of deprivation eventually develop, making it hard to stick to your food plan. You feel angry or miserable, and you go off the diet. Some medications do reduce the experience of hunger somewhat, but only as long as you take them. You will have the same problem with hunger when you stop taking them. More importantly, appetite suppressant pills are not helpful unless your problem is that you feel hunger more intensely than most people. Intense hunger is not the problem for most people. Eating when you are not hungry, but feel deprived, is most often the problem.

The Unavoidable Necessity of Eating

The unavoidable necessity of eating is one of the ways that eating problems differ from problems such as substance abuse. With most addictions, you have the option of choosing to abstain completely. Food is different. If you feel addicted to food, you cannot choose abstinence as your goal. You have to eat several times a day. If you put off eating because you are afraid you might overeat, you end up feeling too hungry and make it even more likely that you will, in fact, overeat. Avoiding eating makes eating even more scary and dangerous.

Point Two: Breaking Food Rules

If you are restricting, you are likely following rules about what or how much you eat. Thus, this is another point at which you make critical eating decisions. Even if you do not overeat, you may become upset with yourself if you eat something that you consider too fattening or if you eat at the wrong time. You may say to yourself, "What the heck," after breaking a food rule, and then overeat or binge. Breaking food rules is an important intervention point in AAT. If you replace food rules with flexible guidelines, then there are no rules to break. For this reason, AAT encourages you to eat whatever type of food you want to eat and work to modify your food preferences instead of relying on strict food rules.

Point Three: Ignoring Fullness

When people are not dieting, they stop eating when they feel satisfied. However, the experience of satisfaction is largely psychological and only partly related to your appetite regulation system. Your biological signals to stop eating are relatively weak, so it is quite easy to ignore them and eat until you feel psychologically satisfied. AAT teaches you to use stomach fullness instead of feelings of satisfaction to decide when to stop eating.

Stomach fullness signals are weak. At first you hardly notice when you start to feel full. Fortunately, the fullness signal does become stronger as you become more full. Unfortunately, for most people, feeling full means feeling close to stuffed.

There are many reasons you lack awareness of early stomach fullness signals. When you focus on the taste of food in your mouth, you are not attending to fullness. In addition, you may have overeaten so often that you no longer recognize early fullness signals. Thus, you only notice strong signals of fullness—the point I call "overfull." Many people do not pay attention to fullness while they are eating, They only notice it after they have become uncomfortably full and realize they would be feeling better had they stopped sooner. Some people prefer feeling overfull. Very full is no longer an unpleasant sensation for them. These people don't feel satisfied until they experience significant stomach fullness. AAT helps you tune back into your stomach sensations.

Point Four: Eating When Food Is Available

Eating when food is available is a very important point of intervention in AAT. In the AAT model, this intervention point does not refer to the times you eat because it is a scheduled eating time. Scheduled meals and snacks are helpful external cues that signal it is time to eat. Eating when food is available refers to all the other times that food is available and you are tempted to eat even though you are not moderately hungry. It is perfectly normal to have urges to eat when you are not hungry, especially when the food is quite appealing. Not eating when food is available can feel uncomfortable in a social situation when others are eating. You may encounter implicit or explicit pressure to eat (or eat more), regardless of your own degree of hunger or fullness. You may consider it rude to refuse food that is offered socially, even if you aren't hungry or don't really want the food.

The real problem with eating when food is available is that you are likely to ignore fullness. You weren't hungry to begin with, so it won't take very much food to go past moderate fullness. Since you don't want to become rigid about your eating, it is okay to eat just for pleasure when special foods are available. Just protect yourself from eating too much on those occasions by making sure to stop at moderate fullness even though you continue to have the desire to eat. AAT teaches you to minimize mindless eating—the times you eat just because the food is there, and it isn't even that special. You can eliminate mindless eating without triggering feelings of deprivation. You can't eliminate all special treats without triggering those feelings.

Eating may be a bad habit that is just plain hard to break. You may have learned that eating makes many tasks less aversive (for example, eating while studying), makes many activities more pleasant (like spending time with your in-laws), or makes an activity less boring (like eating while watching TV). Thus, eating when food is available might be eating for pleasure, might be a habit, or it might serve an emotional purpose. In any case, this kind of eating feels quite normal. Most people do it often. But, eating when not hungry promotes weight gain.

Point Five: Emotional Eating

Emotional eating is the fifth point where you can learn to make different eating decisions. It is a common reason you may have an urge to eat when you are not biologically hungry. Food is naturally soothing, so most people learn to eat to cope with a variety of uncomfortable or distressing emotions. Eating is also a fairly effective distraction and procrastination strategy. Just like eating when food is available, occasional emotional eating is not a problem; both are part of the normal eating path. Emotional eating is only a problem if you do it too frequently, or if you aren't able to stop at moderate fullness. Unfortunately, it is difficult to stop at moderate fullness when you start eating for emotional reasons. When you start eating because you are upset, you want to eat until you get some relief from that feeling. The amount of food it takes to alter emotional states is more than the point of moderate fullness, so you often end up overeating. In addition, when you eat for emotional reasons, you are more likely to choose comfort foods. If you break a food rule, you may then end up bingeing. When you eat for positive emotional reasons, like a celebration, you are also not paying attention to appetite cues when you start eating. Thus, you aren't likely to pay attention to appetite signals that tell you to stop.

Eating can be an effective way to comfort yourself quickly. However, if you worry about your weight, you usually end up feeling even more upset. Plus, if you depend too much on this self-soothing strategy, it will cause problems. Excessive emotional eating is the most common reason people gain weight or fail to lose weight.

For most people, food is a natural antianxiety medication. Food reduces fear and helps you tolerate moderate feelings of anxiety. Food may also make you feel better when you are down or mildly depressed. Once you learn that food is an effective way to alter your emotions, you are likely to use that strategy more and more often. Over time, the association between eating and feeling better becomes very strong. I believe this is what most people mean when they say they are "addicted" to food. When you feel bad, you know that eating will make you feel better, at least for a short period. Thus, you experience intense desires to eat (or even binge) that are similar in many ways to the cravings of addiction. It is extremely hard not to eat when you know that eating will make you feel better right away. Once you start eating, it is hard to stop until the food has masked your feelings. Many problematic eating episodes start as emotional eating. When you eat a moderate amount and you don't feel better, it's very tempting to think that a little more might do it. Emotional eating often turns into overeating or a binge.

In AAT you don't try to eliminate emotional eating completely. Sometimes it feels almost impossible not to eat when you have a strong urge to eat for emotional reasons. In the moment, it is hard to think of any alternative that seems likely to work as well as food—at least not anything as easily available. AAT teaches you how to do emotional eating effectively. You can use food to self-soothe in a responsible way that does not create more harm than good.

Point Six: The What the Heck Response

The what the heck response is most often described as a feeling of intentionally giving up control for a moment, or of not caring what you eat at a given time. This is an important intervention point, because (with the exception of planned binges) you must cross this point to start bingeing. If you break a food rule or overeat, you still have to trigger the what the heck response to turn the episode into a binge. At this intervention point, you can make a different decision. You can choose to tolerate the negative feelings associated with overeating or breaking food rules, and stay on the normal eating path. This means you don't compensate by purging, exercising, or stricter dieting. When you are quite worried about your weight, you are particularly vulnerable to the what the heck response. Any little slip makes you feel like you have blown it. When you feel hopeless, it doesn't matter if you eat more.

The what the heck response is a result of the all-too-human tendency for illogical, all-or-nothing thinking. Events or feelings are categorized as either good or bad, right or wrong, perfect or terrible. When you are subject to this way of thinking, once you decide you are bad, then eating more can't make you feel any worse. Giving up or losing control actually provides an immediate sense of relief from your effort to maintain control, even though you eventually feel more like a failure for having given in.

Point Seven: Plan to Binge (or Overeat)

Many people plan to overeat. Planned overeating may be part of a social occasion, or it may be a special treat. You are likely to have thoughts that justify overeating, such as "I deserve this treat" or "I don't want to put a damper on the celebration by not joining in the feast." Such thoughts are best considered *rationalizations*, meaning that you come up with an excuse to overeat so you don't have to admit that you really want to overeat. Many people plan to overeat on special occasions. Occasional planned overeating is not a serious threat to your weight. The problem with planned overeating is that, though it is planned, you may still feel bad as you are doing it and then give in to the what the heck response. Your planned overeating may turn into an unplanned binge.

Women don't usually plan to binge unless they have completely given up trying to control their weight, or they have a plan to compensate for the binge. It doesn't make any sense unless you truely don't care anymore about the consequences to your weight. Thus, planning to binge is quite different from planning to overeat. Some women stay on the restriction path most of the time but occasionally plan to binge, almost as though it were a shopping spree. They fully intend to compensate by then skipping meals or fasting. However, planned binges are far more common among individuals who also plan to compensate by either purging or by excessively exercising. Appendix A explains how the AAT model can be adapted to include these compensatory behaviors. Those compensatory behaviors need to be treated differently, because they allow a person to escape some of the immediate negative consequences of bingeing. However, they create other, usually even more serious, long-term health consequences.

EATING FROM WITHIN: THE GOAL OF AAT

The rest of this workbook will teach you how to get on the normal eating path, and how to resume effective eating whenever you step off the normal eating path. Once you have adopted the principles of AAT, you will be able to use your internal (primarily stomach-based) appetite signals to make eating decisions that will protect you from some of the temptations of our toxic food environment. I call this "eating from within."

Figure 2.2 shows you what this eating pattern entails. Binge eating has been eliminated, because you have given up food rules and the what the heck response. Occasionally, you may ignore fullness, but you do not then binge or compensate; you use the occasion to strengthen your awareness of what would have felt better—the moderate fullness level.

You will also occasionally be tempted to restrict, as it is normal in this society to prefer to be thinner. However, you will challenge the unhelpful thinking that tries to tell you that restriction is an effective strategy to maintain weight. Instead, you remind yourself that limiting fullness is the key to weight maintenance.

In the next few chapters, I will take you step-by-step through the AAT program. First, you will learn to identify and use stomach cues. Once you are able to follow those cues, you will be able to see more clearly if you have other, non-food problems that are preventing you from making a full recovery. Once you know how to maintain a stable weight through normal eating, you can evaluate your weight goals. Some of you may reconsider your priorities and decide it is more realistic to accept a weight you can maintain with normal eating. Over time, this approach may have a surprisingly positive effect on your weight. However, if at any point you decide to work toward deliberate weight loss, you can do so while maintaining your foundation of eating from within (see appendix C). You need to maintain the basic principles of eating from within while you diet to avoid retriggering binges.

HOW AAT IS DIFFERENT FROM OTHER APPROACHES

Many approaches point out the importance of emotional triggers (emotional eating). Behavioral models emphasize the need to establish better environmental controls to minimize the influence of food cues (eating when food is available). Cognitive behavioral models of eating disorders point out the dangers of excessive restraint and overconcern with weight and shape (the restricted eating path). Addiction models developed the idea of an "abstinence violation" effect, which I have translated here as the what the heck response. The AAT approach adds a new emphasis on the role of biologically-based appetite signals (hunger and stomach fullness). AAT teaches you how to use these signals to your advantage. In addition, AAT points out where you can intervene, that is, where you can start making different decisions.

AAT can be used for a wide range of eating problems. AAT strategies help you establish a more flexible and natural way to manage eating that becomes easier and more automatic the longer you stick to it. Adopting specific but flexible guidelines for making eating decisions reduces obsessing about those decisions. You start making eating decisions quickly and confidently, not agonizing over whether you should or shouldn't eat something.

Figure 2.2: The Goal of AAT—Eating from Within

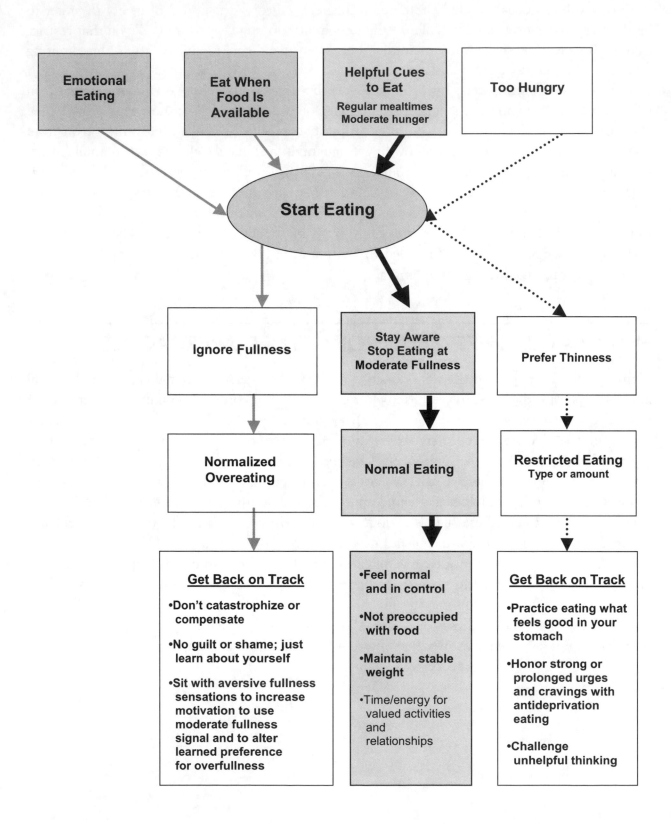

3 Disordered Eating or Eating Disorder?

Appetite awareness training was initially developed to help women diagnosed with eating disorders. However, eating patterns can best be described as a continuum that goes from highly problematic behaviors, such as life-threatening refusal to eat, to completely nonproblematic eating in which a person maintains a healthy weight without significant effort or distress. Most women fall somewhere in between—they may have disordered eating but not an eating disorder. I will briefly describe the criteria that professionals use to make a diagnosis of an eating disorder so you can determine if you would likely meet those criteria. If you think that you might meet the criteria for an eating disorder, you could be developing some potentially serious medical problems, so it is very important to consult a physician who has been trained to evaluate eating disorders. Many of the health consequences associated with disordered eating are not obvious and can only be detected through medical testing. You will not know if you are developing diabetes, are at risk for heart failure, or have thinning bones. See your doctor. Don't put it off.

Whether you have a diagnosable eating disorder or are just engaged in disordered eating makes little difference from an AAT perspective. You will benefit from the program either way. Even if you eat reasonably but you obsess over what you should eat and tend to feel guilty about what you do eat, AAT can help. Those problems are best described as overconcern with weight. Overconcern with weight is at the heart of both disordered eating and eating disorders, but it can be a problem on its own. If this is a problem for you, you may often feel anxious or depressed, and you may become socially isolated. You may complain that worrying about your weight takes up too much of your life.

DO YOU HAVE AN EATING DISORDER?

At the current time, the mental health profession only has two officially accepted diagnoses for specific eating disorders: *anorexia nervosa* and *bulimia nervosa*. The criteria for these disorders are described in the *Diagnostic and Statistical Manual of Mental Disorders IV* (American Psychiatric Association 1994).

A diagnosis of anorexia nervosa means that a person is at an unhealthy weight that, if not corrected, will lead to more significant health problems in the future. A person diagnosed with anorexia nervosa may have previously been at a normal or even above-normal weight for their height. They may have obviously lost weight, perhaps in a short period of time. Or, the person may have always been thin and, at some point, slipped below a minimally healthy level and refuses to gain weight. As you can see, the specific criteria are very stringent so many women who have disordered eating do not qualify for a diagnosis of anorexia nervosa.

- Refusal to maintain a minimally normal weight for age and height (the guideline is a BMI lower than 17.5)

- Intense fear of gaining weight even though obviously underweight

- Distorted thinking (doesn't perceive her own body size accurately or denies that her low weight is a medical risk)

- If female, failure to develop menses at the expected age, or the absence of naturally occurring menstrual cycles for at least three consecutive months; this criteria cannot be evaluated when cycles are regulated by birth control pills

- Individuals with the restricting subtype do not binge eat or purge, but those with the binge-eating/purging subtype do so on a regular basis; their binges may involve normal or even small amounts of food

A diagnosis of bulimia nervosa means that a person uses unhealthy strategies to compensate for binge eating. Again, the specific criteria are quite stringent, so many women do not meet the criteria for bulimia nervosa. The criteria are:

- Episodes of objective binge eating (must be clearly large amounts and entail a feeling of loss of control) at least twice a week for at least three months

- Unhealthy compensatory behaviors (including purging, fasting, or overexercising) at least twice a week for at least three months

- Self-evaluation unduly influenced by body shape and weight

- Does not meet criteria for anorexia nervosa (weight is typically in the normal range)

A third specific diagnosis *binge eating disorder*, is under consideration. This diagnosis means that a person has episodes of objective binge eating at least two days a week for at least six months, but unlike bulimia nervosa, the person does not regularly compensate in unhealthy ways. The binge episodes must create distress or be physically uncomfortable and are often done in secret. People with binge eating disorder may be normal weight but they are often at an unhealthy high weight, and they are at risk for gaining weight if binge eating continues.

A nonspecific diagnosis, *eating disorder not otherwise specified,* can be given to any eating pattern that is distressing and impairs quality of life. Many experts question the usefulness of having the specific eating disorder diagnoses since eating disorder not otherwise specified is the most common diagnosis that is given. Individuals frequently maintain significant levels of distress and disordered eating over long periods of time and their diagnosis may change from one to another. For example, at sixteen a young woman loses significant weight and is diagnosed with anorexia nervosa. With treatment she regains a healthy weight, but starts purging occasionally, when she fears weight gain. By nineteen she meets criteria for bulimia nervosa. She eventually stops purging but remains highly preoccupied with what she eats, eats a very restricted range of foods, and exercises excessively. She no longer meets criteria for a specific eating disorder, but she doesn't feel fully recovered. At age thirty-five, difficulty losing weight after the birth of her second child retriggers restrictive dieting and binge eating, which escalates to the point that she meets the criteria for binge eating disorder.

WHAT ARE YOUR PROBLEMATIC EATING BEHAVIORS?

Use this section to identify the specific eating behaviors that you want to change.

Overeating

How many days per week do you *feel* like you overeat? _____

You may feel as if you have overeaten because you get stuffed, because you have eaten more than you usually eat, or because you have eaten more than you planned to eat.

How often do you have more than one episode of overeating in a single day? _____

How many of your overeating episodes involve objectively large amounts? _____

"Objectively large" means clearly larger than most people would eat in a similar situation. Second helpings, two servings of dessert, or two candy bars are amounts that are quite commonly eaten and are not considered objectively large. Very tall or very active people may eat even more than two servings without considering the amount to be objectively large.

Binge Eating

How often per week do you feel like you lose control while you are eating? _____

How many of those episodes would you estimate involve objectively large amounts? _____

A binge is technically defined by the experience of loss of control at some point while you are eating. A binge does not mean you just feel guilty or ashamed after you overeat; it is more useful if you call that post-eating regret. Loss of control means you want to stop, but you can't make yourself stop. You only stop because the food is gone, your stomach hurts, someone interrupts you, you are able to fall asleep, or you have to leave the situation. Some people feel this loss of control only when they eat objectively large amounts. Other people feel loss of control after normal, or even small, amounts of forbidden foods.

Compensatory Behaviors

How many days per week do you use some type of unhealthy restriction to minimize your caloric intake? _____

How often do you use each of the following strategies?

- Skip meals _____

- Excessive restriction (eat less than 1,000 calories in a day) _____

- Fast (go without eating for eight hours or more) _____

- Take appetite suppressants _____

- Chew and spit out food without swallowing _____

How many days per week do you use unhealthy strategies to prevent calories from being absorbed, reduce water weight, or expend extra calories?

- Exercise excessively _____

- Purge (self-induced vomiting, laxatives) _____

- Diuretic pills/teas/foods _____

These strategies are typically called *compensatory behaviors* because many women use them to compensate for a specific binge or episode of overeating. However, some women do use these strategies as a deliberate way to maintain an unhealthy weight even when they do not believe they have overeaten.

You may have difficulty determining the point at which your exercise should be considered excessive. Do not try to fool yourself into considering exercise appropriate just because you are also doing it for reasons unrelated to weight, such as training for a marathon. Other reasons can be used to justify very intense exercise and mask this problem. Excessive exercise is characterized by doing more than is required for a reasonable training program; not being able to take days off for vacations or when you are ill or need to recover from injuries; or exercise that is done specifically in response to an episode of eating.

ARE YOU OVERWEIGHT?

Overweight is defined by medical standards that indicate the weight at which health risks start to be detected when a large number of people are evaluated. These figures are only estimates for any specific individual. Your doctor can help you determine if you have additional risk factors that you need to consider in deciding what is a healthy weight range for you. The range of BMI used to denote overweight is 25 to 30, and the higher risk category (obesity) is a BMI above 30. However, BMI is only one indicator of an individual's health risk. An individual with a higher BMI who is more muscular may be at less risk than a person with a lower BMI who is less fit.

It is more accurate (and more helpful) to ask whether or not you are over the healthiest weight you could be rather than simply whether or not you are overweight. After all, the question might be rephrased, "Over what weight?" Thus, I refer to the entire healthy weight range as normal weight. Overweight is above that range. I ask you to refrain from referring to yourself as overweight when you simply mean that you feel fat or you weigh more than you want to weigh. While the latter may be true, using the word "overweight" when you are not, in fact, over the normal weight range is quite detrimental. This term triggers negative emotions, which actually make it harder for you to attain your weight goal. You need to say, "I'm in the normal weight range" if that is correct. If you feel compelled to qualify this statement, you can say you are in the high normal range and you can say, "I'd prefer to weigh less." If you are above that range (overweight), simply say, "I'd like to be at a healthier weight." Never say, "I'm fat." Self-criticism is not an effective way to motivate yourself to lose weight. Punishment strategies only work when someone else controls the important negative consequences (like time-outs, fines, or prison terms). Trying to punish yourself backfires when it comes to weight control.

Current thinking, as expressed by leaders of the "Health at Every Size" movement, encourages individuals to focus their efforts on reducing health risks by becoming more physically fit rather than simply attempting to lose weight (Campos 2004; Gaesser 2002). These experts point out that the health risks, particularly those associated with moderate overweight, appear to have been somewhat exaggerated. Regardless of your weight, shifting your focus to achieving a healthier rather than a more culturally desirable weight will help you maintain a better perspective while you work toward your goal.

JUDGING YOUR WEIGHT BASED ON THE BMI

On the next page is the same BMI chart you first looked at in chapter 1.

Figure 3.1:   Body Mass Index

HT	90	95	100	105	110	115	120	125	130	135	140	145	150	155	160	165	170	175	180	185	190	195	200	205	210	215	220	225	230	235	240	245	250
5'0"	18	19	20	21	21	22	23	24	25	26	27	28	29	30	31	32	33	34	35	36	37	38	39	40	41	42	43	44	45	46	47	48	49
5'1"	17	18	19	20	21	22	23	24	25	26	26	27	28	29	30	31	32	33	34	35	36	37	38	39	40	41	42	43	43	44	45	46	47
5'2"	16	17	18	19	20	21	22	23	24	25	26	27	27	28	29	30	31	32	33	34	35	36	37	37	38	39	40	41	42	43	44	45	46
5'3"	16	17	18	19	19	20	21	22	23	24	25	26	27	27	28	29	30	31	32	33	34	35	35	36	37	38	39	40	41	42	43	43	44
5'4"	15	16	17	18	19	20	21	21	22	23	24	25	26	27	27	28	29	30	31	32	33	33	34	35	36	37	38	39	39	40	41	42	43
5'5"	15	16	17	17	18	19	20	21	22	22	23	24	25	26	27	27	28	29	30	31	32	32	33	34	35	36	37	37	38	39	40	41	42
5'6"	15	15	16	17	18	19	19	20	21	22	23	23	24	25	26	27	27	28	29	30	31	31	32	33	34	35	36	36	37	38	39	40	40
5'7"		15	16	16	17	18	19	20	20	21	22	23	23	24	25	26	27	27	28	29	30	31	31	32	33	34	34	35	36	37	38	38	39
5'8"			15	16	17	17	18	19	20	21	21	22	23	24	24	25	26	27	27	28	29	30	30	31	32	33	33	34	35	36	36	37	38
5'9"			15	16	16	17	18	18	19	20	21	21	22	23	24	24	25	26	27	27	28	29	30	30	31	32	32	33	34	35	35	36	37
5'10"				15	16	17	17	18	19	19	20	21	22	22	23	24	24	25	26	27	27	28	29	29	30	31	32	32	33	34	34	35	36
5'11"				15	15	16	17	17	18	19	20	20	21	22	22	23	24	24	25	26	27	27	28	29	29	30	31	31	32	33	33	34	35
6'0"					15	16	16	17	18	18	19	20	20	21	22	22	23	24	24	25	26	26	27	28	28	29	30	31	31	32	33	33	34
6'1"					15	15	16	16	17	18	18	19	20	20	21	22	22	23	24	24	25	26	26	27	28	28	29	30	30	31	32	32	33
6'2"						15	15	16	17	17	18	19	19	20	21	21	22	22	23	24	24	25	26	26	27	28	28	29	30	30	31	31	32
6'3"							15	16	16	17	18	18	19	19	20	21	21	22	23	23	24	24	25	26	26	27	28	28	29	29	30	31	31
6'4"							15	15	16	16	17	18	18	19	19	20	21	21	22	23	23	24	24	25	26	26	27	27	28	29	29	30	30

BMI Category

Below 18—At risk for anorexia
19 to 24—Normal weight
25 to 30—Overweight
Over 30—Obese

Use the BMI chart to answer these questions about your weight:

Based on my BMI, I am:

_____ Below the normal (healthiest) range

_____ In the normal (healthiest) range

_____ Above the normal range (possibly unhealthy)

_____ Above the normal range and I know that I personally have the following health problems that are related to my weight _____

A healthy weight range for my height is _____ .

I consider _____ an acceptable weight range for me.

If you are underweight, are you under pressure to gain weight? _____

If underweight, what is a target weight that you could potentially accept? _____

How distressed do you feel about your current weight?

_____ Occasionally distressed

_____ Frequently distressed

_____ Distressed most of the time

_____ So distressed I often avoid people and activities I might enjoy

What makes it hard for you to accept your current weight? _____

_____

_____

Circle an answer to each of the following questions:

How much of the pressure to lose (or gain) weight comes from you?

None   A little   Moderate   A lot   All of it

How much of the pressure to lose (or gain) weight comes from others in general?

None   A little   Moderate   A lot   All of it

Who are the specific individuals who pressure you in ways that are not helpful? _____

How often do you fear that you will gain weight if you mostly eat what you want to eat?

None   A little   Moderate   A lot   All the time

ARE YOU DISTRESSED BY YOUR THOUGHTS AND FEELINGS ABOUT EATING?

There are many different ways to assess problematic thoughts and feelings, but for our purposes I would like for you to focus on the following three aspects: preoccupation, deprivation, and effort.

Preoccupation

The following questions from the Preoccupation with Eating and Weight Scale (Niemeier et al. 2002) were developed by my research group as a quick way to assess the degree to which thoughts about food create problems for people. Compare your answers to the following norms to help you decide if preoccupation is a significant problem for you. Women without clinically significant weight concerns report thinking about food/eating about 25 percent of the day while women diagnosed with bulimia report thinking about food/eating 50 to 100 percent of the day, and women diagnosed with binge eating disorder typically report thinking about food/eating about 40 to 80 percent of the day. AAT is designed to reduce the frequency of and the distress related to thoughts about food and eating. However, most women find the frequency of their negative thoughts about weight also decreases. When you are convinced that you are doing the very best that you can to attain (or maintain) a reasonable weight, it is a little easier to accept your current weight. When you also realize that dwelling on your current weight only makes it harder to achieve your goal, it is easier to shift your focus to achieving a life worth living rather than attaining a specific weight. If you continue to have very negative feelings about your weight after you have completed this program, it is best to consult a professional to help you challenge the importance that you put on weight as a measure of your worth.

On average, what percentage of the waking day do you spend thinking about food (what you are going to eat, what you are going to keep yourself from eating, or what you have already eaten), calories, fat content of foods, or not being able to eat the foods you want? Place a mark on the line giving your best estimate.

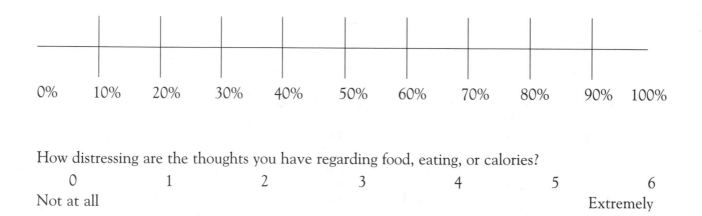

How distressing are the thoughts you have regarding food, eating, or calories?

0	1	2	3	4	5	6
Not at all						Extremely

Once you start having thoughts about food, eating, or calories, how hard is it for you to stop thinking them?

0	1	2	3	4	5	6
Not at all						Extremely

How much do these thoughts interfere with your ability to concentrate on other things?

0	1	2	3	4	5	6
Not at all						Extremely

Deprivation

How frequently and how intensely do you feel deprived, meaning that you feel upset or angry that you can't eat what you want to be eating or resent others who seem to be able to eat what they please?

1	2	3	4	5
Rarely feel deprived	Sometimes	Frequently	Frequently and can be intense	At some level virtually all the time

Effort

How much effort is it taking you to control your eating?

_____ Not more effort than most people

_____ Takes a lot more effort than for other people, but at least I maintain a weight acceptable to me

_____ Takes a lot of effort and I still can't maintain a normal weight range

---

DO YOU HAVE OTHER LIFE PROBLEMS IN ADDITION TO EATING CONCERNS?

Eating and weight concerns can make you depressed and anxious and can damage significant relationships in your life, reducing your social support and your opportunities for fun and intimacy. Consider the following three ways that your eating concerns may be making other problems in your life worse.

Describe any tension or conflict with others that you notice is related to your efforts to manage your eating and weight. _____

_____

_____

_____

_____

Describe any activities or people whom you avoid at times because you are feeling badly about your weight or because you are not willing to be around tempting foods. _____

_____

_____

_____

_____

Describe any activities you value that you have given up in order to have time to manage your weight. Also describe any activities in which your performance has suffered (for example schoolwork, job performance, hobbies, or athletics) due to the time you devote to weight management.

_____

_____

_____

_____

Imagine how your life would be different if you were able to make eating decisions quickly, feel okay about what you eat, and accept your current weight while you continue to work toward a healthier or more desirable weight. What would you start doing with the extra time and energy you would have? _____

_____

_____

_____

_____

While eating and weight concerns usually make other life problems worse, other life problems can also make it more difficult for you to change how you eat. As I will discuss later on,

AAT is designed to be used while you work to resolve other life problems. However, if those problems are too severe or if you are in crisis, you must consider whether or not this is the right time to put your energy into modifying your eating patterns. If you are experiencing an intense difficulty that you expect to be resolved soon, you will probably do better to wait until you can devote more attention to implementing AAT. In AAT, you are training your attention, so initially it takes quite a bit of effort. If your other life difficulties are chronic issues that are not likely to be resolved soon, there is no reason to wait. A better time to start may never come, and AAT may make you feel better so you can handle those other problems better. If you do have significant, ongoing life difficulties, these may limit how much effort you can devote to AAT, so be patient. Your progress may be a little slower than you would like or be slower than others. However, I see many women who are able to recover from disordered eating despite having significant, ongoing life difficulties.

What life difficulties besides your eating are you currently dealing with? _____

_____

_____

_____

Describe how you anticipate these may interfere with your commitment to do self-monitoring and use AAT strategies to change how you eat. _____

_____

_____

_____

Is this the right time for you to start AAT? _____

WHAT IS YOUR MOTIVATION TO GIVE UP DISORDERED EATING NOW?

It may be quite difficult to answer the question asked above. You may know when and why you started worrying about your weight, but it may be less obvious to you why you continue to have such difficulty with your eating. You may not be able to identify what binge eating (or restriction) is currently doing for you. What is making it so difficult for you to give up the current strategies that are not working for you? Consider two possibilities.

The obvious possibility is that you get some short-term needs met by your unhealthy eating behaviors. The AAT model provided in chapter 2 helps you identify some of the positive consequences of binge eating and overeating. You get to enjoy the pleasure of good taste. You may get some attention from your partner or friends, because they worry about your health or feel bad when you are upset about your weight. Or, with restriction, you get to feel thin and in control.

What are some of the positive consequences you might have to give up if you stop disordered eating? _____

_____

_____

_____

The not so obvious possibility is that dwelling on eating and weight helps you avoid facing other, more upsetting or more difficult issues. Your eating or weight concerns may help you avoid complex issues such as dealing with an unsatisfying relationship, a frustrating job, or your fear of going back into the workplace.

What issues do you think you might be avoiding by dwelling on eating and weight? _____

_____

_____

_____

If you have trouble figuring out these answers, just leave the spaces blank. AAT does not require that you understand why you are eating in a problematic manner in order to start changing how you make decisions about eating. As you practice AAT, you will become aware of issues that interfere with your progress. As you stop relying on eating (or not eating) as a way to cope with uncomfortable feelings, you will be able to see more clearly what disordered eating has been doing for you and why it has been too hard to stop your patterns even though they also distress you greatly.

WHAT ARE YOUR IMMEDIATE AND LONG-TERM GOALS?

In this last section, I ask you to establish your own personal goals. If you engage in any *unhealthy eating behaviors*, I recommend that reducing these be your first priority. You will have an easier time changing your *negative thoughts and feelings* about eating and weight once you are eating normally. However, you may feel ambivalent about changing some of your unhealthy eating behaviors. Women usually want to lose weight and stop obsessing about food, but they are often less ready to stop restricting or compensating. I wish it were possible to just help you lose weight or stop thinking about food, but the hard truth is that you will have to change your eating behaviors first. You cannot change your weight or your emotions directly. But you can commit to changing your eating behaviors and you can learn to challenge your unhelpful thoughts. Making those changes is the way to create the changes you want in other areas.

Give the following questions careful thought. What are your long-term goals? What are the real reasons you want to be healthier, think about eating less often, or to lose weight? The latter are immediate, short-term goals. They are better considered a means to an end. What is the end goal you are striving for? A satisfying intimate relationship? A more active social life? Higher self-esteem? Being a healthy model for your own daughter? Being healthy enough to enjoy your retirement and play with your grandchildren?

I want to eat normally because _____

_____

_____

_____

It is important to keep these long-term goals in mind as you work through this program, because they provide the motivation you need to make the difficult changes in your behavior.

HOW TO USE THE REST OF THIS WORKBOOK

Your immediate goals, the eating and weight problems you identified earlier in this chapter, will determine how you should use the remaining chapters in this workbook. Go back and look at your answers. Use that information to decide on the eating behaviors you want to change. Then answer the following questions:

My single most important eating goal is to _____

_____

_____

_____

I will feel comfortable to move on to my next eating goal when I _____

_____

_____

_____

My secondary goals are to _____

_____

_____

_____

You will do best and feel most successful if you focus your attention on achieving one goal at a time. You are likely to make some progress on your secondary goals while you are working toward the most important one, but don't let your attention be distracted from your most important goal.

If your most important goal is to stop binge eating, go to chapter 4 and continue through chapter 8. At that point, if you are satisfied with your progress go to chapter 9, which shows you how to switch to mental monitoring and maintain normal eating for the rest of your life. If you have essentially eliminated binges and would now like to try additional, more deliberate weight loss strategies, skip chapter 9 and go to appendix C. Go back to chapter 9 whenever you are ready to work on weight maintenance.

If your most important goal is to lose weight and you do not binge or use unhealthy compensatory behaviors, start with the exercises in chapter 4 and continue through chapter 8. Since you don't have a problem with binges, you will just be applying the AAT strategies to reduce the size and frequency of episodes of overeating. Once you eat normally most of the time, you are ready to go to appendix C and try out the additional strategies designed to enhance weight loss.

If your most important goal is to stop using compensatory behaviors, read appendix A first. You will need to make copies of the monitoring form in appendix A and use those forms as you work through the exercises in chapters 6 through 8. Chapter 6 will be most helpful if you have large binges. However, if you rarely overeat and you purge primarily after normal to small amounts of food, chapter 8, which addresses altering the types of food you eat, will probably be more relevant. Go to chapter 9 for maintenance strategies once you have essentially eliminated unhealthy compensatory behaviors. I do not recommend that you attempt the specific weight loss strategies in appendix C, because you are particularly vulnerable to retriggering the binge-purge cycle, and you are probably in the normal weight range already. Eating normally and seeing what happens with your weight will better serve you. You need to concentrate on increasing body acceptance rather than achieving a lower weight.

If your most important goal is to reduce preoccupation with thoughts about eating and weight, go to appendix B. The behavior you need to change is excessive restriction. Restriction is difficult to monitor since it is the absence of eating behavior. Thus, the monitoring form in appendix B is designed to help you become more aware of the times you deliberately ignore your hunger and to start identifying the unhelpful thoughts and emotions that make you want to restrict. If you need to gain weight to become healthier, this appendix also shows you how to do so while coping with your fears about weight gain. When you feel ready to switch to mental monitoring, go to chapter 9.

WILL YOU RECOVER FROM DISORDERED EATING?

It is useful for you to identify the ways you will know when you can consider yourself essentially recovered from disordered eating. Don't be a perfectionist and say, "I'll never worry about weight again." Think carefully about what specific changes would allow you to feel that your eating and weight concerns are not significantly different from those of most of your peers. Would it be fewer binges, lower preoccupation with food, or a more reasonable body image? I use the term essentially recovered, because you should not expect your concerns about eating and weight to disappear completely. Given current social pressures, you can expect to have some difficult moments when you get upset about what you eat. You will be tempted to embark on yet another strict diet that you know all too well will set you up for a binge. You will have some relapses. Many times, you will have to deliberately refocus in order to return to the normal eating path. Nonetheless, just as one young woman describes in chapter 9, you can emerge from the maze of disordered eating and be free to put your energy into making a life worth living.

I will know that I am essentially recovered when I _____

_____

_____

_____

THE KIND OF CHANGES YOU CAN EXPECT

Everyone experiences AAT a little differently. Some people take longer than others to tune back into their internal signals. Initially, appetite monitoring feels artificial, but the longer you do it, the more natural the process becomes. As it becomes automatic, you move on to self-coaching. Most people continue to improve the longer they deliberately self-coach. After more than ten years of coaching myself, I still learn new information about how I respond to various foods and I continue to get more comfortable following my own personal guidelines about eating no matter what food is presented or how other people around me are eating. What follows are the stories of the changes two women experienced as a result of AAT.

Glenda's Story
(as told by her therapist, Caroline Aibel, Ph.D.)

Glenda was a forty-five-year-old divorced woman who had two grown children who lived out of state. When she volunteered for a research study evaluating AAT, Glenda reported binge eating episodes three to five times a week without compensatory behaviors. She would also overeat at other times and generally felt out of control around food. Glenda confided that she felt extremely bad about herself, about her lack of control, about her weight, and about her physical health. She did not have supportive social relationships and usually ate alone.

Glenda described her mother as a perfectionist who was not very nurturing and her father as abusive. She was one of five children and reported that her family had a "fend for yourself" mentality. She recalled being teased by her siblings about being fat, although in retrospect Glenda didn't believe she really was fat at that time. However, Glenda felt ashamed about her weight and began eating in secret to hide what she ate. She remembers having definite binge episodes (feeling out of control) starting around the age of twelve.

Glenda had tried many programs that addressed healthier eating and weight loss, but she had never been able to stick with them long enough to lose much weight. She explained that recording her food intake felt awful, particularly when she binged, so she usually wouldn't do it. She was extremely relieved to find out that AAT did not require her to write down what she ate.

After seeing the AAT model, Glenda was able to identify that she was often not aware when she was hungry, and that she was often quite hungry when she started eating. She also recognized that she ate for emotional reasons; often, she knew she wasn't actually hungry. She would ignore fullness deliberately because food was one of her few indulgences, and then experience the what the heck response and continue until she ran out of food or couldn't eat any more. Glenda reported that she was usually "starving or stuffed."

When the appetite monitoring forms were explained, Glenda seemed skeptical that she would be able to gauge her appetite but also excited to try a new way of thinking about eating. The first week Glenda returned with her forms filled out correctly and completely. Curiously, despite having initially said she was always starving or stuffed, almost all her ratings were near neutral. It was clear that Glenda was not aware of her own internal sensations; she did not know what it felt like to be hungry or full unless she really was starving or stuffed. Glenda reported four binge episodes the first week. By examining the binges, Glenda was able to more clearly see her tendency to ignore hunger, eat for emotional reasons (confusing emotions with hunger), and eat by rules that left her feeling deprived. Her goal for the following week was to pay more attention to her internal sensations, particularly stomach fullness.

Over the next few sessions, Glenda found herself increasingly able to distinguish between different gradations of hunger and fullness, and to distinguish between feeling physically hungry and wanting to eat for emotional reasons. Her bingeing decreased in frequency and in the amount of food consumed. She now binged just once or twice a week and was usually able to cut the binge short (she would eat a half a pan of brownies rather than the whole pan). In becoming more attuned to her internal states, Glenda was able to talk about the guilt and shame she experienced about feeding herself. As Glenda began to better understand her relationship with food, appetite, and the way feeling deprived was related to her childhood abuse experiences, she started being able to limit eating to scheduled meals and snacks and times when she truly felt hungry. Between the sixth and fourteenth week of treatment, Glenda only had two binges, and by the fourteenth week she was binge free.

Glenda had always exercised moderately, usually by walking. Around week ten, she decided to increase the intensity of her exercise so that she would not have to rely so heavily on reducing her intake in order to start weight loss. She first increased the strenuousness of her walking; then she added some weight training. To enlist more social support for exercising, Glenda started walking with a friend once a week and signed up for a Pilates class.

As Glenda stopped using food as the only way to comfort herself, she noticed how isolated she had become and realized that feeling alone and not connected to other people was a significant trigger for eating. By week thirteen, Glenda was willing to start working on reaching out to create more meaningful relationships. Feeling better about herself now that she had her eating under control, Glenda found that interacting socially was easier and more rewarding than it had been in the past. Her therapist encouraged Glenda to find other ways to fill the space that food and binge eating had previously occupied in her life. Glenda decided to reengage with her creative side by attending Ikebana classes (Japanese flower arranging). These classes had the added bonus of fostering some new friendships.

Glenda transitioned from written monitoring to mental monitoring around week fifteen. By the end of treatment (after twenty-four weeks), Glenda reported occasional overeating but no binges, and she had lost a modest amount of weight. She was pleased and surprised that she could "eat like a normal person and not gain weight." She knew that the key to preventing relapse (for her) was to stay conscious of her body's response to food and to stay connected to other people. As part of her relapse plan, Glenda agreed that should she end up bingeing, she would analyze the situation right away, write down the emotions that were involved, and commit to eating normally at her next scheduled mealtime. Glenda reported feeling confident in her ability to remain binge free.

Glenda decided that, with her history, she would be too vulnerable to feelings of deprivation if she tried even a moderate weight loss diet, so she decided she would just continue eating normally and continue with her exercise program and see if she would gradually lose a bit more weight.

Karen's Story (as told by her therapist, Lara Ray, MA)

Karen was a twenty-five-year-old woman who came to the clinic saying she had eating concerns and generally wasn't happy with her life. She had recently moved to the area, and in her efforts to establish a new set of friends, found herself frequently drinking more than she intended and getting involved in more sexual activity than she intended. Bingeing and overeating had been an issue for her since she was ten years old. She hid food from her parents and later from her roommates. When she binged, she ate large amounts of "forbidden" foods. She remembered at least five episodes when she had eaten so much she had become physically sick and ended up vomiting, although she denied intentionally doing so. For the past two years she reported bingeing two to three times a week. She restricted during the week, so she had been able to keep her weight in the high normal range. She was most likely to binge eat after she had been drinking, as her inhibitions were generally lower. She reported that when her eating was out of control, her life felt out of control as well.

Karen wanted to work first on her problems with eating. She agreed that the AAT model might work for her because she "had a lot of unsuccessful experiences with dieting and she had a tendency to get a little obsessive when asked to count calories." For the first three weeks Karen had difficulty getting herself to complete the written forms even though she liked the idea of tuning back into her internal signals. She began to see that her difficulty with doing the forms was similar to a more general difficulty she had with making a plan and sticking to it. In the moment, she usually "went with her feelings" and often ended up regretting things she had done (or had put off).

For several weeks, Karen worked on following through on commitments. As she was able to monitor more of the time, she started feeling more in control of her eating and was then more motivated to continue monitoring For the next six weeks she continued to monitor, paying particular attention to the what the heck response that triggered most of her binges. She identified the excuses that she used in the moment to give herself permission to go ahead and eat more (or binge), and she learned to challenge those excuses.

By the end of twelve sessions, Karen had established a regular schedule of meals, which reduced her problems with getting too hungry. She eliminated binges by making conscious decisions to eat when she knew she would feel deprived if she refused to have what she wanted. At this point, she phased out the written forms. She began coming in every two weeks and established a relapse prevention plan. By the time she terminated therapy, Karen had not had a binge episode in over two months. She had recently experienced some distress related to a romantic relationship that was not going well, but she was happy to report that the distress did not lead to emotional eating. She had also just accepted a new job and felt like her life was generally going well. She was still surprised that she had been able to change her eating so much in such a short period of time since she had had problems with food for so long. She attributed her success this time to thinking about food and eating in a different way—she focused on what she wanted to eat and what really felt good after she ate it, not about what she could or couldn't have. In the past, she would start feeling deprived when she tried to diet, which just made her feel rebellious and triggered more binges.

Discover Your
Stomach Signals

As you know, the goal of AAT is to rely primarily on internal appetite cues (hunger and fullness) to regulate eating. Appetite-based eating is a positive and effective way to stop binge eating, reduce your preoccupation with food, and maintain a stable weight. But how do you get started? Unfortunately, just telling yourself to eat when you are hungry and stop when you are full is not that helpful. AAT provides a new tool that teaches you how to eat this way: *appetite monitoring*. This means you write down how hungry you feel before you start eating and how full you are when you stop eating. Appetite monitoring is quite different from food monitoring, which many of you have already tried, either as part of an intervention or on your own. Writing down everything you eat can be helpful, and it is the most widely used weight-loss strategy. However, I have found that appetite monitoring is a more effective way to get you to focus on what is really important—what is happening inside when you eat—instead of focusing on what foods you should or shouldn't eat. When you first try to monitor your appetite signals, you may feel uncomfortable. People are not used to thinking about eating in this way. At first, many people think that they can't do appetite monitoring or that they aren't doing it right. However, appetite ratings are based on how you feel, so however you rate your feelings is the right way. You can't do it wrong. Within a couple of weeks, you will feel confident about making these ratings and be on your way to normal eating.

Many therapists and counselors believe that you must first figure out why you are eating too much (or eating when you aren't even hungry) before you can change the way you eat. I agree that disordered eating is not just about food, but it is about the process of eating. Thus, AAT takes the opposite approach. First, you learn a new strategy for making decisions about eating. You get started on the normal eating path, regardless of why you have been having difficulties with food. Then, each time you get sidetracked from the normal path, you identify what happened and how to get back on track the very next time you eat. If you have been tuning out your appetite signals in order to diet or binge, appetite monitoring helps you rediscover your internal cues. If you are already aware of your appetite signals but you find it hard to follow them, appetite monitoring provides clear, positive prompts that encourage you to challenge the unhelpful thoughts and excuses you use to rationalize disregarding those cues.

WHY YOU MUST MONITOR YOUR APPETITE

You may ask why you need to use written monitoring to get on the normal eating path. You probably think, "I can just read the book. I get the basic idea, so I'll just start doing it." Some people can do that, but most people need a bit more help. When you first understand why you are doing something, especially something that isn't working well for you, psychologists say you have developed *insight*. Insight helps motivate you to make the changes you need to make. However, insight often isn't enough. Many people know why they binge or overeat and know how they should be eating, but they are still not able to change their patterns.

Appetite monitoring gives you a specific method, a tool to help you change how you eat. It focuses your attention on each episode of eating in your day in a new way. People usually focus on the food they eat—mostly on the taste or the calories of the food. Appetite monitoring draws your attention to what makes you start and stop eating, not what you choose to eat. If you learn how to start and stop eating effectively, you can cope with any kind of food that is put in front of you. You have a strategy for deciding if and how much you are going to eat. At first, you must rate hunger and fullness on paper to ensure you are paying attention to your internal experiences. Once responding to your appetite cues becomes automatic, you will be able to phase out the written ratings and just do them in your mind.

Appetite monitoring feels quite different from food monitoring. If you stick with it for a few weeks, you will be surprised how much it changes the way you think and feel about eating. At first, I purposefully ask you not to write down what you eat, because I want you to focus all your attention on how your stomach feels. Some people have very negative reactions to writing down the foods they eat. It is okay if you don't ever want to monitor the foods you eat. However, AAT gives you the option of adding some food monitoring later on if you find it necessary to lose weight. AAT just doesn't rely on food monitoring as a central component of the program.

Understanding the principles of AAT is important. You need to understand why it is such a good idea to eat according to your appetite cues. But understanding is not enough to get you to do it. Take a deep breath and make a commitment right now to do the self-monitoring exercises in this workbook. You must use written monitoring for at least four weeks. At that point, some people are ready to switch to mental monitoring. However, many people need to do written monitoring much longer, especially if they decide to do the weight loss part of the program. Commit to four weeks. It is the minimum for effective results. After that you can decide for yourself if you wish to continue written monitoring or monitor mentally.

INTERNAL AND EXTERNAL CUES THAT CONTROL EATING

Before we move into the appetite monitoring portion of this chapter, I would like to give you some information about why people generally start and stop eating, what hunger is, and how AAT approaches hunger. Let's start by explaining appetite cues. Many cues influence your decisions to start and stop eating. Table 4.1 provides examples of common cues that influence eating.

Table 4.1: Eating Cues			
	Internal appetite-related cues	**Internal cues not related to appetite**	**External cues**
Cues to restrict	Prefer feeling hungry or empty Dislike feeling full	Thoughts/feelings about eating or weight: ■ feel fat/bad ■ fear weight gain ■ need to feel powerful or in control ■ rules about forbidden foods	Weight/shape reminders: ■ social comments ■ clothes feel tight ■ trying on clothes ■ comparing yourself to others ■ thin ideal in media
Cues to start eating	Feeling hungry	Feeling deprived Cravings Desire (urge) to eat Thoughts about enjoying, or deserving food	Regular mealtime Food available Food talk or pictures Situations or activities associated with eating Social prompts or pressure
Cues to stop eating	Feeling full	■ Rules about how much food is appropriate or allowed ■ Feeling satisfied; don't want any more	Serving size/ packaging No more food available Leave the situation Social norms or concerns about what others are thinking

External cues are signals that occur in your environment. The most common external cues are food, people, places, and advertising. An external cue, like walking past a candy jar, may directly trigger an urge to eat—you may pick up the candy without thinking much about it. More often, however, an external cue triggers a thought or feeling (for example, "I want that candy") that triggers an urge to eat. *Internal cues* are signals that come from within you. The most common internal cues are thoughts, rules, beliefs, feelings, and physical sensations. Many of these cues do not encourage a moderate, healthy eating pattern, but some can be helpful.

AAT is based on the idea that *internal appetite-based* cues (hunger and fullness) are particularly dependable guides to eating in a way that is healthy and feels normal. Internal cues not related to appetite are not typically helpful; these cues either encourage you to overeat or they encourage you to restrict when you are actually hungry. External cues are not based on your appetite. However, some external cues are helpful because they encourage you to eat in a way that supports your internal appetite-based cues. For example, scheduled mealtimes keep you from getting too hungry, and individual serving packaging encourages you to stop eating at the end of a serving. When you use internal appetite-based signals in conjunction with helpful external cues, you will be protected from many of the cues that encourage you to restrict and to overeat.

TANK B AND TANK P

The experience of hunger is tricky. When you feel hungry, you may or may not have a biological need for food. You may know that you aren't truly hungry, but you still want to eat. Anita Johnson (1996) developed the following metaphor to explain how hunger can trick you. Your body operates as if you are a car with two gas tanks. Tank B (biological hunger) is the tank for nourishing your physical body. It needs to be filled with food. Tank P (psychological hunger) is the tank for nourishing your spirit. Food doesn't fill Tank P, so you don't feel satisfied even if you eat. Hunger signals coming from Tank P indicate that you have psychological needs that aren't being adequately met.

When you can't tell the difference between biological and psychological hunger, you are likely to try to satisfy psychological hungers with food. Eating is an easier and simpler solution than trying to meet complicated psychological needs. Food may temporarily mask the discomfort of unmet psychological needs, but it takes a lot of food to silence a psychological hunger signal. Since no amount of food really fills Tank P, you are likely to feel "hungry" again soon no matter how much you eat.

AAT increases your awareness of the physical sensations associated with biological hunger, so you get better at recognizing when your desire to eat is primarily psychological. When Tank B is empty, this is true hunger. This signal appropriately tells you to eat. When Tank P is empty, you get a *false hunger signal.* Using food to meet other needs is not very effective; it doesn't change anything that is going on in your life. To boot, if you eat too much you become overweight, which just adds another problem to your life.

HUNGER AS AN ALARM SYSTEM

The experience of hunger can still be tricky even when you are biologically hungry. Hunger is not your enemy, but it is a very powerful force. You have to understand how biological hunger works in order to manage it effectively. The easiest way to understand this phenomenon is to recognize that hunger is set up to work as an alarm system, not as an indicator of how much your body needs food. The first feelings of hunger serve as an early warning system—they are not very loud. I call this moderate hunger. When you ignore these early signals, they usually turn off for a while because your body knows that there is no urgency to obtain food. Long ago, this system was adaptive; it might take a while to obtain food, so early hunger signals were important. Now that people have easy access to food, this early signal is not really necessary. It's not surprising that people learn to ignore moderate hunger when they diet. It is quite possible to ignore your hunger for a while if you are sufficiently distracted. You may choose to wait until dinner, because you know that food will be available soon. However, if dinner is delayed, your hunger signal will eventually reappear. Your hunger signal gets stronger each time it returns until you have to eat in order to turn it off.

Some people learn to tune out their hunger signals so well that they are rarely aware of them. Psychologists describe this as *dissociation,* which means you have put something out of your conscious awareness. When you have been tuning out hunger, you may not feel very hungry even though your body needs nutrients. In other words, you can need food even when you don't feel very hungry. Once you start to eat, your attention is refocused on sensations associated with hunger, so you are likely to get back in touch with how hungry you are. People usually eat too fast and have trouble controlling the amount they eat when they are truly hungry. Your biological drive to eat kicks in once you start to eat, and this pressure makes it harder to maintain control and stop when you want. If you do eat more than you intended, you feel like you lost control; that feeling is very scary if you are worried about possible weight gain or you are trying very hard to lose weight.

As you may have experienced, if hunger is ignored too long, the signal eventually gives up and shuts off. This is also an adaptive biological response, because hunger is just a signal to look for food. You will get daily hunger signals even if you are overweight. However, if there is truly no food available or if you refuse to eat, the signal becomes useless; it may as well turn itself off. Interestingly, people have different responses to self-imposed fasts. Some people gorge when food is again available, while others have trouble eating and have to start with small amounts. It is not clear why people respond differently to breaking a fast, but if you do become underweight, your biological signals will eventually come on strong in an effort to encourage you to eat to restore any weight lost. This is one of the reasons that fasting is not an effective weight-loss strategy.

The fact that feelings of biological hunger can go away temporarily makes it even harder to distinguish true hunger from false alarms. When you refuse to respond to hunger signals, you eventually feel deprived. You can also trigger deprivation feelings by restricting types of food even if you consume adequate calories. Regardless of how it is triggered, a sense of deprivation is an emotion; it is one of the psychological hungers that can trigger false alarms. When you feel deprived, you keep thinking that you feel hungry. You must learn to respond differently to deprivation triggered by daily hunger (inadequate daily intake) or low weight (inadequate stores) than to deprivation triggered by restricting food type too severely or by restricting other (nonfood) pleasurable indulgences.

THE AAT WAY TO MANAGE HUNGER

Since it is difficult to judge your hunger, you need specific guidelines to manage hunger effectively. First, set up a regular eating schedule. A schedule is the best way to avoid triggering a false hunger alarm. For most people, the best schedule is three meals and two snacks at fairly equally spaced intervals during their waking hours. You may find that you need more or fewer scheduled eating times, but start with this pattern to see how your body responds. Some people are hungry in the morning and need to eat fairly soon after they get up. If they get up early, they may need a midmorning snack to make it until lunchtime. Other people don't feel hungry early or don't get up too early, so they may eat a late breakfast and not need a snack before lunch. Most people need a midafternoon snack—you don't want to be too hungry at dinnertime. If you stay up late, you may need to schedule an evening snack.

If you currently eat more than six times a day (a pattern called *grazing*), you will need to gradually reduce the number of times you eat. Call three of your episodes meals even if you prefer to use a mini-meal strategy (small meals and substantial snacks). If you currently eat less than three times a day, you need to increase the number of times you eat. If making this change is difficult, you don't have to do it all at once. You can change gradually, but it helps to get started right away. If you find it hard to eat breakfast, start with a very light breakfast and have a substantial midmorning snack.

You may need to adjust your schedule after you get back in touch with your hunger cues. When you start to eat less in the evening, you may become more aware of feeling hungry in the morning. Once you understand the difference between biological and psychological hunger, you may become aware that your need for an evening snack is mostly psychological, and you may be able to eliminate it some of the time. When you train your body to expect food at certain times, your hunger signaling system learns that it can depend on you to provide food at regular intervals without being prompted. You will then have fewer false hunger alarms and be better able to detect them when they occur.

Second, follow the *two-hour rule*. Each time you eat, eat enough so that you are not likely to be biologically hungry for at least two hours. For most people, this will be at least 200 calories. I don't want you to count calories, but it is important to understand that one piece of fruit is not an adequate snack. It will not keep you from being hungry for two hours. You need to eat enough that if you get an urge to eat within two hours, it will be clear that you are dealing with a false alarm. When you know your hunger is a false alarm, you will find it easier to decide to distract yourself and wait for the next scheduled time to eat.

Third, you need to rate your hunger every time you are about to make a decision to eat. Rating your hunger is the way to draw your attention to this signal. You need to learn to identify the early warning signal—moderate hunger. As you learn how your body responds to different amounts and types of food, you can better plan your eating schedule to avoid getting too hungry. Most importantly, rating your hunger makes you stop and decide if what you feel is biological hunger (Tank B) or is a false alarm (Tank P). People are usually surprised to find out how often they don't feel biologically hungry; they just have an urge to eat. Hopefully you will find that you get hungry at about the same time you have scheduled meals. If not, you will need to alter your scheduled eating pattern so it better matches your particular pattern of hunger. Right now, just learn to recognize and rate your hunger. Your job is to avoid getting too hungry before you eat. Later on, you will learn strategies to deal with cravings and urges to eat when you are not even moderately hungry.

Let Your Stomach Be Your Guide

You must commit to using stomach fullness as your cue to stop eating, because this cue is the clearest and most reliable. It will work no matter what you are eating. Moderate fullness is indicated by the first sign of stomach distention. It is a weak signal because it was designed so that it could be ignored when overeating might be useful.

You are moderately full when you first feel that your stomach pushes out or presses against your waistband. If you have trouble identifying this signal, you may find it helpful to put your hand on your stomach before you eat and check it several times as you eat. At first, the moderate fullness signal may be hard to detect, but virtually everyone we have trained learned to do so within a couple of weeks. Some people find it helpful to wear clothes that have a waistband. The pressure can be a helpful reminder of stomach distention. However, you will get to the point where you do not have to rely on a waistband. If you choose to do this, it is important not to wear a very tight waistband, as that may encourage you to eat too little. If you don't eat enough each time you eat, you may get too hungry before the next scheduled time to eat. You may have to eat too frequently. A grazing pattern creates its own set of problems.

When you listen more to your stomach and less to your mouth, you will find it easier to stop after moderate amounts of food. Your mouth is focused on taste, so you may end up feeling deprived if you don't eat as much as you want. Your stomach signal is based on fullness, not taste. Your stomach signal is the secret to eating less without feeling too deprived. You don't debate the issue or try to justify eating more. By using stomach signals, you take the decision to stop eating out of the psychological realm. If you focus on getting psychologically satisfied, anything less feels negative. When your goal is just to get full, you can feel good about stopping at moderate fullness.

When you stop at moderate fullness, you have usually eaten enough to keep you from getting too hungry before the next scheduled time to eat. You haven't eaten a lot, however, so you can't wait too long. You certainly can't skip meals. When you decide to use moderate fullness as your cue to stop eating, you have to be a bit more careful in order to avoid getting too hungry. In the past, you may have eaten only two or three large meals a day. When you are stopping at moderate fullness each time you eat, you may have to eat four or five times a day.

To detect moderate fullness, you have to pay attention while you are eating in order to notice as soon as you start to feel full. At first you may not be able to stop as soon as you notice moderate fullness. With practice, you will get better. Paying attention to your internal sensations while you eat is called *mindful eating*.

Mindless and Mindful Eating

Mindless eating is a problem because it adds calories without providing much pleasure or satisfaction. This is the easiest kind of eating to get rid of, because it doesn't have many positive consequences. You aren't getting much out of it. Thus, stop mindless eating before you try to stop the more difficult episodes such as emotional eating. The way to stop mindless eating is to eat mindfully. Eating mindfully means eating slowly and paying close attention to the taste of food in your mouth plus the feel of food in your stomach. Regardless of why you start eating, pay attention while you eat. By eating mindfully and monitoring fullness, you can prevent many eating episodes from turning into overeating episodes through ignoring fullness. Sometimes you may still ignore fullness deliberately because you are enjoying the taste, but you are less likely to eat as much food that you don't enjoy.

Use Your Stomach as a Stop Sign

Imagine there is a fairly obvious red stop sign in your neighborhood. However, there's a blind curve right before the sign, so the police have put up a warning sign before the curve that says "Stop Sign Ahead." They want to alert drivers who may be unfamiliar with the neighborhood and may fail to see the stop sign in time. After a while, you no longer pay any attention to the warning sign. Suppose the police stop patrolling this area and there is little traffic. Soon you don't bother to stop. Applying this analogy to eating, you no longer notice your moderate fullness signal. Often, you fail to stop even at the regular stop sign (clearly full). You usually stop when the food is gone although you might stop earlier if you get really full.

Appetite awareness training is designed to do two things. The first thing is to reinstate the importance of the stop sign. In essence, the police start patrolling the neighborhood, so you start stopping at the stop sign. You don't feel particularly negative about this since you used to stop at the stop sign all the time. You know there is a good reason to stop there; stopping may prevent an accident. You had just been getting away with not stopping before, and now you can't. To help you remember to stop, AAT also puts up a new, bright orange, very large warning sign. This is the moderate fullness signal. Now you pay attention and stop eating at this point as much of the time as you can. When you can't stop there, at least you stop at the regular stop sign (clearly full). You avoid getting uncomfortably full or stuffed.

WRITTEN APPETITE MONITORING

Consider how long you have been eating the way you do now. With any well-established habit, you need something to help break the automatic pattern. Fortunately, it won't take that long to learn a new way to eat. An external cue, one outside of your mind, is the most effective way to de-automatize your reactions. Written appetite monitoring will help you do just that. The external cue (your monitoring form) reminds you to attend to your internal cues. Later, when listening to your internal cues has become automatic, you can drop the external cue and rely solely on awareness of internal cues. Most people require at least four weeks of written monitoring to break old habits. Some people who have a long history of disordered eating or need to lose substantial weight need to do written monitoring for four to six months before they feel sufficiently confident to switch to purely mental monitoring. This chapter includes a sample monitoring form. As you work through the book, you'll need to make multiple copies of the blank forms and use the copies for self-monitoring. You can also download more forms from my Web site (http://psych.colorado. edu/~clinical/lcraighead/). Now, renew the commitment you made at the beginning of this chapter and follow the instructions below to start monitoring your appetite.

For the next week, pay close attention to your internal appetite cues every time you eat. In subsequent chapters I will ask you to add other information as you add other strategies to help you stay on the normal eating path. For now, just pay attention to your stomach sensations.

Your goal this first week is to stay on the normal eating path as much as you can. Try to eat so that all your ratings are in the gray area (not too hungry and not too full). However, you should not expect to be able to do this all the time just yet. Your first task is just to recognize the two key points: moderate hunger (2.5 on the 7-point scale) and moderate fullness (5.5 on the same scale). Don't worry if you have trouble deciding on your exact rating within the gray area. The difference between a 4 and a 4.5 is not important.

INSTRUCTIONS FOR MONITORING YOUR APPETITE

Start each day with a new page (circle the day of the week).

Before your meal or snack complete the following:

1. Record as a separate episode each instance of eating that involves a meaningful amount. You do not have to record water, diet drinks, gum, or other minimal amounts (like a few hard candies). Include drinks that have substantial calorie content, especially alcoholic drinks. Alcohol may be a trigger for loss of control.

2. Record the time you start eating.

3. Circle whether the episode was a meal (M) or a snack (S).

4. Mark an X on the line indicating how physically hungry you feel when you start eating. If you forgot or weren't able to record before you ate, just do it all afterwards.

After your meal or snack, complete the following:

1. Mark an X on the line to indicate how physically full you feel when you stop eating. Each line of the appetite scale (1 to 7) should now have two Xs on it. The N (4) stands for a neutral sensation—not hungry, but not feeling any sense of stomach fullness. You need to cross over N each time you eat so you get some sense of satisfaction even though you don't eat as much as you might want.

2. Put a stay by "Ate Mindfully" each time you remember to eat mindfully (slowly and enjoying the taste).

3. Start thinking of eating as occurring in clear episodes as a way to counter the tendency to graze. Grazing is the only way you can eat a lot more than you need but never feel overfull. Your goal is normal eating. Normal eating means eating at least three and, preferably, five times a day. If you eat more than five times, just write down any additional snacks at the bottom of the page.

4. In the "Feel" box, star "Pos" if you ended up feeling positive about what or how much you ate. Circle "Neutral" if you didn't have strong feelings. Circle "Neg" if you ended up feeling negative; write down how you felt (guilty, deprived, etc.). At times you may feel bad even if you do not overeat; explain why you feel negatively.

Normal eating means that your appetite ratings (Xs) are all in the gray area and you feel neutral or positive about each episode of eating.

Monitoring Your Appetite

Notes to Self:
Describe your physical sensations and explain negative feelings

Day: M T W Th F S Sun

Time
7:00

Ⓜ
S

Too Hungry — — X̲ _ _ _ X̲ _ _ N (3 4 5) **Ignored Fullness**
1 2 3 4 5 6 7
Ate Mindfully*

Feel
Pos*
Neutral
Neg

felt good--

no stomach distension

Time
12:00

Ⓜ
S

Too Hungry — _ X̲ _ _ _ X̲ _ _ N **Ignored Fullness**
1 2 3 4 5 6 7
Ate Mindfully

Feel
Pos
Neutral
(Neg)

ate chips--didn't plan to

wasn't too full but still

felt guilty

Time
4:00

M
Ⓢ

Too Hungry — _ _ _ X̲ _ X̲ _ _ N **Ignored Fullness**
1 2 3 4 5 6 7
Ate Mindfully

Feel
Pos
Neutral
(Neg)

treats at work--should have

left--felt overfull didn't

feel good

Time
6:00

M
Ⓢ

Too Hungry — _ _ _ X̲ X̲ _ _ N **Ignored Fullness**
1 2 3 4 5 6 7
Ate Mindfully

Feel
Pos
Neutral
(Neg)

ate while fixing dinner

bad habit--really mindless

mad at self--felt stupid

Time
7:30

Ⓜ
S

Too Hungry — _ _ X̲ _ _ X̲ _ _ N **Ignored Fullness**
1 2 3 4 5 6 7
Ate Mindfully

Feel
Pos
Neutral
(Neg)

ate dinner anyway--not

hungry--couldn't put stuff away

without finishing leftovers

Goals:
Eat scheduled meals/snacks.
Avoid getting too hungry.
Resist urges to eat when not hungry.
Stop at moderate fullness.
Explain negative feelings.

Monitoring Your Appetite

Notes to Self:
Describe physical sensations and explain negative feelings

Day: M T W Th F S Sun

Time	**Too Hungry**			N			**Ignored Fullness**	**Feel** Pos Neutral Neg
M S	1	2	3	4	5	6	7	

Ate Mindfully

_____
_____
_____

Time	**Too Hungry**			N			**Ignored Fullness**	**Feel** Pos Neutral Neg
M S	1	2	3	4	5	6	7	

Ate Mindfully

_____
_____
_____

Time	**Too Hungry**			N			**Ignored Fullness**	**Feel** Pos Neutral Neg
M S	1	2	3	4	5	6	7	

Ate Mindfully

_____
_____
_____

Time	**Too Hungry**			N			**Ignored Fullness**	**Feel** Pos Neutral Neg
M S	1	2	3	4	5	6	7	

Ate Mindfully

_____
_____
_____

Time	**Too Hungry**			N			**Ignored Fullness**	**Feel** Pos Neutral Neg
M S	1	2	3	4	5	6	7	

Ate Mindfully

_____
_____
_____

Goals:
Eat scheduled meals/snacks.
Avoid getting too hungry.
Resist urges to eat when not hungry.
Stop at moderate fullness.
Explain negative feelings.

RECALIBRATING YOUR APPETITE

Once you have started monitoring your appetite, you will notice some interesting things. Your ratings of hunger and fullness are subjective. Only you can assess your internal state. In the beginning, your sense of these points will probably be a bit distorted. Due to the normalized overeating in our environment, you may not feel full as soon as you are biologically full because you think full means psychologically satisfied. By paying close attention, you can recalibrate your "appetite meter" so that it will more accurately reflect the true state of hunger in your body (Tank B) and not your psychological hungers (Tank P). The amount of food it takes for you to feel full typically decreases over time. This is not a problem! It is a sign of progress. For example, you may initially feel moderately full after three slices of pizza. After several weeks of monitoring, you may notice that actually you feel full after only two slices. Your appetite meter has been recalibrated; you feel full with smaller amounts than you did before.

Limit Amount, Not Type, of Food

In AAT, you should never limit the types of food you eat in any drastic way. AAT focuses on amount, because amount needs to take priority over type. The boundary on amount protects you even when you choose to eat high-calorie foods; you still only eat a moderate amount. Further, you are less likely to trigger feelings of deprivation if you can have whatever type of food you want. Many diet strategies encourage you to fill up on low-calorie, high-volume "diet" foods. This strategy assumes that you won't then want higher-calorie foods. However, you can never have enough of what you don't want. Some people end up bingeing on low-calorie foods like apples or brown rice. Bingeing feels bad no matter what food you eat. If you try too hard to substitute low-calorie foods you don't want for foods you do want, you will feel deprived. Often you eventually eat the higher-calorie food anyway.

For example, Mary was driving home from a moderately stressful visit with her future in-laws. She felt like having some comfort food and really wanted a cheeseburger for lunch. However, she wanted to stick to her diet, so she had a salad instead. She didn't feel satisfied, so she ate some rice cakes and fruit that she had in the car, stopped again to get some frozen yogurt, and later had several diet cookies. But she still had the cheeseburger on her mind and eventually stopped early for dinner and binged on a cheeseburger plus fries, a shake, and two candy bars. She had spent all afternoon thinking about whether or not she would give in and eat the burger. If she had just eaten the cheeseburger with a salad for lunch (before she even wanted any fries), she would have eaten fewer total calories and avoided the aversive preoccupation all afternoon that eventually led to loss of control.

Substituting lower-calorie foods can be a useful strategy. However, this strategy needs to be secondary. It only works if you don't end up violating your amount boundary. For example, half a box of diet cookies adds up to more calories than four regular cookies. Wait to start substituting low calorie foods until you are very certain you can maintain your amount boundary.

Why Not Monitor Food in Addition to Appetite?

In the first weeks of AAT, I ask you specifically not to write down the amount or type of food you eat. I want you to focus on how food feels inside you, not on the food itself or how many calories or fat grams it has. There are many reasons for this. First, any focus on food is external, and it distracts you from how the food feels inside you, which is more important. You may have preconceived ideas about how much you should eat, what a regular portion is, and how much other people eat. When you focus on the food, you tend to go by these notions rather than figuring out how certain amounts of food feel inside you. Portion sizes in this country are generally misleading. If you go by what is served, you are likely to be more than moderately full most of the time. If you go by the tiny serving sizes specified on the back of packages, the amount is likely to be too small and you may not get even moderately full. You can't go by what other people eat, because people vary in size and activity level. Serving sizes provided on packages or in restaurants make no distinction between a six-foot two-inch competitive athlete and a four-foot eight-inch sedentary computer programmer. Thus, you cannot rely on external guidelines to tell you how much to eat.

To avoid feelings of deprivation, you need to eat what you *want* and to *enjoy* what you eat as much as you can. When you monitor the types of food you eat, it is very hard not to focus on calories or fat and end up labeling foods as "good" or "bad;" then you fail to enjoy the food. Some of you will decide you don't ever want to write down what you eat. However, if you do want to work on a healthier or lower-calorie diet in addition to stopping at moderate fullness, chapter 8 will show you how to incorporate some food monitoring to address those concerns.

5 Take Back Your Power

The last chapter was designed to help you increase your awareness of internal appetite cues—the stomach signals you are training yourself to use to make more effective decisions about eating. You were given two AAT guidelines. First, eat regular, scheduled meals and snacks, but do not eat outside these regularly scheduled eating episodes unless you become moderately hungry before the next scheduled time to eat. In doing this, you avoid being too hungry when you start eating, and you make it easier to follow the second guideline, which is stop as soon as you notice moderate fullness. You probably found out that eating with your appetite wasn't quite as easy as it sounds. You probably noticed many occasions when you had an urge to eat yet you knew very well you were not hungry. Today's environment is full of powerful cues that encourage you to eat all kinds of wonderful foods. These external cues are often the trigger for such urges. The self-monitoring exercise presented in this chapter is designed to help you increase your awareness of the unhelpful external cues that make it difficult to eat normally. You can challenge the power of these external cues by making conscious decisions about when you are going to start and stop eating. Take back your power; make your own eating decisions!

HOW THE ENVIRONMENT INFLUENCES YOUR EATING

You can often point to something specific that happened in the environment that triggered an urge to eat (or an urge to restrict/not eat). When you take control of your eating decisions, you will be able to respond more effectively to external cues that encourage you to eat. The environment influences your attitudes about eating and weight in both direct and indirect ways.

For example, social norms and the overall tone of media messages promote a thin ideal for women and support the stigma associated with being overweight. You probably don't realize how much of an effect these messages have on you. Such messages (You should be dieting!) make it very difficult to maintain a healthy attitude about weight and dieting. They generate negative emotions and unhelpful thoughts that promote unhealthy eating behaviors.

Living in an environment that encourages unhealthy attitudes about food, weight, and exercise makes it more likely that you will also have spontaneous negative thoughts and feelings about eating even when there is no obvious environmental cue. When you have internalized the culture's negative attitudes about weight, it doesn't take a specific event to trigger urges to restrict (not eat). I will show you how to challenge those spontaneous (uncued) urges later on. Right now I just want you to become more aware of the many environmental cues that are influencing your eating decisions.

INCREASING AWARENESS OF EXTERNAL CUES AND SHIFTING THE BALANCE OF POWER

You are already aware of the more obvious external cues. You know that the presence of tempting food can create strong urges to eat. You may also realize that sometimes you feel pressured or obligated to eat (or to eat more than you would like) because of social circum-stances. Social norms tell us a lot about when and how much food should be offered. Accepting or not accepting food that is offered can carry significant social meaning. Packaging and serving sizes are also important external cues that influence how much you eat. There are various other signals to eat that can present themselves based on your circumstances. AAT helps you respond to these external cues differently. You must first become aware of those cues; then you can make conscious decisions about how you are going to respond to them. This strategy is your best defense against mindlessly following environmental signals.

Over the course of the next week, each time you start to eat, ask yourself these questions:

- Why am I eating right now?

- Is it mealtime?

- Is it because I am hungry?

- Am I responding to something in my environment, or to people in my environment?

- Or, did the desire to eat just pop into my mind?

Likewise, each time you stop eating ask yourself:

- Am I stopping now because I am moderately full?

- Did the serving size or the packaging provide a helpful external signal to stop?

- Am I stopping because I think other people might notice if I eat more?

I believe you will be shocked to discover how much of the time you can identify some external cue, and how infrequently the reason you start (or stop) eating is based primarily on hunger or fullness. For most of us, the environment has clearly taken the upper hand in regulating when, what, and how much we eat.

You will never become immune to the effects of the environment, but you can shift the balance of power. When you eat without making a conscious decision to do so, it is mindless eating. Mindless eating is the easiest kind of eating to give up, because it is not doing that much for you. The way to eliminate mindless eating is to commit to making a conscious decision each time you start to eat and to using moderate fullness as your cue to stop, instead of eating until the food is gone.

AAT asks you to plan regular, scheduled meals and snacks. These scheduled eating times are external cues to eat, but these are helpful cues because they keep you from getting too hungry. Planned meals and snacks also help reduce the number of times each day you have to make a decision about whether or not to eat. Most of the time, you just follow your schedule. You only have to make a decision when urges to eat come up at other times. The schedule reduces obsessing about when to eat.

When you notice an urge to eat (outside of planned times), you can then make a conscious decision to eat or to handle the urge another way. The first step in making a conscious eating decision is to figure out what made you want to eat. It is possible you have become truly hungry, in which case you might choose to eat an extra snack. On the other hand, you may have just had a false alarm. False alarms are much easier to detect when they occur within the context of a regular schedule. Perhaps someone brought cookies into the office. You notice the presence of the cookies makes you want to eat. You have just identified an external cue that could dictate your eating choices if you weren't mindful of it.

TAKING CHARGE OF YOUR EATING

When you take charge of your eating, you decide how you are going to respond to urges to eat triggered by environmental cues. You might ask, "Wouldn't it be easier to change my environment?" Make whatever changes you can, but in the long run, you will be most successful if you learn to regulate from within. When you are in charge, you can make positive eating decisions regardless of the environment. You may choose to put yourself in more healthy eating environments; that will make it easier for you. However, in today's world you must be prepared to make effective decisions when you are in an unsupportive environment.

Specific diets or food plans establish a whole set of cues; you decide to use these to regulate your eating. Thus, a diet creates a new, but usually temporary, eating environment that makes it easier to restrict. You buy certain foods, get rid of others, change how you cook, and generally avoid eating out. You tell others you are on a diet so they won't pressure you to eat. Introducing these environmental changes helps you reduce your intake, but you must be prepared to make the changes permanent. Otherwise, when you go off the diet, you will return to your prior eating patterns. AAT teaches you the skills necessary to make effective eating decisions from within.

This puts you in a position to permanently empower yourself and regain control of your eating. Let's look at how you can attain those skills.

Monitoring Helpful and Unhelpful External Cues

In the coming week, as you monitor your internal appetite cues (rating hunger and fullness and noting mindful eating), you will also start monitoring conscious decisions to start and stop eating, and the times you choose to eat, not when your environment dictates. The form in this chapter asks you to indicate if you were aware and made a conscious decision each time you ate and each time you stopped. In addition, I want you to note on the form any helpful or unhelpful external cues you noticed (besides regularly scheduled eating times).

If you see a food commercial or someone brings donuts to the office, and you then feel an urge to eat, write these circumstances down as unhelpful cues. On the other hand, if you buy chips in an individual bag, this is a helpful cue. If you buy a large bag of chips, it is harder to eat a few and leave the rest for tomorrow. A small bag prompts you to eat less. When you finish, you have to think about it to get more.

One thing you are likely to notice is that most of the time you stop when you finish whatever was served or there is no more food. Eating this way is fine if you have gotten very good at predicting your fullness response. If you know exactly how much lunch to pack or how much dinner to order, serving sizes will help you. However, external stop-eating signals are a problem when they do not support your internal appetite signals, and this happens quite often. External signals can encourage you to keep eating past moderate fullness even when internal signals tell you to stop. Go ahead and use external signals that help you, but don't use them in a effort to trick your appetite. For example, packing a very small lunch because you know it will be easier to stop even though you won't be moderately full is not a healthy way to use external cues.

Social norms also serve as external signals. For example, if you attend a formal, sit-down dinner, you are unlikely to ask for a second helping. The serving provided is probably quite adequate, but even if it were a bit too small, you would probably not have a strong urge to have more. You might rave about how good the food was, but you wouldn't think of asking for seconds. But what happens when you eat dinner at a friend's house and she serves your favorite dish family style? You take a moderate portion initially, and as soon as you are finished she offers you more. You were already primed to want more since the food was sitting right there and it is difficult to turn down your favorite dish. It is it even more difficult to refuse if she insists. So, you have a second helping.

Decisions to stop eating work the same way. You may feel quite satisfied with two cookies when only two are left in the box. But if you open a new box of cookies, you are less likely to feel like stopping after two. Monitoring external cues and making conscious decisions about your eating allows you to start taking your power back.

INSTRUCTIONS FOR MONITORING EXTERNAL CUES

1. Continue to monitor your appetite as you did last week.

2. Your goal is to make a conscious decision (CD) each time you start to eat and each time you stop eating. Being conscious of your decisions to eat will reduce eating mindlessly in response to external cues. Each time you are aware that you make a CD, answer the question yes. If you were not aware, just leave it blank because you want to focus on the positive, not to increase self-criticism. Describe any external cues (food or people) that are helpful in reminding you to follow your internal appetite cues (help you resist eating just because food is available or help you to stop eating at moderate fullness).

3. Circle Food Available (Food A) whenever this creates a problem (triggers an urge to eat when not hungry or the desire to eat past moderate fullness). When you have a mild to moderately strong urge to eat when you are not even moderately hungry, try to resist the urge; distract yourself or get away from the food. However, when a strong urge is triggered by special food that is available, it may be more effective not to fight it. Whenever you predict that you are going to feel deprived if you don't eat a particular food, make a conscious decision (CD) to have that food and enjoy the treat without getting stuffed. When you do that, write ADE (Anti-Deprivation Eating). This is effective eating because it is likely to prevent binges.

You are not always going to be aware and able to make a conscious decision to eat. You are just trying to shift the balance of power so that you decide when and how much you eat more of the time. Don't criticize yourself when you fail to make a conscious decision about eating. Just feel good about each time you can manage to do so. Conscious decisions eliminate a lot of mindless eating that you won't really miss.

Monitoring External Cues

Day: M T W Th F S Sun   **Notes to Self:**

Time	**Too Hungry**		N			**Ignored Fullness**	**Feel** Pos Neutral Neg	CD to start? CD to stop?
M	1	2	3	4	5	6	7	
S			Ate Mindfully			FoodA		

Time	**Too Hungry**		N			**Ignored Fullness**	**Feel** Pos Neutral Neg	CD to start? CD to stop?
M	1	2	3	4	5	6	7	
S			Ate Mindfully			FoodA		

Time	**Too Hungry**		N			**Ignored Fullness**	**Feel** Pos Neutral Neg	CD to start? CD to stop?
M	1	2	3	4	5	6	7	
S			Ate Mindfully			FoodA		

Time	**Too Hungry**		N			**Ignored Fullness**	**Feel** Pos Neutral Neg	CD to start? CD to stop?
M	1	2	3	4	5	6	7	
S			Ate Mindfully			FoodA		

Time	**Too Hungry**		N			**Ignored Fullness**	**Feel** Pos Neutral Neg	CD to start? CD to stop?
M	1	2	3	4	5	6	7	
S			Ate Mindfully			FoodA		

Unhelpful External Cues/People
(Triggered urges to eat when not hungry
or desire to keep eating past 5.5 on the scale)

_____

_____

_____

Helpful External Cues/People
(Encouraged you to stop at moderate
fullness)

_____

_____

_____

EATING ASSERTION

People in your environment may not support you in taking charge of your eating. Thus, if you choose to take back your power and eat from within, you may need help with eating assertion: asserting your rights to regulate your own food intake and to enjoy what you choose to eat. Other people may feel hurt, unappreciated, or negatively evaluated by your choices. They may not understand why you have to eat this way, and they may even be moderately inconvenienced at times. You need to explain what you are doing and stand your ground when others expect you to join in social eating that doesn't work for you.

The skills for assertive eating are the same skills needed to be assertive in other areas of your life. I will briefly introduce assertion skills here. However, if you are having difficulty with these skills, I recommend further reading or consultation with a professional to provide encouragement and support as you learn to become more assertive in taking charge of your eating decisions.

Empathic Assertion for Family and Friends

Your family and friends may want to be helpful even if they are not. They may have no idea how to be helpful, or they may have their own ideas about what will help you. Usually, they think they know what you need better than you do. They may criticize or nag you to eat less, which just makes you feel resentful and hurt. Sometimes, they may offer you food and encourage you to eat. The latter might be a well-meant attempt to convince you that your weight and shape are not as important to them as you seem to think. However, such actions undermine your efforts to take charge of your own eating and feel better about yourself. Fortunately, many of these people will respond very well to empathic assertion. *Assertion* is learning how to effectively get what you want out of a situation, while *empathic assertion* attempts to get your needs met while maintaining the best possible relationship with the person you are dealing with. Here's how to do it.

Step one: Make sure you understand your eating rights. Read the rights listed below:

1. I have the right to take charge of my eating and exercise.

2. I have the right to not feel hungry no matter what my weight is.

3. I have the right to ask for (not demand) reasonable accommodations from others that will help me to exercise and eat based on my own needs.

4. Not exercising my rights can be hurtful in the long run, both to my sense of self and to my relationships with other people.

5. When I don't let other people know what could help me, it is really a form of selfishness. I am denying them the opportunity to experience a more mutually rewarding relationship.

6. I have the right to set boundaries and to limit my relationships with other people when they are not able to support me appropriately.

7. I am responsible for my behavior and my feelings. I am not responsible for how others choose to feel when I am appropriately assertive about taking care of myself.

8. I will be happier in the long run if I exercise my rights appropriately.

9. _____

    _____

10. _____

    _____

You will note that there are a couple of empty spaces at the bottom of this list. Add other rights if you can think of any that are specific to your situation. Getting clear about your rights is critical. You will not be able to stand up to others if you are not clear about your rights, or if you do not believe in those rights.

Step two: When you make a request, be very specific about what you need from that person or what you want them to stop doing. The following list may be helpful:

■ Ask people to allow you to make all your food decisions.

■ Explain the basis for how you are trying to eat so they will understand it.

■ Ask people not to offer food to you even when they are hungry or want to eat. Assure them you will ask for food if you want some.

■ Ask people to allow you to serve yourself whenever possible and to order for yourself.

■ Ask them to substitute nonfood items or activities unrelated to eating when they give you treats or gifts.

■ Indicate that it's fine to ask you to eat out with them, but that they need to let you know where they plan to go or to ask for your input on where to go.

■ Ask people to respect your food decisions even if they do not understand them or agree with them.

■ Ask them not to ask if you are really hungry or not yet full.

■ Ask them not to question your choice of foods or make suggestions about what you should eat.

- Ask people to agree to a mutually assertive relationship regarding food and exercise. Explain that you will feel freer to ask for their help if they will agree to tell you when they can't help or if your request isn't convenient. They don't need to explain or have an excuse. You understand it will not always be possible for them to be helpful.

- Let them know whether or not you welcome offers to share entrees or desserts, or if that sort of offer puts pressure on you to make food choices you wouldn't otherwise make.

- Let them know that you value their companionship and understand that eating is an important way to connect socially, so they don't need to avoid asking you to join them for food occasions.

- Be very clear about the kinds of comments about weight and appearance that are helpful and those that are not. Positive comments about appearance (not weight specific) may be helpful. However, you should make this choice for yourself. Some people dislike comments about appearance altogether. Comments (even in fun) about weight are never helpful. Even comments that are intended to be positive can be interpreted negatively by people who are sensitive about weight issues (such as "You've lost so much weight.").

A vague request to be more supportive is not useful; another person's idea of being supportive may not be what you have in mind. Do not expect other people to read your mind, even if they know you very well. You must be willing to tell people exactly what will help you, even if you think it sounds silly or seems like it should be obvious to them.

Do not assume that people are unwilling to change. Most people who have difficulty being assertive have unrealistically negative expectations about what others are willing to do. Give others the opportunity to change and start helping you. Some people may choose not to change, but you may be pleasantly surprised to find out how many people are willing to help when you ask in an empathic, nonthreatening way and when you remain willing to remind them patiently while they overcome old habits. If someone wants to change but is having a hard time, ask how you can help them do so. Many people set up a code word or phrase ("remember AAT" would work well in this case). This is an easy and good-humored way to remind someone that they are pressuring you to eat or making you feel guilty about having a food treat.

Step three: Make sure you understand where the other person is coming from. Instead of getting (or staying) angry, try to find out why they keep doing something that is bothersome to you. Give them the benefit of the doubt—especially when you know they do care about you. Are they feeling threatened that you will become more confident or feel better about yourself? What is their own experience with food, and what does that experience make them believe is the "right" way to eat? In the space below, make a list of significant others who could help you as you try to eat from within. Write down what they could do that would help, as well as anything they are currently doing that is not helpful to you.

_____

_____

_____

_____

_____

Step four: Rehearse what you want to say ahead of time. Use the format illustrated in the sample below.

I understand that you only want the best for me but when you (make comments about what I order or plan for dinner) I feel (criticized and defensive) and it is harder for me to stay committed to following my own appetite signals. It will help me if you (refrain from commenting on what I eat until I feel more confident making my own decisions).

Step five: Think about the best time and place to bring up your requests. The first time you bring up a specific issue, it may be best to have a more formal, extended talk. Explain that you are trying to learn a new pattern of eating that has been proven to help many people, and ask specifically for their help and support. Explain the basics of AAT, and invite them to ask you for an explanation whenever they do not understand what you are doing. You will probably need to repeat your requests many times before you are able to establish a new way to interact with these individuals about food issues. Nonetheless, an initial, formal request for help is a good way to get started.

Strong Assertion for Saboteurs

You may find that a few individuals actively sabotage your efforts to eat from within. Sometimes you have to be very persistent. When such people see that you are determined to follow this program, they may stop hassling you. Also, as you gain confidence in using your internal signals, you may find that comments from those individuals bother you less and less.

If empathic assertion does not work, you may have to resort to stronger versions of assertion. Strong assertion includes two additional components. First, express your anger or resentment very explicitly; for example, "When you tell me not to eat something, I feel angry and I resent being treated like a child. I recognize I have issues about eating, but I need to resolve those issues myself. What you are doing is making my problems worse." Second, (if necessary) specify a consequence if the person continues to undermine your efforts. For example, "When you bring ice cream home, it is harder for me to stay in charge of my eating. If you want ice cream, please eat it while you are out. I will tell you when I feel strong enough to manage having it in the house. Until then, if you bring ice cream home, I will throw it out."

I do not recommend strong assertion unless you absolutely have to use it. Strong assertion can damage a relationship, and it can escalate other conflicts you may have with the person. However, at times, strong assertion works amazingly well. Sometimes it turns out that the person is more of a bully whose bark is worse than their bite. When you make it clear that you will not tolerate poor treatment (teasing and the like), they back down. Surprisingly, you will sometimes even get an apology; for example, "I was really just kidding. I didn't realize it hurt your feelings that much." However, don't count on that. Sometimes, you have to be satisfied that the person just stops the offensive behavior.

This week, take notes on your self-monitoring forms when someone else undermines your efforts. If you find that you have a serious "saboteur," especially one you cannot avoid easily (for example, your spouse), don't be too hard on yourself. When you have to deal with a saboteur, you may not initially be as successful as you would like in following your internal signals. Try to limit the time you spend with unhelpful individuals. If you cannot avoid the person, you may need to seek out extra help from other friends or a counselor to buffer the negative effects of a saboteur and get the support you need to follow the AAT program.

Reduce Binges to Mere Overeating

You have now tackled three of the intervention points identified earlier in this book: becoming too hungry, ignoring fullness, and eating when food is available. Your new skills are helping you stay on the normal eating path more of the time. In this chapter, you will learn strategies to eliminate your largest and most distressing eating episodes, those usually called binges, by eliminating the what the heck response. Binge episodes differ from ordinary (what I call normalized) overeating by the way you feel while you are eating. You may feel out of control either because you are eating forbidden foods or because you are eating amounts you consider excessive. The critical point is that you feel out of control. You may binge only when you are alone, because you probably don't want other people to know about these episodes. Eating a lot at a social occasion may feel less like a binge because others may also be eating large amounts.

WHAT EXACTLY IS BINGE EATING?

Overeating is very common, and no one can specify the exact point at which overeating becomes *binge eating*. I use the term *getting stuffed* to indicate episodes in which you end up feeling clearly stuffed. Some people use the term binge to mean they ate a forbidden/treat food (or at least more of it than planned), so they didn't really feel in control of what they were eating. Psychologists typically define a binge as any episode in which you experience loss of control; an objective binge means the amount was also clearly large while a subjective binge means the amount was not clearly large—it might have even been quite small. Unfortunately, loss of control is, itself, hard to define. It means different things to different people. Thus, some people find it useful to use the term binge, but others don't like to use that word. Also, some people feel okay about occasionally eating to the point that they feel stuffed. AAT avoids the problem of defining precisely what is a binge by asking you to separate your ratings for physical fullness from your ratings of your psychological feelings.

AAT encourages you to accept as reasonable (normal eating) any amount of any food as long as you do not go past moderate fullness. You mark negative feelings on your form to indicate when you feel bad psychologically about how much or the type of food you choose to eat. It is important for you to become aware of how often you do not allow yourself to enjoy food even when you are eating normally (not going past moderate fullness). This is your cue to challenge the unhelpful thoughts that try to tell you that food is bad or that you should have eaten less than you did. Within AAT, your goal is to first eliminate episodes in which you get stuffed, regardless of whether or not you feel loss of control. Then, chapter 8 will show you how to deal with negative feelings about the types of food you choose.

Why do some episodes of eating feel particularly distressing? The distress comes from having two very strong but conflicting feelings at the same time. Psychologists call this *ambivalence*. In this case, you have an intense desire to eat and you also feel strongly that you should not be eating because of your concern about weight. You resolve this conflict (for the moment) by tuning out your conscious awareness of the thoughts that say "Don't eat!" or "Stop eating!" so you are able to eat. I call all variations of this tuning out of some of your feelings, the what the heck response. As soon as you tune back in, you realize that you feel very distressed. You may experience this whole phenomenon as simply regret (after eating) or as having loss of control (during). Some women use the term "bingey" to indicate something in between, the times they don't feel totally out of control but it doesn't quite feel the same as normalized over-eating. In AAT, it doesn't matter because all highly distressing episodes need to be eliminated. From now on, for simplicity, I will refer to all unusually distressing episodes as binges, although some of them may be more accurately described simply as getting stuffed.

The AAT strategy to eliminate binges is to use conscious decisions (CDs) to eat to counteract your tendency to dissociate (tune out) parts of your awareness. Instead of pushing away your urge to eat/binge, you must give yourself conscious permission to eat the type of food you really want. You can eat a small amount, a moderate amount or even a substantial amount. You just don't give yourself permission to get uncomfortably full or stuffed. It sounds too simple but it works. All you have to do is be willing to give yourself conscious permission. That conscious decision undermines any sense of loss of control. The catch is you have to be willing (I'll say more about that later).

At first, you are likely to overeat to some extent, but gradually you will become more able to stop before you feel uncomfortable, then ultimately before you even feel completely full. For example, one of Dr. Dicker's clients had strong urges to binge on chocolate chip cookies. When she first gave herself permission to eat them, she could only stop after eating at least ten of them. As she refused to tune out and stayed conscious of her stomach as she ate them, she was able to gradually reduce the number of cookies it took before she could stop. Her binges went from ten, to about eight, to about 6 to about 4, at which point even she agreed it was not accurate to call it a binge. Eventually, she was even able to enjoy occasionally eating cookies because she felt confident that she could stop at moderate fullness.

Unplanned Binges

Most of the time people don't plan to binge. You just overeat, for whatever reason, and the overeating turns into a binge through the what the heck response. This response resolves the conflicting feelings described above. When you think "what the heck," you are tuning out your awareness of the thoughts that say "stop eating" so you can keep on eating. You may or may not stay tuned into the taste of the food, but you are tuning out what is happening in your stomach. AAT helps you stay tuned into your stomach so you won't go past the point where your stomach feels uncomfortably full. In this chapter you will learn to challenge the what the heck response, because it can turn mere overeating into a binge. Your goal is to reverse this process and first reduce your binges to mere overeating. Chapter 8 will then help you to reduce overeating and eating types of food that make you feel "bad."

Emotional eating is another point at which eating can turn into a binge. Emotional eating is simply a description of the reason you start eating. Emotional eating means you wanted to eat in order to change something about the way you were feeling. When you start eating for emotional reasons, you have three options: you can stop at moderate fullness, you can keep eating past moderate fullness so you end up overeating, or you can plan to binge.

Emotional eating is quite normal. Virtually everyone eats for emotional reasons at times. For example, you may want ice cream (or a special treat) when you feel a bit lonely or down. A person who doesn't binge will eat a normal portion, or they might overeat (go for a special, large sundae). However, such people do not feel out of control, and they do not eat such a large amount that they feel uncomfortably stuffed. A person who binges often uses food for the same reasons that other people use food. Eating makes you feel better. Eating can be used to buffer the experience of pain or to overcome fatigue or boredom. However, people who binge typically eat excessive amounts in their (usually not too successful) effort to change uncomfortable feelings. Chapter 7 will help you reduce the frequency of emotional eating.

Planned Binges

For some people, a binge does not merely moderate the intensity of uncomfortable feelings, it creates an altered state of consciousness. People who experience this state typically say they become numb or oblivious to other things during a binge. They may lose track of time or forget to do something important. They may forget part or all of what actually happened during their binge. Sometimes, people binge in order to get to sleep; food helps them attain this altered state. People who plan to binge always have a reason. They are deliberately seeking an altered state, which they know from their past experience they can get from bingeing. Planned binges are part of the emotional eating path, because the only reason you would plan to binge is to alter your emotional state in some way. Chapter 7 will help you reduce planned binges. Right now, concentrate on reducing unplanned binges.

Emotional Eating Can Work for You; Binge Eating Never Works

People who don't binge often feel better after emotional eating. They feel comforted, less anxious, or perhaps pampered. However, the times they don't feel that much better after their food treat, they don't continue to eat in a vain effort to get the food to do something more for them. When emotional eating works for you, I call it *effective emotional eating* (EEE). You will learn how to do this in the next chapter.

Binge eating never works. A person who binges does not feel better after a normal amount, so they continue to eat until the food is gone or they feel so stuffed that they have to stop. When you binge, you feel worse afterward, never better.

A BINGE IS A TEMPER TANTRUM

I believe that a binge is best understood as a temper tantrum. A tantrum is rarely the most effective way for a child to get what she wants, but she does it anyway. Sometimes a tantrum appears to be deliberate, but most of the time tantrums don't seem to be a very conscious choice. They just happen. A child has a temper tantrum when she can't come up with any better strategy to get what she wants. If you understand what makes a child have a temper tantrum, you will understand the nature of binge eating.

What kind of situation leads to a child's tantrum? She wants something in a store or asks to do something and is refused. If the child is not able to negotiate skillfully (or is not even allowed to express her angry feelings), she feels powerless. She becomes very angry and frustrated. If she does not have good skills to regulate her emotions, she will not be able to stay calm and continue thinking about alternative ways to try to get what she wants. Her emotions will override her logical thinking processes. At that point, she just has a fit. She is just expressing her feelings; she is no longer focused on getting what she wants. In fact, having a tantrum usually ensures that she will not get what she wants, and often she will be punished. When she is calm, she can tell you she knows she won't get her way with a tantrum. However, while having the tantrum, this awareness is tuned out. She is not able to use information that she normally knows to make an effective decision about how she should act. She acts only on the basis of her feelings of frustration.

Parents describe children who have tantrums as out of control. When the tantrum starts, it is useless for parents to attempt to explain the basis for their refusal, or to threaten punishment. The strategy recommended for parents is to ignore the child until she calms down. If necessary, they are to remove or restrain the child. Discussions about alternatives, consequences, and more effective problem solving must wait until later, after the child has calmed down.

All children have some temper tantrums in their early years. However, only a few children continue to have tantrums, because most parents do not tolerate tantrums. Their children learn that tantrums don't work. More importantly, effective parents teach their children other ways to regulate their emotions and to negotiate for what they want. A child will continue to have tantrums if her parents often give in and allow her to get her way. However, some children continue to have tantrums even though their parents almost never cave in. Such children persist because they have failed to learn any strategies that work better. Until they are taught skills and strategies that work better, they will keep having tantrums.

The solution for binge eating is similar. You already know that binge eating doesn't work. You always feel worse afterward. You may even get punished for binge eating (by gaining weight), but you continue. The solution is to learn better skills. Figure out why you are resorting to a tantrum and learn strategies to meet your needs more effectively than by bingeing. Only then can you give up binge eating as a coping strategy. At that point, your urges to binge will diminish.

What drives a binge is not as obvious as what a child wants when she has a tantrum; it is different for each person. You have to figure out exactly what your binges are telling you. Listen to your body talk. Each time you binge, imagine that you are having a temper tantrum. Then ask yourself what is it that you want. What you are trying to get or what you are trying to avoid.

Deprivation Binge

The most obvious type of binge is a *food deprivation binge*. You are at a special occasion and you want some specific food. However, you absolutely won't allow yourself to have any. You try pushing away the deprived feeling, but if it keeps coming back you may give in. When you do, you are likely to binge rather than eat a normal portion. Often, the feeling of food deprivation is quite vague and it may build up gradually, over a period of time. If you are restricting a lot, especially restricting types of food, or if you restricted a lot at some point in your past, a vague feeling of deprivation can be easily triggered whenever you don't allow yourself to have food (or something else) that you want. A deprivation binge is when you (not someone else) are the agent who is refusing to give yourself what you want. When other people are eating what you want to be eating, you are likely to feel even more deprived. However, other people do not directly make you feel deprived. You do that to yourself.

Depriving yourself of certain foods is the most obvious type of deprivation, but there are other types as well. When you binge, you may believe it's all about the food. You may not be aware that you are feeling deprived in other ways. If you can't tell the difference between biological hunger (Tank B) and psychological needs (Tank P), you may think that food is really what you want. As you continue to monitor your appetite sensations and identify your emotions, you are likely to discover feelings of deprivation that go beyond the realm of food. Often it is not food that you really want; food is simply the best available substitute.

The AAT guidelines are set up to reduce food-specific deprivation. You are instructed to eat what you want, because forbidding specific foods triggers more intense feelings of deprivation than limiting amounts. You are also asked to make conscious decisions to choose anti-deprivation eating when food is available and a strong urge has been triggered, even though you know you are not biologically hungry. When you don't allow yourself some of a favorite food when it is available, you are likely to end up feeling deprived, if not immediately, then later on. When you choose anti-deprivation eating, you stay tuned into your stomach sensations, so you can notice (and stop at) moderate fullness instead of overeating or bingeing. In chapter 8, you will learn some ways to modify your preferences for types of foods. When your preferences change, deprivation becomes less of a problem because you are more often eating what you want.

Frustration Binge

The second type of binge is a *frustration binge*. Frustration occurs when you do not have control over getting what you want. Feelings of frustration are not as easy to eliminate as feelings of deprivation. You may experience frustration as a sense of bitterness or resentment that you do not have the resources or skills to negotiate successfully for what you want. You may experience frustration as anger if other people are deliberately preventing you from getting or doing what you want. You may experience frustration as depression if you want something that it is not possible to have (like a different body type or a different mother), or if what you want is to undo something that has already happened (like a car accident or a divorce). In those situations you may feel quite hopeless, because you know for certain that it is not possible to get what you want.

Feeling powerless or hopeless is the main ingredient of the frustration binge. When you feel powerless, you lose motivation to stay focused on getting what you really want. You recognize at some level that a binge is not going to solve your real problem and even that it's likely to make your weight problems worse. However, you settle for what you can get, namely, food. You try to numb your pain by tuning it out. Binges are one way to express feelings of frustration; they just aren't a very effective way to express those feelings. Nonetheless, it is important to point out that binges are a much less destructive way to express your feelings than some other strategies that people adopt—drugs or alcohol, for example. When you stop binge eating, you need to make sure you find positive alternative ways to cope with frustration. You don't want to end up doing something that has even more negative consequences than bingeing.

Leftover Binge

Some binges do not seem to be expressions of current feelings of deprivation or frustration. They seem to be more like a bad habit that is left over from an earlier time when you did have significant emotional issues. You may not be able to identify any particularly intense emotions at this point even though you still have a strong urge to binge. You only know that you feel bad if you are prevented from bingeing. *Leftover binges* often follow a pattern, such as bingeing in the evening after eight o'clock or only on weekends. You may plan these binges so that they occur at certain times, particularly when you are going to be alone. You experience some sense of control over these binges in that you can put them off, but you can't seem to give them up altogether. If you feel as though most of your emotional issues are currently resolved, you are probably puzzled by why you continue to have urges to binge.

Leftover binges are due to emotions, but the emotions that trigger them are different from the emotions that trigger other binges. The emotions that trigger leftover bingeing are relatively weak. You probably had quite intense emotions when you first started binge eating (perhaps while going through a divorce or coping with a trauma or family conflicts). Once binge eating has been established as a way to cope with negative feelings, even minor disappointments or vague feelings of discontent can be enough to trigger a leftover binge. Long-standing feelings of being a failure in managing your weight can be enough, in themselves, to maintain leftover binges. If you don't know why you have the urge to binge, self-monitoring will help you identify your feelings. If you are still having a hard time understanding what you really want, you may find that talking to a counselor will help to clarify your feelings and uncover the other needs you have masked through binge eating.

SEPARATE PSYCHOLOGICAL ISSUES FROM EATING DECISIONS

When other life problems are mixed up with making eating decisions, it is hard to deal effectively with either issue. When you start working on changing your eating, another life problem may become more pressing. You may switch your attention to that issue and forget about the eating for a while. When you try to focus on other issues in your life, you may experience such distress about your eating that you end up going back to it. In this way, eating problems can serve as an excuse for not dealing with other important concerns, or other concerns can serve as an excuse for not dealing with eating problems. You end up stuck. You do nothing effective about changing either one, or you end up alternating between managing your eating and dealing with other life issues. This on-and-off-again pattern may be associated with weight loss and subsequent regain.

In AAT, you are asked to rate physical stomach sensations (hunger and fullness) separately from your emotions. You practice making eating decisions based on your stomach, which keeps you on the normal eating path regardless of how good or bad you are feeling emotionally. You learn to challenge your thoughts when you try to use emotions or stress as an excuse to get off the normal eating path or to stay off once you get sidetracked.

How is it possible to focus on eating and other issues at the same time? It's possible because normal eating does not require the same level of attention and effort as restricting/dieting do. In the past, you may have been so focused on weight loss that you didn't give yourself the option of sometimes just maintaining your weight. You won't always have the energy and attention necessary to lose weight, but you can always eat normally. Then you won't gain weight, despite whatever else is going on. Eating normally breaks the yo-yo dieting cycle. You are not always actively working to lose weight, but you are always actively working to maintain your weight. You can choose to work toward weight loss during periods of time when you can make it a high priority.

Reducing the Power of Emotions

Sometimes your emotions will get in the way, and you will get sidetracked from the normal eating path. However, by shifting more of the power to your stomach, you can reduce the power of your emotions. You learn to challenge the thoughts and feelings that get in the way of staying on the normal eating path. In AAT, you are allowed to decide to eat for emotional reasons; you just have to acknowledge what you are doing and work to stop at moderate fullness.

At this stage in the program, you don't have to understand your emotional reasons for bingeing. You don't have to know why you want to eat when you aren't hungry. Just use stomach fullness as your signal to stop, regardless of why you start eating. As you continue in the program, you will likely recognize that some of your problem episodes are due to emotional eating. However, not all of your problems with food are emotional. When you eliminate the other paths that lead to bingeing or overeating, you will be better able to see whether or not you have emotional issues that need to be addressed before you can make further progress.

UNDERSTANDING THE WHAT THE HECK RESPONSE

The key to reducing binges to normalized overeating is to stop the what the heck response. During this coming week you must put your attention on the thoughts and feelings you have at the time that you lose (or give up) control and start to binge. These are the thoughts and feelings that allow you to tune out your awareness of the negative consequences of bingeing so that you can continue to eat. Any time you overeat or you break a food rule, you are vulnerable to having a what the heck response. The way you think and feel about having overeaten (or having broken a rule) determines whether you allow this event to turn into a binge. Each time you notice a what the heck response, try to identify which of the following types of unhelpful thinking were involved.

All-or-Nothing Thinking

All-or-nothing thinking is the basis for the feeling of relief or release that many people experience when they binge. This unhelpful way of thinking involves the all-too-human tendency to think in terms of polar opposites. Events, people, and food are labeled either "good" or "bad"; you are either a "success" or a "failure." When you think in terms of all or nothing, anything you eat that is not exactly what you planned is "bad." This dichotomous thinking is not helpful, because it undermines your ability to stop in the early stages of a binge. Once you have crossed a certain line, you can't redeem yourself (in your own eyes), so you are released from making any further effort to stop eating.

To challenge this dichotomous way of thinking, you must change your definitions of success and failure. You have to start thinking that any time you are able to stop short of a full-fledged binge is a success. Remind yourself how calories work in your body. Each calorie adds the same amount of energy as the one before it, so you benefit from stopping at any point. Some calories provide more healthy nutrition than others do, but right now that is not important. Right now, you just need to stop thinking there is some magic point where all is lost so you might as well go all out. When you force yourself to think about calories as continuous (not dichotomous) information, you have a huge incentive to stop whenever you can. For example, stopping after one pint of ice cream is in fact very positive if you used to eat a quart. Training yourself to think this way will take you a long way toward overcoming binges based on all-or-nothing thinking.

Magical Thinking

Magical thinking is a way you trick your conscious mind into being unaware of reality for a period of time. As children, we all did a lot of magical thinking. We believed we could (or might have) caused something to happen just by thinking about it. Or, we believed that if we wanted something badly enough, we would get it. Children don't always make a clear distinction between fantasy (what they wish for) and reality (what is). It is a slow and usually painful process to learn that one's thoughts are not as powerful as one would like. It is also painful when you learn that something you strongly believed in does not turn out to represent reality.

Adults resort to magical thinking much less often than children, but it can still show up when you really don't like the harsh reality that you are in. You can escape reality for a moment by suspending your rational thought processes. It is fairly easy to suspend one's awareness of the caloric nature of food. The connection between taste, calories, and weight is certainly not that obvious in the moment you are eating. Magical thinking allows you to make excuses that justify continuing to eat. The most problematic rationalization of this kind you can make is to believe it will be easier to wait and get back on track later (tomorrow, after the holiday, or when your in-laws leave). You know rationally that calories don't work that way, but you want them to. Waiting to get back on track doesn't make sense rationally; every calorie you consume in the meantime counts.

Denial

Denial, or the "I don't care" way of thinking, is another way you keep yourself from facing the painful reality that you do care about your weight, even though you don't want to stop eating right now. When you say you don't care, you are temporarily discounting something that is very important to you. Some people really do not care that much about their weight, but those people are not reading this book. When you say you don't care, yet you continue to feel bad about your weight and keep going back to dieting, then you really do care, and it's not helpful to pretend that you don't. You must challenge this way of thinking. When you say, "I don't care," you cut yourself off from whatever motivation you might have to cut a binge short. Thus, when you catch yourself saying this, refocus and challenge it. The most effective way to challenge denial is to acknowledge both sides of what you really feel; for example, "I do care about my weight, but I'm feeling hopeless" or "I do care, but I'm feeling like the goal isn't worth the effort." Then you can deal with your real (ambivalent) feelings instead of pretending you don't have them.

Feeling Hopeless or Angry Triggers Unhelpful Thinking

Hopelessness is a feeling that triggers unhelpful thinking patterns. If you fall into this pattern, you typically feel resigned throughout the binge episode. You don't get much of a positive feeling of relief at any point during the binge. However, you also don't believe you will feel any better if you stop eating, so you undermine any motivation you might have to stop. Hopelessness results from thinking that exaggerates the negative. You take any slight slip as compelling evidence that you will never be successful in managing your weight in the long run. Once you have concluded that you won't succeed, further effort seems futile. Hence you binge.

The strategy you need to use to challenge hopelessness is to recognize that it is a consequence of all-or-nothing thinking. With eating behavior, there is never a reason to be hopeless. Some things you can't change (at least not easily or inexpensively); for example, your facial structure or eye color. You can't take back something hurtful you have said. But eating behavior is something that you can change, because it is something that you have to do every day. You don't even have to wait very long to have another opportunity to change. You will be making another eating decision within a few hours. Of course, changing your eating may not change your weight or shape quite as much (and certainly not as fast) as you would like, but you can always make a different decision the next time you have to eat.

To combat hopelessness, your goals need to be based on your behavior, not your weight or shape, because the latter can only be changed indirectly. You will feel hopeless if you set a goal that may not be attainable. If you notice you are feeling hopeless, reevaluate your goals. Right now, your goal is simply to stop a little earlier in every binge episode than you did before. This is something you can do.

It may surprise you to discover that you alternate between feeling hopeless and feeling angry or at least rebellious. Because of (unhelpful) all-or-nothing thinking you may go back and forth, instead of finding a more constructive (middle path) stance regarding your personal struggles with eating and weight. When you dwell on thoughts that life is unfair, you are likely to feel angry or hopeless. The most useful challenge I have found for this type of unhelpful thought is a quote in an inspirational book by Wheeler (2003).

She writes. "It turns out that life is quite fair. You have things that others do not have, and others have things that you do not have" (p. 82). She also reminds you that "You can either ride the waves or be pounded by them—it's up to you" (p. 34). Use your wise mind to accept the fact that you may well have a more difficult time achieving (or maintaining) a weight acceptable to you than do some (if not many) other people. The issue for you is not what deck of cards you've been dealt, but how well you play your hand. You have only two choices in life you can; cultivate an attitude of gratitude and play as well as you can, or you can just grow old, angry, and bitter (adapted from Hollingsworth 2001, p. 82).

Once you stop bingeing, your overeating will gradually reduce as well, because your preference for the way your stomach feels will change. Right now, just do whatever it takes to stop short of the completely overstuffed feeling you get from a binge.

TRANSFORM URGES TO BINGE WITH CONSCIOUS DECISIONS TO OVEREAT

Now that you have learned about the nature of your binges and how the what the heck response works, it is time to learn how to transform your binge into mere overeating by making conscious decisions about the way to eat. When you make a conscious decision to eat, or even overeat, you are not bingeing. You have not lost or given up control; you are able to stay aware and watch what the food is doing or not doing for you.

You will be able to give up binge eating entirely once you develop better strategies to meet your food and nonfood needs. At that point, you will no longer have to rely on willpower to fight urges to binge. When you use willpower, you always have to be on your guard. When you use self-observation to teach yourself that overeating is a less negative option than bingeing, you have mastered a new strategy. Eastern philosophies refer to this strategy of expanding your awareness as using your *wise mind*. Using your wise mind means you use all the information available to you about all of the possible options you have to make the most effective decision. Marsha Linehan (1993) describes this process as committing to doing what works, even when you don't feel like doing it. Unlike willpower, using your wise mind gets easier and easier over time. Eventually, your urges to binge weaken and usually disappear, because your wise mind knows that bingeing never really works.

Using your wise mind to limit the size of a binge may sound ridiculous. You may be thinking, "I already know that binges don't work, but that hasn't stopped me from binge eating." Some behaviors can be changed with intellectual insight alone, but eating is a behavior that does not respond readily to this kind of insight. AAT teaches you to use experiential learning to support your intellectual insight. You must be wholly convinced that choosing overeating is a more effective alternative than taking the chance of triggering a binge. You gain this experiential (whole-body) knowledge by focusing not on the food itself, but on what the food is doing inside you. This is why I emphasize that you have to actually do self-monitoring. You can gain intellectual insight just by reading the book, but you have to do the monitoring to gain the experiential knowledge needed to actually change your behavior.

Willpower

When you have an urge to binge that is moderate, willpower (not doing what you feel like doing) may work, but when the urge is strong, this is unlikely to work. One problem is that willpower requires a tremendous amount of effort. Another problem is that even when willpower seems to work, you often end up feeling deprived later on and the urge to binge returns—

stronger than before. When you try willpower and still end up bingeing, you feel discouraged and hopeless. It is better to avoid those feelings, because they can trigger emotional eating or the what the heck response. It is okay to try willpower if you want, but if the urge is strong or the urge comes back after you have tried to distract yourself from it, you need to use a different strategy. Making a conscious decision to eat what you want (or even overeat) takes the power out of your urge to binge. You have permission to eat; you don't need to binge. Remember, willpower hasn't been working very well for you; otherwise you would not be reading this book!

Challenge Your Fear of Weight Gain

It is difficult to make conscious decisions to eat (or even overeat) when you are worried about your weight. If you are trying to restrict in order to lose weight, how can you give yourself permission to overeat? You have to remind yourself that you have agreed to wait to lose weight until you have eliminated binges. Making conscious decisions to overeat will not cause you to gain weight. The reason for this is that you are going to be making a conscious decision to overeat only occasionally—only when you have a strong urge to binge. The rest of the time you are going to stay on the normal eating path and stop at moderate fullness. Overall, you will not be eating any more total calories per week than you did before you were making conscious decisions to eat. In fact, most of you will end up eating considerably less than when you were refusing to eat what you wanted and ended up binge eating at least some of those times.

HOW TO RESPOND TO URGES TO BINGE

In the coming week, I would like you to try the following strategy when you notice an urge to binge.

First, in your mind rate the urge on a 7-point scale from 1 (mild) to 7 (very strong). If the urge is no more than moderate (5 or below), try to distract yourself with a positive alternative activity, preferably one that is incompatible with eating or is very interesting and engaging. However, when you have a strong urge to binge (6 or 7), make a conscious decision to eat (or overeat if necessary) instead of binge. In other words, do not fight with a strong urge, because you may end up losing control. Instead, you take control and you make a decision; for example, I want cookies, so I will have cookies, but I will stay tuned into my stomach. I may even have to overeat, but under no circumstances will I continue once I feel uncomfortable stomach sensations. When you have a strong urge to binge, you are doing well if you are able to stop anywhere short of feeling stuffed.

Stay focused on your stomach so you can stop as soon as eating no longer feels good. I call this the *point of diminishing returns*. This is the point at which you realize the food no longer tastes as good as before or your stomach starts to feel uncomfortably full. Your stomach is the first place in your body that is going to register discomfort with large amounts of food.

Some people find it helpful to indicate the size of their binges so they can see that they are, in fact, reducing amounts. If you think that would be helpful, put an "S" (small), "M" (medium), or "L" (large) beside the B (indicating binge) on your monitoring form. Each time you limit the size of a binge to less than is typical for you, put a happy face on your form to identify this as a success. You need to give yourself positive feedback for each small step you make in the right direction. When you see that you are able to cut short a binge, you gain confidence in your ability to use AAT strategies.

Reducing amounts in binges is surprisingly easy for many people. Most people have never set this as a goal. Instead they respond with all-or-nothing thinking—either you binge or you don't. Now, you are challenging that thinking. There is no magic point at which eating more doesn't matter.

INSTRUCTIONS FOR THE MONITORING WHAT THE HECK RESPONSE

1. Continue to monitor your appetite cues as you have been doing and circling Food A whenever that plays a significant role in a problematic episode.

2. Your goal this week is to challenge the what the heck response to prevent, or at least cut short, a binge. You may have to make a CD to eat (ADE), or you may have to stay tuned in and stop at the point of diminishing returns. If you are successful in resisting the urge, put a star by Urge-NoBinge (U-NB). If you are not able to resist, circle Heck and B (for Binge).

3. In the space beside the appetite ratings, write down any unhelpful thoughts or excuses you gave yourself that encouraged you to keep on eating past moderate fullness. Use your wise mind to challenge them.

4. Starting this week, you have a daily summary to help you remember the priority of your goals. Check NoB? if you had no binges. Check All Normal Eating? if you were able to stay within the gray all day (even if at times you felt negatively about what or how much you ate.) Use ADE as needed to keep deprivation from rising to a high level.

CHALLENGING EXCUSES AND OTHER UNHELPFUL THINKING

In addition to choosing antideprivation eating to prevent binges, you must challenge the unhelpful thinking that encourages you to tune out and continue eating. Thoughts can be smoke screens, tricks that your mind plays to block out some of your awareness for the moment. Imagine a magician, whose career is built on diverting your attention to an interesting decoy in order to trick you. Your mind acts like a magician. You have to figure out how your mind diverts your attention from important aspects of your awareness and subsequently convinces you to binge.

Monitoring the What the Heck Response

Day: M T W (Th) F S Sun

Notes to Self:
Write down unhelpful thoughts/excuses. Use your wise mind (WM) to challenge all-or-nothing/magical thinking, denial, hopelessness, rebellion.

Time 11:00	**Too Hungry** ___ X ___ N ___ ___ ___ X ___ ___ **Ignored Fullness**	
(M) S	1 2 3 4 5 6 7	**Feel** Pos Neutral (Neg)
	Ate Mindfully FoodA U-NB* B (Heck)	

skipped breakfast and got too hungry--overate & felt hopeless-- wanted to blow the whole day

Time 4:30	**Too Hungry** ___ ___ ___ X ___ X ___ ___ ___ **Ignored Fullness**	
M (S)	1 2 3 4 5 6 7	**Feel** Pos* Neutral Neg
	Ate Mindfully* FoodA U-NB B Heck	

WM says: it won't be easier to start over tomorrow--just get back on track--have your snack so you aren't too hungry at dinner

Time	**Too Hungry** ___ ___ ___ N ___ ___ ___ ___ ___ **Ignored Fullness**	
M S	1 2 3 4 5 6 7	**Feel** Pos Neutral Neg
	Ate Mindfully FoodA U-NB B Heck	

skipped dinner--had snack so wasn't that hungry & thought I could make up for big lunch (magical thinking)

Time 9:00	**Too Hungry** ___ X ___ N ___ ___ ___ ___ X **Ignored Fullness**	
M (S)	1 2 3 4 5 6 7	**Feel** Pos Neutral (Neg)
	Ate Mindfully FoodA U-NB (B) (Heck)	

started out to just have some ice cream--finished the container did Heck and all-out binge

Time	**Too Hungry** ___ ___ ___ N ___ ___ ___ ___ ___ **Ignored Fullness**	
M S	1 2 3 4 5 6 7	**Feel** Pos Neutral Neg
	Ate Mindfully FoodA U-NB B Heck	

_____
_____
_____

Goals:
Choose anti-deprivation eating (as needed).
Challenge excuses to binge.
Stop at point of diminishing returns.
Reduce size of binges.

Daily Summary:

No B? ____

All normal eating? _____

Deprivation: Low   Med (High)

Monitoring the What the Heck Response

Notes to Self:
Write down unhelpful thoughts/excuses. Use your wise mind (WM) to challenge all-or-nothing/magical thinking, denial, hopelessness, rebellion.

Day: **M   T   W   Th   F   S   Sun**

Time	**Too Hungry**			N		**Ignored Fullness**
M						
S	1	2	3	4	5	6 7
			Ate Mindfully			FoodA
			U-NB		B	Heck

Feel
Pos
Neutral
Neg

_____
_____
_____

Time	**Too Hungry**			N		**Ignored Fullness**
M						
S	1	2	3	4	5	6 7
			Ate Mindfully			FoodA
			U-NB		B	Heck

Feel
Pos
Neutral
Neg

_____
_____
_____

Time	**Too Hungry**			N		**Ignored Fullness**
M						
S	1	2	3	4	5	6 7
			Ate Mindfully			FoodA
			U-NB		B	Heck

Feel
Pos
Neutral
Neg

_____
_____
_____

Time	**Too Hungry**			N		**Ignored Fullness**
M						
S	1	2	3	4	5	6 7
			Ate Mindfully			FoodA
			U-NB		B	Heck

Feel
Pos
Neutral
Neg

_____
_____
_____

Time	**Too Hungry**			N		**Ignored Fullness**
M						
S	1	2	3	4	5	6 7
			Ate Mindfully			FoodA
			U-NB		B	Heck

Feel
Pos
Neutral
Neg

_____
_____
_____

Goals:
Choose anti-deprivation eating (as needed).
Challenge excuses to binge.
Stop at point of diminishing returns.
Reduce size of binges.

Daily Summary:

No B? _____

All normal eating? _____

Deprivation: Low   Med   High

Look for your excuses to binge. See if these excuses make sense when you are thinking rationally about the way food and calories actually work in your body. The following are a few excuses people commonly make for continuing to eat past even comfortable fullness:

- I might as well finish the package.

- I can't throw this out.

- I paid for it, so I should eat it.

- It will be easier to start over tomorrow.

Excuses are the way you buy some time before you have to get back on track after you overeat or binge. There are always going to be times when you ignore fullness and get off track. Getting off track is not a serious problem, you just have to get back on track. Staying off track is the problem. Becoming aware of your excuses helps you decide to get right back on track. Getting back on track means not compensating—no skipping the next meal. It means eating the next regularly scheduled meal, even if you eat only a small amount since you may not be hungry.

The types of unhelpful thinking discussed previously can often be detected in the excuses you use. For example "I don't care" devalues your long-term goal so you can give in to a short-term desire. It's a version of denial.

With magical thinking, an excuse may sound reasonable on the surface, but it doesn't reflect reality. You say "A little won't matter" or "A little more will make me feel better."

With all-or-nothing thinking, you fail to recognize that reality is not black and white. In reality, there are always many shades of gray. To challenge this form of unhelpful thinking, identify the two most extreme versions of your thought. For example, if you are thinking, "Losing weight is too hard; I'll never be able to do it," the extreme opposite thought is, "Losing weight is so easy, anyone can do it." Use your wise mind to look for a more reasonable, balanced thought that will encourage you to stay (or get back) on track. For example, you might change the excuse of "I have a slow metabolism" to "Weight loss is hard, but not impossible, and weight maintenance is actually easier than I thought it would be. Even if I am busy or stressed, I can eat normally and not gain weight."

CHANGING YOUR PREFERENCE FOR OVERFULLNESS

With AAT, you don't have to rely so heavily on willpower to eat less. When you are tuned into your stomach sensations, you are likely to notice that the stuffed feeling you used to like doesn't really feel that great. Once you give up getting stuffed, you then notice the more subtle uncomfortable feelings associated with overfullness. Most people who pay close attention notice that comfortably full actually feels slightly better than overfull. This awareness alters your preference from overfull to full. Altering your preference from full to moderate fullness is more of a challenge; your body naturally wants to get full. Stopping at moderate fullness is not aversive, but it is more of a learned preference than an innate one. However, you can cultivate a preference for moderate fullness. The program in this book is helping you do just that.

ARE YOU READY TO GO TO THE NEXT CHAPTER?

The amount of time necessary to essentially eliminate urges to binge varies considerably depending on the severity of your initial binge-eating problem. Some people are able to move on to the next part of the program after a week or two of challenging the unhelpful thoughts and excuses that allow bingeing. However, many individuals need to do this for several more weeks before they are ready to move on and address emotional eating.

You do not need to wait until your binges are completely eliminated to go on to the next chapter. If most of your binge episodes start out as emotional eating (or are planned binges), it is likely to be helpful to go ahead and start addressing why you look to food to change your feelings.

You are ready to go on to the next chapter when:

- You are eating normally much of the time (staying in the gray) even though you may not always feel positively about what kinds of food you are eating and you may still have to put in some effort to stay mindful while you eat and stop at moderate fullness.

- You can usually identify why you start eating. You choose to eat in order to prevent getting too hungry and to prevent feelings of deprivation.

- You have eliminated much of the mindless eating that you didn't enjoy.

- You are giving yourself credit when you avoid a binge by marking U-NB on the worksheet. Your urges to binge have started to decrease in frequency or intensity.

- You have noticed some change in the amount of food it takes for you to feel satisfied. Sometimes you actually feel good when you stop at moderate fullness. Sometimes you notice that overfullness doesn't feel quite as good as it used to.

7 Effective Emotional Eating

In the last chapter, you worked on not allowing overeating to turn into a binge; you learned to challenge the what the heck response. Now, you are going to work on reducing the power of emotions to trigger urges to eat (or to binge). Eating is not the only way you can make yourself feel better. You can develop alternative (nonfood) ways to change your emotional state so you have more options when you feel like eating for emotional reasons.

If you eat normally most of the time and do not binge, you will be able to maintain a stable weight even if you occasionally eat for emotional reasons. However, if you want to lose weight, you may need to work harder to reduce the frequency of emotional eating. Emotional eating is the main reason people are not able to reduce their calories on a consistent enough basis to lose weight. For most people, dieting is a roller-coaster ride. There are great days when you stick to your diet plan, but other days when you can't. You get discouraged when you can't stick to your plan. As long as you have a reasonable diet plan (you don't get too hungry), the biggest problem is emotional eating. When you start eating for emotional reasons, you are likely to choose comfort foods, which are usually higher in calories, and you are likely to eat past moderate fullness. You aren't thinking about food as a way to alleviate hunger; you are using food to feel better.

In this chapter, you are going to learn several strategies you can use to cope with your emotions without having to eat. You will learn to challenge unhelpful thoughts that generate or maintain negative feelings. You will learn to use alternative activities to distract yourself from moderately strong urges to eat. You will also learn strategies to increase your tolerance for simply experiencing negative feelings without eating. Most importantly, you will learn to limit how much you eat whenever you do start eating for emotional reasons. The latter is what I call *effective emotional eating*. Effective emotional eating is particularly useful when you want to eat for positive emotional reasons. Celebratory eating is a significant problem for your weight, because it is usually done in social situations where alcoholic beverages and particularly tempting foods are available. On those occasions, you have to deal both with your desire to enjoy the occasion more fully (an emotional trigger) and your desire to enjoy the special food (a food available trigger). Furthermore, alcohol makes it harder to stay aware of stomach sensations. It is much easier to tune out body awareness when you are drinking.

UNDERSTANDING EMOTIONAL EATING

Emotional eating is eating to fill psychological needs (Tank P is empty). When you experience this type of an urge to eat, you may be quite aware that you don't really feel hungry; you just feel like eating. At times, you may have a craving for a particular treat food. Even more puzzling are the times that you feel hungry even though you know you have recently eaten a reasonable amount of food, so you can't be biologically hungry. From early on, we have all been given food for many reasons besides hunger: to express love or approval, to show hospitality, or to help us cope with negative experiences. Eating gets associated with feeling better. Now, when you feel bad you may also "feel" hungry. You know you will feel better if you eat, so you think you must be hungry.

Eating, especially eating treats, is a naturally pleasant experience, and most people feel a little better after they eat. Research has shown that giving babies sugar pacifiers helps them tolerate painful medical procedures better than plain pacifiers. Children who are given lollipops to suck while getting injections report less pain and distress. As everyone knows, "a spoonfull of sugar makes the medicine go down." At a minimum, eating is good distraction. Unfortunately, food is limited in how much it can do for you psychologically, and its psychological effects don't last very long. If you often feel hungry or have urges to eat when you know you aren't biologically hungry, you may notice some of the following patterns:

- It is hard for you to get a feeling of satisfaction from food; you often want more than typical amounts.

- You may only feel satisfied when you feel stuffed; that may be the only time it is obvious to you that you can't possibly be hungry.

- Even when you get satisfied, you feel hungry unusually soon compared to others.

- When you try to diet, you have difficulty because you can't tell the difference between biological hunger (need for food) and psychological hunger (need to deal with emotions). Or, you ignore urges to eat when you know you aren't truly hungry, but then you feel deprived, which leads to overindulging later on.

The AAT Mind-Set About Emotional Eating

In AAT, binge eating and getting stuffed are *never* viewed as effective coping strategies, because you always end up feeling worse. Thus, AAT has you eliminate eating large amounts first, even if you have to allow yourself more treats or comfort foods in order to do so. In contrast, eating for emotional reasons is viewed as an acceptable coping strategy provided that you are able to stop at moderate fullness and that you don't use this strategy all the time. Overuse of eating to cope with emotions is one of the main reasons a person gains weight, or fails to lose weight. Once you rarely binge (or get stuffed), you are ready to start looking more closely at the emotions that make you want to eat when you are not really hungry.

Dealing with the many emotions that can trigger urges to eat is complicated, and it can feel overwhelming. AAT has a single guideline for dealing with emotional eating: Stay tuned into your stomach no matter why you start eating. Your stomach is quite reliable and will not lead you astray. However, when you decide to satisfy emotional needs with food, you have to be very careful. It is much harder to stop at moderate fullness. This chapter teaches you how to use food effectively when you just can't come up with a better alternative.

Over time, you are going to develop better self-care skills, and when you do, you won't need to eat for emotional reasons as often as you do now. In the meantime, use your stomach fullness signal to protect yourself from excessive emotional eating that will only amplify your weight concerns. Now, imagine you have an urge to eat and you know it stems from emotions, not true hunger. This is how you talk to yourself using an AAT mind-set:

> *This is Tank P hunger. If I can't think of an alternative, or if I try several alternatives and still have a strong urge to eat, I will make a conscious decision to choose self-soothing eating. Eating a moderate amount of something I really want can be an effective way to nurture or soothe myself until I can figure out more effective ways to manage my feelings. To use food as effectively as I can, I need to figure out what type of food I really want. What food is most likely to help me change my emotions. However, if I don't feel better after one serving of the food I really want and I am tempted to eat more, then I have to change gears. At that point, I must accept that food is not going to work in this situation, and that eating more is guaranteed to make me feel worse. I am not going to do something that I am fully conscious will make me feel worse almost immediately. I will use problem-solving skills to come up with some additional alternatives, or I will practice tolerating my distress without eating.*

Can You Ever Eliminate Emotional Eating?

You don't need to completely eliminate emotional eating. You can learn to use food more effectively to feel better occasionally without relying on it to fix all your feelings. Deciding to have a treat may be the most viable option you have in certain situations. However, you do need to eliminate using emotions as an excuse for getting stuffed (or a binge). Challenge your excuses when you find yourself using emotions to justify that kind of eating. For example, "I'm so upset; I can't help it. I've had such a hard day, I deserve it." There is never a good enough reason to get completely stuffed. You will feel worse, not better.

What About Your Underlying Emotional Issues?

Many approaches to emotional eating are designed to help you resolve your underlying emotional issues so you won't feel the need to eat so intensely. In contrast, AAT starts by taking decisions about eating out of the emotional realm. How much you "want" is no longer the basis for your eating decisions. Instead, you choose to use hunger and fullness to decide when to start and stop eating. Rather than simply giving in to emotionally-driven urges to eat, you instruct yourself in the following way:

> *It doesn't matter if I feel anxious, upset, or bored, or I am celebrating and enjoying food. I have made a commitment to stop as soon as I feel stomach distention. At that point, food has done all the good it can do for me. Continuing to eat will detract from whatever good the food can do for me and will create more negative feelings. In the moment, it may be hard for me to remember that I will feel worse later. That is why I use my stomach as a stop sign instead of allowing my mind to make excuses to eat more. Of course I don't want to stop eating. Right now, I think more food will make me feel better. But I know that is magical thinking. I wish more food would make me feel better, but it won't. Getting stuffed always makes me feel worse.*

You may find that you do have emotional issues and that you must address these before you are able to make further progress with AAT. You may be able to address these yourself, or you may need the help of a peer counselor, personal coach, or professional counselor. You can probably stop gaining weight without resolving other emotional issues. However, you are likely to find that you have to address those issues if you want to reduce emotional eating enough to lose a substantial amount of weight. You must first learn to manage your emotions without bingeing or overeating before you try to lose weight. Otherwise, emotional eating is going to sabotage your efforts. Once you can do that, chapter 10 describes how to use AAT as a foundation for weight loss.

HOW DO YOU HANDLE URGES TO EAT FOR EMOTIONAL REASONS?

In the last chapter you learned to manage urges to binge by making conscious decisions to eat what you really want to eat. Staying conscious of your decision to eat allows you to challenge the what the heck response. Choosing anti-deprivation eating is the way you keep deprivation low when you have a strong urge to eat. When you fail to prevent deprivation, you set yourself up for emotional eating. Deprivation is one of many emotions that can trigger urges to eat (or plans to binge).

As discussed in the last chapter, when you have a strong urge to binge you may not always be able to stop at moderate fullness. You may end up eating to the point of diminishing returns, the point at which eating no longer feels good. It is a success whenever you can cut a binge short of getting stuffed, regardless of where that point happens to be. However, when you have a less intense urge, just an urge to eat, you have more options. You can try distraction, urge surfing (acknowledging and observing your urge to eat without acting on it), or tolerating the feeling without eating. Alternatively, you can decide to "use" food but to do so effectively (stop at moderate fullness).

In this chapter I will focus mostly on the later strategy, how to do effective emotional eating (what I call EEE). The other alternatives require skills that Marsha Linehan calls emotion regulation skills. If you have trouble developing or using those skills, you may benefit from her skills training manual (Linehan 1993) or you may need the help of a professional counselor. Linehan's skills training manual was first developed to help people cope with borderline personality disorder, a severe problem with regulating emotions, but the skills taught in it have been found effective for a wide array of problems.

Deprivation Leads to Emotional Eating

If you have been dieting a long time, particularly if you have been following a strict diet, you are likely to have a backlog of deprivation feelings. These deprivation feelings may go away fairly quickly once you start following AAT guidelines, because you'll realize you're allowed to eat what you want and get moderately full. It is difficult to construe that as deprivation. However, if you have been highly sensitized to the feeling of deprivation, it may take several months of normal eating for your general feeling of deprivation to diminish. Let's look at an example of the way past deprivation may be related to current urges to eat (or binge).

Jill, a college student, came to the eating clinic because she had such strong urges to binge that she felt completely out of control. Though she had not yet become overweight, she feared that she would if she couldn't stop bingeing. She correctly recognized that her sense of loss of control was the result of several years of severe restricting she had done when she was required to maintain an ultrathin weight for her modeling career. She had stopped modeling and given up deliberate restriction over a year before coming to the clinic. She had anticipated that she would want to eat a lot more at first, but she became alarmed when her urges to binge remained strong after a year of not dieting. She was scared of her urges to eat and felt that they had to be controlled. By monitoring her appetite, Jill realized her history of severe deprivation made her unusually sensitive to any attempt to forbid herself to eat something she wanted. She learned to use anti-deprivation eating deliberately to minimize her feelings of deprivation without getting stuffed. After two months, the intensity of her deprivation feelings lessened. She found she was able to eat normally, and her urges to binge essentially disappeared.

With AAT, you will still feel tempted to eat when your favorite treats are available, but you'll know that you must eat treats sufficiently frequently so that your general deprivation level remains low. Then, the urges are not overwhelming. You don't have to binge. You can choose to eat treats sometimes, especially as part of your scheduled meals and snacks, and you can choose not to eat treats at other times.

Deprivation is even trickier when it has little to do with refusing to eat the foods you want. If you feel deprived but you can't identify any specific food you crave, your sense of deprivation probably comes from not allowing yourself adequate pleasure in other areas of your life rather than simply from restricting the kinds of foods you eat. You may be very hard on yourself or you may deprive yourself of simple indulgences that would reduce your need to get pleasure from food. If you decide that nonfood deprivation is a significant aspect of your emotional eating, you may benefit from seeing a professional to help you figure out why you deprive yourself in other areas and how you can start enriching your life in nonfood ways so you can rely less on food.

How Emotional Eating Relates to the Other Problem Paths

If you check in and you don't feel hungry and you can't identify an obvious external cue, your urge to eat has to be coming from Tank P. However, you may not be able to identify what you feel at the moment, or what change in your emotions you expect to achieve by eating. Difficulty managing uncomfortable emotions is the most significant cause of eating disorders. I use the word "uncomfortable" to point out that your feelings may not be extremely intense; they may just be a little uncomfortable. These milder feelings are often the most difficult to identify, which also makes them difficult to manage differently.

From the AAT point of view, emotional eating is only one of the ways you get sidetracked from the normal eating path. When you start following AAT guidelines, you realize that eating when food is available, allowing yourself to get too hungry, ignoring fullness, and the what the heck response account for many of your problem eating episodes. Perhaps you thought that emotional eating was your main problem because emotion-driven eating episodes typically feel the most upsetting. You are more likely to remember episodes that are triggered by intense emotions. However, you will make progress faster by first taking care of all the other problem pathways, the ones that are a bit easier to handle. Once you have reduced the other problem paths, you may find that you don't have as many emotional eating episodes as you once thought. In any event, emotional eating is easier to deal with once some of the smoke has been cleared. So, before you try to reduce eating for emotional reasons, you will do well to deal with the other problem paths first.

EFFECTIVE EMOTIONAL EATING: A STRATEGY TO LIMIT THE HARM DONE

When nonfood alternatives are not easily available or are not working for you, you are encouraged to make a conscious decision to allow yourself self-soothing eating. This strategy (limit the harm done) is similar to the strategy you learned in the last chapter, where I asked you to make a conscious decision to eat (or even overeat) in order to prevent a binge later on. Effective emotional eating means you give up using emotions as an excuse to get stuffed. Each time you are successful in using food to soothe yourself without getting stuffed, you limit the harm done and you gain confidence in your ability to use, not abuse, food.

Imagine you are planning to celebrate a special occasion with friends. Or, you are tense and need to calm down. In the moment, you can't come up with a better plan, so you decide you will eat something. However, you stick to the AAT principles, so you commit to stopping at moderate fullness even if you would like more. If you are not able to stop at moderate fullness, at least you stay aware as you are eating so you can identify the point of diminishing returns and stop as soon as you feel uncomfortable. Using conscious decisions to eat teaches you what amounts of which special treat foods will work to make you feel better. You also learn to notice when the pleasure of eating diminishes, the point at which food has done all it can do for you and you need to try some other strategy. When you feel worse after having a treat, you know you have not used food effectively. Let's look at an example of effective emotional eating.

Liz knows that when she has had a particularly stressful day at work, she has an urge to binge as soon as she walks into her house. If she comes home and tries to make dinner, she overeats as she cooks and often keeps snacking for the rest of the evening. She has learned to make a conscious choice on those days to stop and eat dinner on the way home. She starts with soup because it makes her eat more slowly and the heat relaxes her tense stomach. She eats a normal-size dinner and has a special treat, a small piece of her favorite fudge. Usually she goes a little past moderate fullness, but when she gets home she is feeling okay and she does not have strong urges to eat more. In short, she has used food effectively.

Liz is also working on alternative ways to reduce stress at work. She has signed up for an assertion training class so she will be better able to set appropriate limits and communicate effectively with her boss. She has started a weekly yoga class. In the long run, these strategies will reduce how frequently she feels so stressed that she has the urge to binge, but in the meantime she knows how to manage her urges to eat for emotional reasons without getting stuffed.

Managing Emotional Eating and Life Stress

You may manage your eating pretty well as long as life is going well but you may not be able to maintain your focus on eating when something significant comes along to disrupt your routine. It may not matter if the change is positive (like going on a vacation or moving to a new house) or negative (like illness, injury, or family problems). You probably feel as though you only have enough energy and attention to cope with one area of your life at a time. So you alternate between working on your eating and dealing with other issues. This either-or approach leads to yo-yo dieting and a pattern of weight loss and regain.

The AAT philosophy is to deal with both eating and other life issues at the same time. You choose to maintain normal eating regardless of what else is going on in your life. You never stop being aware of your eating. You are able to maintain normal eating even under duress because the basic principles are simple. Whether there is too much food available or you are dealing with emotions that trigger eating, you just stay tuned into your stomach and allow it to tell you when to stop. You never give yourself an excuse to get completely stuffed. If you are very upset, you may need to eat, but as long as you don't get stuffed you are not likely to gain weight. You learn that you can weather emotional storms and special occasions without triggering binges or gaining weight.

YOUR STEP-BY-STEP GUIDE TO MANAGING URGES TO EAT

Food can be an effective way to cope with emotions, but when hunger is not the reason you want to eat, food is rarely the most effective strategy you could choose. Use the following exercise to learn strategies to make better eating decisions when you want to eat but it is not time for a regularly scheduled meal or snack. These strategies are not intended to resolve long-standing issues. These strategies just get you through the moment without bingeing or overeating. This exercise does help you start identifying any long-term issues that you need to address, but you can't fix those issues in the moment. For those issues, you need to develop a longer-term strategy. The next time you have an urge to eat go through these steps.

Step one: Rule out biological hunger. Every time you have a desire to eat, ask why?

Is it close to my regular time for a meal or snack? _____

Am I physically hungry? _____

If the answer to either question is yes, eat the type of food you want to eat but make sure you do not go past moderate fullness.

If the answer to both questions is no, ask yourself:

Am I craving a certain food? If yes, what is it? _____

If no, which statement feels more true at this moment?

_____ I have a definite urge to eat food.

_____ I really just want something to do to try to change my emotional state.

Step two: Rate the intensity of your urge to eat (1 to 7).

If your rating is weak (3 or below), try distraction. Get rid of any tempting food or leave the environment. Then practice ignoring any slight feeling of deprivation you experience.

If your rating is moderate (4 to 5) you can try distraction, but you may be more successful if you consciously practice urge surfing. Urge surfing is acknowledging that you want to eat and just observing your desire to eat without acting on it. You watch the way the urge initially increases, peaks, and starts to decrease. Urge surfing helps you realize that an urge is just a feeling and reminds you that you don't have to act on every feeling you have. The intensity of an urge will fade on its own if you acknowledge it instead of trying to suppress it or pretend you don't have the urge. Challenge your unhelpful thinking. It is not awful that you must refrain from acting on an urge. You do this all the time with urges that are not related to food. With practice, you can learn to tolerate moderate urges to eat when you aren't biologically hungry.

If the urge is strong (6 or 7) or persistent (keeps coming back), don't fight with it. Acknowledge it and make a conscious decision to eat. Remember, you have already acknowledged that you are not feeling physically hungry so you know you are only eating for taste. When you eat for taste, you need to obtain the most pleasure possible from whatever calories you take in. Thus, it is critical that you eat the type of food you want and that you eat slowly and mindfully. You need to enjoy what you eat to the fullest so the food is able to do its job, which is to make you feel better.

Alternatives for Urges to Eat When Not Hungry

Activities designed to alter physical sensations and emotions directly so you can self-soothe without eating:

- Take a nap or go to bed early.

- Practice breathing exercises (e.g., somato-respiratory integration exercises), meditation, or prayer.

- Listen to a relaxation audiotape.

- Watch a yoga video.

- Do some physical activity (like walking, stretches, or exercise).

- Take medication if pain is the feeling you are trying to reduce.

- Sing, listen to music, or dance.

- Get a massage or learn self-care techniques to reduce arousal (self-massage for feet or hands or use a theracane; alternative practices such as jin shin and acupressure).

- Take a hot bath, sauna, or hot tub.

Activities that are highly positive or engaging so they distract you or provide pleasure without eating:

- Watch a movie.

- Go shopping (window-shop if you can't afford to buy).

- Talk on the phone.

- Go visit someone.

- Play video games, surf the Web, or e-mail a friend.

- Write letters or write in a journal.

- Read for pleasure. Read inspirational and self-help books. (They give you new ideas to consider and boost motivation.)

Activities that are incompatible with eating:

- Get (or give yourself) a manicure or pedicure.

- Tend to your garden.

- Do some knitting or needlepoint.

- Paint a picture.

- Create crafts.

- Develop new hobbies (like photography, origami, or flower arranging).

List any other activities that work will for you: _____

_____

Step three: Identify and challenge thoughts that are encouraging you to eat even though you know you aren't hungry. What thoughts cause you the most difficulty?

- ☐   I deserve a treat.

- ☐   I want to celebrate.

- ☐   I want to avoid doing something else (procrastinate).

- ☐   I feel bored.

- ☐   Food will help me keep doing something I don't want to be doing (like studying).

- ☐   Food will make me feel better.

- ☐   Other: _____

Ask yourself:

Can I find a nonfood way to treat myself or celebrate? _____

Can I do something else to distract myself? _____

Am I willing to try a nonfood way to feel better? _____

Can I ask someone else to distract me or help me feel better (get support)? _____

Identify and challenge the excuses you give yourself that keep you from trying some activity other than eating. What excuses cause you the most difficulty?

- ☐   I can't think of anything else that will work.

- ☐   I don't have time for anything else.

- ☐   I've tried other things and they never work.

- ☐   I think I should be able to tolerate urges without having to distract myself.

☐ I think others will notice or comment on what I am doing.

☐ I don't like to ask others for help; it makes me feel weak or inferior.

☐ I think I will make others uncomfortable or diminish their pleasure in eating.

☐ I might be considered rude or unsociable if I don't join the eating.

☐ I just don't want to do what I know will work; I feel rebellious and unwilling.

☐ Other: _____

Identify what interferes when you try to tolerate an urge to eat without acting on it. What makes it too hard for you to just tolerate distress?

☐ Not eating triggers an uncomfortable feeling of deprivation. (Try finding a nonfood indulgence.)

☐ Not eating makes me anxious or restless. (Try using another strategy to reduce this more directly.)

☐ Not eating makes it harder for me to make myself do something I really need to do. (Give yourself permission to procrastinate but in a nonfood way, or set up a nonfood reward for yourself if you will just go ahead and do what you are putting off.)

☐ Not eating makes me feel angry and rebellious. (Practice using nonfood ways to express these feelings such as journaling, art, and talking about your feelings.)

☐ Other: _____

Remember the most important guideline when you are trying to find nonfood alternatives: *Don't try harder; try different.* Most of you already try hard not to eat when you know you aren't hungry. Lack of effort is not usually your problem. Lack of creativity or being stubborn is more likely the problem. You may be bullheaded and refuse to try alternatives that might work because you think you shouldn't have to do them. After all, you know many other people who don't have to do them. So, you keep doing the same old things that don't work. Instead, open your mind. Put aside your pride and stop comparing yourself to everyone else. Just figure out what works for you right now. There is always something else you can try. You just have to be willing. It is hard to develop the mind-set of being willing. You have to cultivate a willing attitude; it doesn't come naturally. I refer you to Marsha Linehan's skills training workbook (1993) if you need more help learning to do what is necessary to get the results you want. You can apply the principles in it to help you cultivate a willing attitude. Another helpful resource when you just don't feel like doing what you know would help is Winget's (2004) book about "getting a life."

HOW TO MONITOR EMOTIONAL EATING

Using food effectively is a necessary skill. Overusing food is the problem.

Anita Johnson (1996) suggests that the type of food you crave can give you a clue about your feelings. Certain foods are typically associated with certain types of feelings. For example, many people want crunchy foods when they are angry, but want creamy or rich foods when they need comfort.

Your associations between certain foods and specific emotions have been established through your unique experiences with food, so the meaning of the food you want may or may not be the same as what that food would mean to someone else. If you can't figure out why you want the particular food you want, think of situations or events from your past that typically involved that food. Then identify the feelings you were having in those situations. Those feelings are most likely to be the feelings you have now when you crave that food.

Many strong associations between feelings and food are established during childhood. For example, you may be feeling a bit insecure or left out of some group activity, and find yourself wanting to eat. You want the taste of homemade cookies. You remember that as a child your mother gave you homemade cookies when you came home from school. If you were upset she would listen to your problems as you ate the cookies and you would feel reassured that things would work out. As an adult, you may have trouble acknowledging when you feel insecure. You may just know you really want some cookies.

If you frequently use food to avoid feelings, you may have trouble identifying those feelings. You may think you just like to eat and that's all there is to it. If you often put a "?" on your worksheet, consider what kinds of uncomfortable feelings you may be avoiding. As you practice digging a little deeper into uncomfortable feelings, you will get better at tuning in to what you are feeling when you want to eat for emotional reasons.

INSTRUCTIONS FOR MONITORING EMOTIONAL EATING

1. Continue to monitor your appetite cues as you did last week. Continue to circle FoodA and/or Heck when appropriate. Continue to write down and challenge unhelpful thinking and excuses that encourage you to eat past moderate fullness.

2. Your goal this week is to reduce emotional eating. Circle EmEat if you overeat (or binge) and you were eating for emotional reasons (to celebrate or to cope with uncomfortable feelings). Each time you mark EmEat, describe the emotions that made you want to eat. If you can't describe your feelings, put a ? Note Effective Emotional Eating (EEE) or Anti-Deprivation Eating (ADE) when you use these strategies effectively to self-soothe or prevent deprivation without getting stuffed or bingeing.

3. Continue to complete the daily summary.

Monitoring Emotional Eating

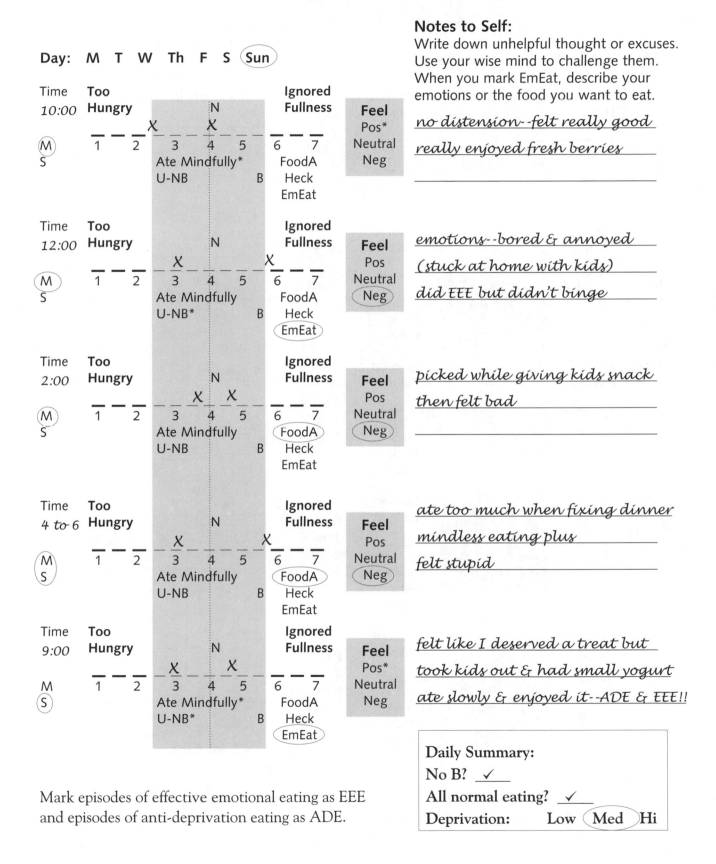

Notes to Self:
Write down unhelpful thought or excuses. Use your wise mind to challenge them. When you mark EmEat, describe your emotions or the food you want to eat.

no distension--felt really good
really enjoyed fresh berries

emotions--bored & annoyed
(stuck at home with kids)
did EEE but didn't binge

picked while giving kids snack
then felt bad

ate too much when fixing dinner
mindless eating plus
felt stupid

felt like I deserved a treat but
took kids out & had small yogurt
ate slowly & enjoyed it--ADE & EEE!!

Daily Summary:
No B? ✓
All normal eating? ✓
Deprivation: Low (Med) Hi

Mark episodes of effective emotional eating as EEE and episodes of anti-deprivation eating as ADE.

Monitoring Emotional Eating

Notes to Self:
Write down unhelpful thought or excuses. Use your wise mind to challenge them. When you mark EmEat, describe your emotions or the food you want to eat.

Day: M T W Th F S Sun

Time	**Too Hungry**	N	**Ignored Fullness**	**Feel** Pos Neutral Neg
M S	1 2 3 4 5 6 7 Ate Mindfully U-NB B		FoodA Heck EmEat	

_____
_____
_____

Time	**Too Hungry**	N	**Ignored Fullness**	**Feel** Pos Neutral Neg
M S	1 2 3 4 5 6 7 Ate Mindfully U-NB B		FoodA Heck EmEat	

_____
_____
_____

Time	**Too Hungry**	N	**Ignored Fullness**	**Feel** Pos Neutral Neg
M S	1 2 3 4 5 6 7 Ate Mindfully U-NB B		FoodA Heck EmEat	

_____
_____
_____

Time	**Too Hungry**	N	**Ignored Fullness**	**Feel** Pos Neutral Neg
M S	1 2 3 4 5 6 7 Ate Mindfully U-NB B		FoodA Heck EmEat	

_____
_____
_____

Time	**Too Hungry**	N	**Ignored Fullness**	**Feel** Pos Neutral Neg
M S	1 2 3 4 5 6 7 Ate Mindfully U-NB B		FoodA Heck EmEat	

_____
_____
_____

Mark episodes of effective emotional eating as EEE and episodes of anti-deprivation eating as ADE.

Daily Summary:

Binge? _____

All normal eating? _____

Deprivation: Low   Med   Hi

HOW TO IDENTIFY UNDERLYING LIFE ISSUES

Forcing yourself to label your emotions when you mark emotional eating is the first step toward effectively identifying any life issues you may need to confront. You will notice which emotions keep turning up when you want to binge or get stuffed. Then, you can identify the underlying issues that you need to tackle directly, not mask with eating. AAT can limit the harm done by emotional eating, but AAT strategies do not address other emotional issues. Those issues will keep triggering emotional eating until they are adequately addressed.

Many people find it useful to set aside regular, specific times to think about what is not working or what is missing from their life, and to make concrete plans to get started on changing their situation. I recommend you set aside fifteen minutes each evening for some undisturbed thinking time about why you choose to use food instead of changing what you don't like about your life. Or, you can set aside an hour a week to have, in essence, your own therapy session. During this time, stay focused on the task of making a plan to address long-term issues; do not get sidetracked thinking about problems you must deal with this week. If you feel stuck or it is too painful to face these issues on your own, consider seeking professional help. Even if you have a friend who wants to help, talking with a counselor may work better. A counselor is trained to remain more objective while helping you sort out your feelings and allow you to come to your own conclusions. It's hard for a good friend to remain objective and refrain from giving you advice.

Use the following questions to start the process of figuring out your emotional issues and developing long-term plans to deal with those issues.

MY LONG TERM PLANS

What do I need to do in the long run to reduce my need to use food to feel better? How am I going to keep my Tank P full enough so that I don't need to eat so often to fill my psychological needs? What underlying emotional issues do I think I may need to tackle? Check all that apply.

- ☐ Lack assertiveness (You are not able to make time for self or you have difficulty setting boundaries with others.)

- ☐ Feel deprived regarding food (You feel it's unfair that your genes or metabolism make it harder for you to attain a reasonable weight than it is for others.)

- ☐ Feel bitter (You feel life has been unfair to you in other, nonfood ways.)

- ☐ Lack financial resources

- ☐ Life lacks adequate alternative pleasures

- ☐ Life lacks adequate social contacts or activities

☐   Family demands or conflicts

☐   Work too demanding or stressful

☐   Health problems

☐   Other psychological issues (depression or anxiety)

☐   Difficulty staying organized and focused on a plan of action

☐   Significant others not supportive

☐   Guilt

☐   Dwelling on things from your past that can't be changed (for example, past losses or trauma)

What keeps you from addressing these issues?

_____

What is your plan to start addressing these issues?

_____

_____

_____

Do you need to seek professional help to address these issues?

_____

Most of my clients find they can stop binge eating and stabilize their weight even when they have significant unresolved life issues. They learn to stop at moderate fullness most of the time no matter what. This strategy may sound like a version of "just say no," but it isn't. You are able to stop bingeing because you have discovered a more positive reason to stop; you stop as soon as your stomach feels uncomfortable. As you monitor your appetite, the difference between eating that is an effective coping strategy and eating that makes you feel worse becomes quite clear. This awareness makes it easier to stop using food ineffectively, but it doesn't eliminate emotional eating altogether. In fact, giving up binge eating takes away one of the strategies you use to cope with or avoid uncomfortable emotions. The good news is that it is easier to deal with your other issues once they are clearly exposed rather than disguised as disordered eating. The bad news is you still have to deal with them.

Mary's story is an example of the way larger life issues relate to disordered eating. Mary lived alone, held down a demanding and stressful nursing job, and was primarily responsible for her elderly mother, who lived in town. Her mother was demanding, difficult, and critical about

Mary's weight, despite the fact that she, also, was overweight. Mary learned to use the AAT guidelines and regained a sense of control over her eating. Within ten weeks, she had essentially stopped bingeing and getting stuffed. This improvement put a stop to her pattern of weight gain, but she continued to have many episodes of emotional eating in which she wanted comfort foods. She had to make conscious decisions to eat to self-soothe quite often, but she no longer got uncomfortably full or stuffed.

Mary was able to identify that her triggers for emotional eating were times she didn't stand up for herself at work or with her mother. Mary didn't set adequate limits that would allow her to plan her eating and take care of her own needs first. While she was now able to maintain a stable weight, Mary realized she needed to address her larger life problems before she could consider attempting weight loss. She looked into resources for assertiveness training and found a class that started in a few weeks. She also started looking for a new job, recognizing that finding a better job situation might take a while. In the meantime, she continues to practice normal eating and pays close attention each time she feels good about what or how much she eats. She does not give up and wait to improve her eating until she resolves her larger life issues. At some point, she will feel ready to consider more deliberate weight loss strategies.

ARE YOU READY TO GO TO THE NEXT CHAPTER?

Learning to deal effectively with emotions (especially feelings of deprivation) is a lifelong process. When you know how to do effective emotional eating and how to use anti-deprivation eating, you are better prepared to cope with the challenges of eating in today's environment. You will get better at normal eating the longer you practice AAT. I encourage you to use this chapter's worksheet to monitor for at least a week. Many people with long-standing emotional issues with food need to continue using this written monitoring for extended periods of time. Make copies and use this worksheet until you feel comfortable that you can avoid getting stuffed regardless of the situation. If you want to take AAT one step further, go on to chapter 8, which teaches you how to modify your preferences so it is easier to choose healthier types of food more of the time.

8 Food Awareness Training

If you feel pretty good about your ability to stop at moderate fullness but you still feel bad when you eat certain types of foods or you have not achieved a weight acceptable to you, this chapter offers some additional help. *Food awareness training* makes it a little easier to choose healthier or lower-calorie foods. From an AAT perspective, the best foods are foods that have relatively fewer calories per unit of volume. AAT encourages you to try low-calorie-density foods, such as vegetables, because these foods create stomach fullness sensations with the least amount of calories. You can achieve moderate fullness, feel pretty satisfied, and still limit calories. These foods tend to promote health as well.

Many people notice that their food preferences naturally start to change in a healthier direction as soon as they start paying attention to stomach fullness. At this point, you no longer want to get stuffed, even when you choose to eat your favorite foods. You are too aware of the discomfort you feel in your stomach after you have had too much of any type of food. Many people decide to stop at this point. You can just continue eating normally and see what effect it has on your food preferences and your weight. However, if you want to encourage weight loss, you can do more than stop at moderate fullness. You can practice food awareness training.

EXTENDING YOUR AWARENESS TRAINING

Food awareness training asks you to extend your awareness of stomach fullness to include more global bodily sensations that occur when you eat different types of foods. These sensations include gastrointestinal symptoms such as bloating, abdominal distress, heartburn, and slightly queasy feelings as well as changes in attention and energy. You may notice that you get hungry or feel tired sooner after eating high-sugar foods than after eating high-protein foods. You may also notice differences in your psychological state depending on the types of food you choose. These feelings might be positive, such as a sense of well-being and self-efficacy after you make certain food choices, or they might be negative, such as a sense of annoyance, guilt, or shame after making other food choices. Awareness of these consequences can serve as motivation to choose alternative foods that you will feel good about eating. You can significantly amplify the power of these sensations through focused attention in the same way that you learned to pay attention to sensations of stomach fullness.

In food awareness training, you do not set limits or goals for calories or fat grams, and you do not follow a specific food plan. You simply commit to trying alternative, low-calorie-density foods, carefully evaluating how you feel after eating different foods and developing your own personal food guidelines based on these previously ignored (or at least minimized) sources of information. Then, you practice deliberately consulting your food guidelines each time you are making a decision about what type of food to eat. This deliberate consultation brings you to a new level of mindful eating. Now, you not only make a conscious decision to start eating, you also make a conscious decision about what you are going to eat (after consulting your food guidelines). Your personal food guidelines summarize your particular reactions to specific amounts of specific types of foods. You continuously gather new information about how you react to foods each time you eat. As you become more aware of the connections between what you eat and how you feel, you revise your personal guidelines. Your guidelines allow you to make fast and accurate predictions about how you are likely to feel if you make a particular food choice. You can take this information into consideration and make a wise decision about what to eat. These guidelines help you stop obsessing over what you should or shouldn't eat. You can stop making choices that don't end up feeling good.

FOOD AWARENESS VERSUS DIETS

I encourage you to try this approach to food awareness because it is easier than following a diet. However, if you try food awareness and you still cannot achieve the weight loss you desire, and if you predict you can handle greater limitations on the types of foods you are allowed to eat, you can also try any of the many specific diets designed for weight loss. You may have to try several diet plans to find one that you can tolerate. As discussed in appendix C, almost any diet can be modified so that you can maintain the basic AAT guidelines.

You should also be aware that specific diet plans are just a set of rules that tell you what or how much to eat. When you use these kinds of rules, you may trigger deprivation; you may end up breaking the rules and trigger the what the heck response. Rules don't teach you how to make your own decisions about food. Thus, if you decide to follow a specific diet plan for a while, come back to this chapter when you are ready to make the transition back to eating from within and to make your own food choices.

If you try specific diets, you may find that the additional limitations placed on what you can eat trigger feelings of deprivation and urges to binge that you thought were gone for good. If this happens, please stop immediately and come back to this chapter. You will need to stay with this slower, less restrictive strategy and gradually modify your food preferences through increased awareness of the consequences of different foods for your whole body.

MAKING DECISIONS ABOUT THE TYPE OF FOOD TO EAT

Eating decisions are complicated. You have to decide when, how much, and what type of food you want to eat. You already know when to eat (scheduled meals and snacks and when you feel hungry) and how much to eat (not more than moderate fullness). Up to this point in the program, you have been encouraged to eat whatever types of food you want. Choosing what you want to eat usually means choosing what will taste best. Unfortunately, many of the foods that taste best are high-fat or high-calorie foods. Furthermore, many of these foods are also calorie-dense foods, like fudge. High-calorie-density foods may trick your fullness signals. You might consume a lot of calories before you feel the moderate fullness signal. Thus, the goal of food awareness training is to help you modify your food preferences so you choose low-calorie-density foods more of the time.

Maintain the Fullness Boundary

Success in reducing total calorie intake depends on your ability to maintain the fullness boundary while you experiment with low-calorie-density food alternatives. People naturally tend to eat larger amounts when they eat low-calorie-density foods. This phenomena is probably largely psychological; you think you can afford to eat more of those foods. However, it may be partly biological since your body prefers to maintain a stable weight. When you reduce the calorie density of what you are eating, you may instinctively feel like you need to eat a little more to compensate for getting fewer calories. To lose weight, you must trick your weight regulation system by not allowing that kind of natural compensation. Your goal is to keep the amount (the volume of food you eat) the same, but reduce the calories. Only then can you achieve significant calorie savings while maintaining a feeling of moderate fullness. However, you mustn't restrict calorie-dense foods too severely, because you may trigger feelings of deprivation. Maintaining your fullness boundary allows you to eat some high-calorie-density foods without fearing loss of control. You know you are going stop at moderate fullness no matter what type of food you eat. However, substituting low density foods helps weight concerns as long as you don't start feeling deprived.

Balance the Power of Taste

Taste, or rather anticipated taste, is not a good signal to use when deciding when to eat. If you start eating whenever tasty food is available or whenever you think about tasty food, you will likely develop a weight problem. Taste is also not a good signal to decide when to stop eating. Most foods still taste good at the moderate fullness point. If you rely on taste as your signal to stop, you will eat until the food no longer tastes good, or until the food is gone.

How should you use taste? Since taste is a very powerful and natural signal, it is better to respect that signal and work with it rather than try to trick it. If you limit the variety of foods you eat or eat lots of bland, diet foods that don't taste very good, you might eat less for a while. But avoiding tasty foods does not feel normal and it ultimately leads to feelings of deprivation.

Fortunately, you don't have to ignore taste completely. It is perfectly okay to use taste as one of the signals you use to decide what type of food you are going to eat; doing so protects you from developing feelings of deprivation. Food awareness training simply teaches you to balance the power of the anticipated taste with accurate predictions about how that food is going to make you feel once it gets past your mouth. Most people don't naturally think much about how they are going to feel after they have eaten. Since weight gain doesn't show up immediately, fear of weight gain is often not adequately compelling in the moment that tasty food is available. Food awareness training forces you to pay attention to more positive and immediately compelling reasons to make healthier food choices. You want to feel good after you eat. You don't really want to feel uncomfortable or upset after you have eaten. When you consider the more immediate consequences of your food choices, high-fat, high-calorie foods lose some of their appeal and low-calorie-density foods become more appealing.

Combining Taste and Feel to Make Eating Decisions

Imagine your coworker brings in donuts one morning, but you also have fresh fruit salad available for your usual morning snack. You have a decision to make. If you just consider taste, you are likely to choose the donuts, and you may eat several if you eat until they stop tasting good. If you consider how you will feel in twenty minutes, you are likely to make a different decision. If you predict you will feel deprived if you don't have a donut, you may choose anti-deprivation eating. However, you will choose to eat one or, at the most, two donuts, because you are committed to stopping at moderate fullness. After several weeks of food awareness training, you may have some new information available to you. You may have become quite clear that you feel better the rest of the morning when you eat fruit salad than when you have donuts. You may have discovered that you get too hungry before lunch when you eat donuts. You may learn you get a real drop in energy an hour after eating donuts. When you consider all this information, you may choose to eat only one donut or to eat just the salad some of the time (and not feel deprived later on). This is the model you want to use when selecting what types of foods to eat. Balance taste against how you will feel later in the day, and make your choice based on both pieces of information.

MONITORING HOW FOODS FEEL

Since most people focus on taste while they are eating and tune out their body, you will need to shift your attention from your mouth (taste) to your stomach and to other bodily sensations (the feel of the food in your body). This shift does not ensure that your preferences will change, but it does provide opportunities for your preferences to change. With time you will get better at predicting how you are going to feel after you eat high-fat, high-calorie foods, and you may find that this knowledge reduces your preferences for those foods.

In order to achieve this alteration in preferences, you need to monitor how different types of food feel in your body. You do not need to monitor taste; you are already quite aware of how foods taste. You may also be quite aware of your negative thoughts as you contemplate eating high-fat, high-calorie foods, but those often fail to be adequately compelling to guide your choices. What you need to monitor is how you feel shortly after you eat specific foods. This will give you positive reasons to make healthier choices. Starting this week, wait twenty to thirty minutes after you have stopped eating before you fill out the monitoring form. At that point, check in with your whole body, rate fullness as usual, then notice your feelings and evaluate the types of foods you ate as "Worth it" or "Not worth it."

You may decide a food was worth it for any number of reasons. The food may have both tasted good and felt good (such as strawberries). You may have chosen anti-deprivation eating and it worked well. You may have chosen effective emotional eating and it worked well. As long as you still feel good about your food choice a half hour later, it was worth it.

Likewise, you may decide a food was not worth it for any number of reasons. You may have been disappointed. Perhaps you thought the food was going to taste better than it did. You may not feel so good (physically) afterwards and decide the initial good taste wasn't worth the negative feelings. You may have eaten mindlessly and gotten no pleasure, only calories. Whenever you check in and realize you would now be feeling better if you had eaten less or if you had chosen a different food, then the food you ate was not worth it. Some people find it helpful to make notes about why they rated particular foods worth it or not worth it, but that may not be necessary for you. It is fine if you just categorize each food as worth it or not.

When you only eat one food, for example a snack of cookies, it is easy to decide if that food was worth it or not. When you eat several foods in a single episode, for example at a scheduled meal, you must consider each food separately. You may conclude that some of the foods were worth it (the burrito and salad) and some were not (the chips). If all the types of foods felt good but you ate more food than felt good, don't bother to write down all the foods. This is not a problem of food type. This means you need more practice stopping at moderate fullness. Write "just too much" in the column labeled "Not worth it." This will remind you to focus more on amount than type.

Using awareness to modify food-type preferences does require some effort. It requires more effort than simply stopping at moderate fullness. However, in the long run, modifying food preferences makes it easier for you to choose healthier foods. From now on, each time you decide to start eating, consider how each option will likely taste (in your mouth) plus how it will feel later on (in your stomach). Then use your wise mind to make a balanced decision that works for your whole self, not just your mouth. Use the Monitoring Food Type form until this process becomes automatic. Once again, you will need to make copies of this form.

INSTRUCTIONS FOR MONITORING FOOD TYPE

1. Continue to monitor your appetite and continue to circle "Eat Mindfully" as you have in previous weeks. Food A, Heck, and EmEat have been removed from your form

because you are now focusing on food type. Pencil those in whenever they cause a problem to remind you to get back on the normal eating path.

2. Your goal this week is to increase your awareness of food type by staying mindful of your stomach and your whole body's response to food after you have swallowed it. Make your ratings twenty to thirty minutes after you have finished eating. At that point, you are clear about how the foods have made you feel. Evaluate each type of food you ate as Worth It or Not Worth It, and write it down in the appropriate column. As long as you still feel good about what you ate it was worth it. If you now wish you hadn't eaten it, you will be able to identify why it was not worth it and what type/amount of food might now be feeling good. You must preserve this *moment of clarity* by updating your written Personal Food Guidelines. Otherwise, this awareness (insight) tends to fade quickly and you are not likely to be able to use it next time you are making choices about what you are going to eat. Be careful not to turn your Personal Food Guidelines into a new set of food rules. They do not tell you what foods are good or bad, rather they remind you how you felt the last time you ate certain types or amounts of food, so you are more likely to make a fully informed (wise mind) decision about what you are going to eat the next time.

3. Continue to complete the daily summary to remind you to maintain those goals while you become more aware of food type.

PERSONAL FOOD GUIDELINES

At the end of the first week, take your daily monitoring forms and use the information about how different types of food felt to establish your personal food guidelines. These guidelines are written summaries of what you have learned about how you respond to different types of foods. You can deliberately consult these guidelines each time you decide what to eat. Revise these guidelines each week as you identify new feel-good foods and notice which foods are not worth it. Keep your guidelines up-to-date, as your feelings and preferences are going to be continuously evolving. Out-of-date guidelines will not give you accurate predictions, and you need to be as accurate as possible in predicting how you are going to feel after you eat a particular amount of a particular food. At first, it is helpful to point out each time you make an accurate prediction and you actually experience the expected consequences. As you learn to trust yourself, using the guidelines will start to feel more automatic. You are likely to notice that you can make eating decisions more quickly now that you have guidelines. You don't obsess about what to fix at home, what to order when you are out, or what to select at a party. Remember, these personal guidelines about food just supplement the basic guideline of AAT. The most important AAT guideline remains *stop when you are moderately full no matter what food you decide to eat.* The following example illustrates how personal guidelines work.

Monitoring Food Type

Day: M T W Th F (S) Sun

Before eating: Use wise mind to balance anticipated taste and feel of foods.

Worth It	Not Worth It

Time 10:00 — Too Hungry ... N ... Ignored Fullness
X (at 3), X (at 5)
1 2 3 4 5 6 7
(M) S — Ate Mindfully* — Heck

Worth It: grapenuts, milk, blueberries

Time 12:00 — Too Hungry ... N ... Ignored Fullness
X X (at 3, 4)
1 2 3 4 5 6 7
M (S) — Ate Mindfully — Heck

Not Worth It: muffin—wasn't that good (FoodA)

Time 1:00 — Too Hungry ... N ... Ignored Fullness
X (at 3), X (at 5)
1 2 3 4 5 6 7
(M) S — Ate Mindfully — Heck

Worth It: tuna salad, tomatoes, crackers
Not Worth It: 5 crackers would have been fine—didn't need to eat 10 crackers

Time 4:30 — Too Hungry ... N ... Ignored Fullness
X (at 3), X (at 5)
1 2 3 4 5 6 7
M (S) — Ate Mindfully — Heck

Worth It: powerbar

Time 7:00 — Too Hungry ... N ... Ignored Fullness
X (at 3), X (at 5)
1 2 3 4 5 6 7
(M) S — Ate Mindfully* — Heck

Worth It: soup, sushi, salad, glass of wine
Not Worth It: fried wontons? 2 drinks at bar pretzels at bar (FoodA!)

Information for personal food guidelines: Maybe OK to eat fried wontons—it's my favorite appetizer but split appetizer, I would have felt better--watch out for crackers, it's hard for me to stay mindful with them--bread or roll might feel more filling--Drink with dinner--not before

Daily Summary:
No B? ✓
All normal eating? ✓
Deprivation: (Low) Med Hi

Monitoring Food Type

Day: M T W Th F S Sun

Before eating: Use wise mind to balance anticipated taste and feel of foods

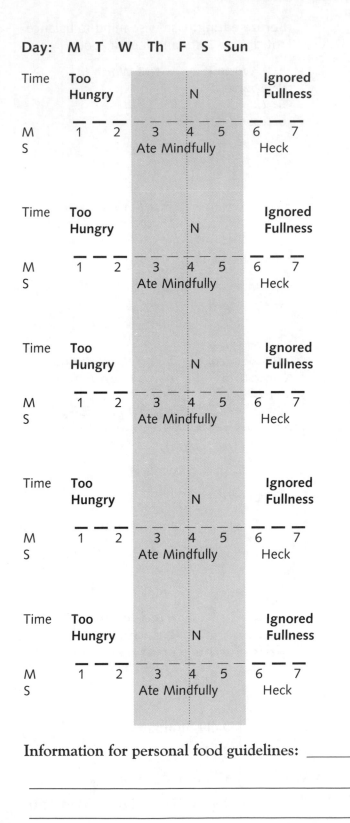

Time	**Too Hungry**	N	**Ignored Fullness**
M S	1 2 3 4 5 6 7	Ate Mindfully	Heck

Time	**Too Hungry**	N	**Ignored Fullness**
M S	1 2 3 4 5 6 7	Ate Mindfully	Heck

Time	**Too Hungry**	N	**Ignored Fullness**
M S	1 2 3 4 5 6 7	Ate Mindfully	Heck

Time	**Too Hungry**	N	**Ignored Fullness**
M S	1 2 3 4 5 6 7	Ate Mindfully	Heck

Time	**Too Hungry**	N	**Ignored Fullness**
M S	1 2 3 4 5 6 7	Ate Mindfully	Heck

Worth It	Not Worth It

Information for personal food guidelines: _____

_____

_____

Daily Summary:

No B? _____

All normal eating? _____

Deprivation: Low   Med   Hi

Developing and Revising Personal Food Guidelines

One Sunday you eat three donuts instead of your regular breakfast because your husband brought home a box when he picked up the paper. When you check in, you realize you went past moderate fullness because the donuts tasted so good. Perhaps you also noticed other things about how you felt after the donuts. The second donut probably didn't taste quite as good as the first one and the third one may have started to taste too sweet. You didn't feel very good an hour later. The pleasure of eating this food was short and the negative feelings lasted much longer. In retrospect, you rate the donuts as not worth it.

After this experience, you develop the following personal guideline to help you make future decisions about donuts: When I consider taste and stomach sensations, I recognize the main pleasure is in the first donut. I think I would have felt okay if I had had one donut along with a yogurt. I wouldn't have felt deprived, and I would have felt better the rest of the morning.

You try this guideline the next time your husband brings home donuts. You check it out. You do feel much better, but you notice it was very hard for you to stop after the first donut. You made sure your children ate the rest of the donuts, or perhaps you threw them out. After this experience you revise your guideline again. You explain to your husband that you appreciate that he thought of you and that an occasional treat is nice, but it would help you if he only brought home one donut for you to eat.

As you continue to pay attention to how you feel when you eat donuts, you may eventually notice that donuts don't taste quite as good as they used to, and you wonder if you might prefer something less sweet for a treat. You ask your husband to substitute a scone or a muffin for the donut so you can see how eating that food feels. The scone may (or may not) have that many fewer calories than a donut, but it may feel better. You might then try an alternative food that tastes good, feels good, and has fewer calories (perhaps a low-fat muffin). The important point is to stay tuned in and pay attention to how you feel each time you eat. You will need to continually update your personal food guidelines as you learn more and more about how you respond to food type.

Pure Pleasure Foods

The most effective foods are options that combine good taste with good feel. However, it is okay and sometimes necessary to eat for pure pleasure. Eating for pure pleasure means eating based solely on how the food tastes, not on how it feels in your body. When you have cravings or you are presented with very special foods that are not always available, you may choose to eat just for the taste. Earlier in this book, I referred to this kind of eating as anti-deprivation eating because the main reason you would eat purely for taste is to prevent feeling deprived if you refuse to allow yourself a treat you really, really want.

Within AAT, it is fine to eat pure pleasure foods as long as you don't get stuffed. Normal eating allows for some of this kind of eating, though ideally it is done at meals or snacks, not just because pure pleasure foods happen to be available. It is not necessary for you to eliminate all eating for pleasure in order to maintain a stable weight. You are not going to gain weight when you occasionally eat moderate amounts of pure pleasure foods.

However, when your goal is to lose weight, it may be necessary to minimize the number of pure pleasure foods you eat, because they are usually high-fat, high-calorie foods. When you are in weight-loss mode, you want to save calories whenever you can, so you mostly choose low-calorie-density foods. Choose pure pleasure foods only when you predict that refusing to have what you want will set you up to eat more calories later on. The better you can predict how you will feel later, the more effective you will be in minimizing the number of treats you require.

WHAT FOODS HELP YOU LOSE WEIGHT?

The widespread consensus among experts on weight management is that there is no single "best" food plan for losing weight. Individuals can be successful in losing weight in many different ways. Successful dieters eat many different types and combinations of foods. If there was one magic diet plan that would work for everyone, nutritionists would definitely have figured it out by now. Many different food plans will work if you actually eat what the plan says to eat. However, we all know that the critical aspect of long-term weight management is to develop a plan with lots of foods you like. If you try to eat a lot of foods you don't like, you will go back to the foods you like when you stop the diet. Clearly, low-calorie-density foods are the foods most likely to promote weight loss, but you must find food options that you like and are willing to eat over the long run.

Your body and your life circumstances are going to change over time, so you are likely to need to adjust your food choices many times throughout your life. This is why AAT does not tell you what foods to eat; it just encourages you to try low-calorie-density options. AAT tells you to use feedback from your stomach and your body to continually reevaluate your food choices instead of relying solely on taste to make those decisions. By keeping your personal food guidelines up to date, you can adapt to any situation and figure out what kinds of foods among those that are available will work best for you.

Should You Avoid Tempting Food?

When you are trying to lose weight, it is reasonable to avoid exposure to tempting high-fat, high-calorie foods to some degree. It is easier to make low-calorie-density choices when you don't have highly tempting options easily available. However, you also must learn to eat high-fat, high-calorie foods in moderation. If you always avoid those foods, you remain vulnerable to binge eating or overeating. You need to feel safe around all food. Avoiding foods doesn't change your preferences for them. Food awareness training teaches you to use your stomach and body signals to balance the power of taste so you can actually change your food preferences over time.

Stop the Good Food/Bad Food Game

Many people on diets try to ignore taste when they decide what to eat. They develop rules about "good foods" and "bad foods." Rules about what foods are good or bad for you have the potential to become a problem. You may react badly when you break a rule (feel guilty or depressed) or you may start feeling controlled by the rules and become angry and rebellious. In either case, you are likely to end up engaging in the what the heck response. Food awareness training shifts your focus away from the food itself to the way you feel when you eat that food. Foods are not inherently good or bad, but different foods have different purposes. Some foods give you immediate pleasure; they taste really good. Some foods make you healthier or make you feel better. Your job is to make decisions that balance your needs for pleasure and health. It is tempting to label high-fat, high-calorie foods as "bad for you" instead of deciding how to best use those foods to meet your needs. Labeling a food as "bad for you" turns out to be the worst possible strategy for changing your preferences for it. It doesn't make you want it less. Using self-critical thoughts to keep from eating high-fat, high-calorie foods (for example, by anticipating guilt) is also not a great idea. When tasty foods are forbidden, it just points out how much you really want them. That is not going to reduce your preference for them. It only increases you vulnerability to the what the heck response.

Using positive thoughts to help you choose low-calorie-density foods is a better option. Positive thoughts do not create the same problem as self-criticism. Anticipating feeling proud of yourself can help you make better food choices. However, positive thoughts alone aren't usually enough. That's why the power of positive thinking is not enough to make people lose weight. Positive thoughts work much better when they are backed up by your whole-body awareness that you feel better physically when you eat more low-calorie-density foods.

The reason you need to become more aware of your bodily sensations is that thoughts come from your mental self. As I have mentioned before, your physical self doesn't communicate cognitively. Your physical self doesn't really listen to your thoughts. Your physical self only learns from experiences directly. When you shift your awareness from what you should do to what actually feels good, you are putting your mental and your physical self on the same page. When both aspects of yourself are focused on achieving the same outcome, your actions are more likely to reflect your wise mind instead of your self-critical (negative) mind.

HOW DO FOOD PREFERENCES CHANGE?

A choice is something you do. A preference is simply a statement about what you would like to do. You have already been making choices to limit how much you eat by stopping at moderate fullness, whether you prefer to or not. Hopefully most of you now prefer to stop there. Once a preference has been modified, less effort is required to make that choice. It feels automatic not punitive. Now you are choosing to try low-calorie-density foods, whether or not you prefer them. As you pay attention to your whole body, you are likely to notice that you actually feel better when you eat these foods your food type preferences may change. It is then easier to choose low-calorie-density foods more of the time.

Food preference can be judged on two criteria. You can judge a food based on whether or not you like it. (For example, "I don't like broccoli" or "I like ice cream.") Or, you can judge food based on how much you like one food over another. For example, "I like ice cream more than broccoli, but I like fudge even more than ice cream." When you have to make a decision about what to eat, you usually have several options; thus, relative preference is usually more important than absolute preference. You probably rarely choose to eat foods you don't like at all.

With food awareness training, your absolute preference may or may not change. You might find that you don't like donuts any more. You may find that you actually do like sweet potatoes. But your relative preferences are quite likely to change. As you consider feel as well as taste, you will notice that the overall effect of donuts isn't as positive as you once thought, and you may realize you enjoy fresh fruit a lot more than you used to. You still may not choose to eat fresh fruit every time donuts are available, but you are likely to choose fresh fruit more often than you did before because your preference for donuts relative to fruit has weakened.

The smaller the difference in how much you like the various options you have available, the easier it is to choose the "healthier" option (at least some of the time), without triggering feelings of deprivation. Be accurate when you talk to yourself about your preferences for types of food. Don't try to trick yourself into saying you don't like the taste of something when you actually do. It is better to say, "I love the taste of fried chicken, but I prefer the feelings I have after a turkey sandwich, so I'm going to choose the sandwich for lunch today."

Attending to previously ignored consequences of food is the mechanism by which your food preferences change. Food preferences evolve all the time, whether or not you are paying attention. Without guidance, your preferences will tend to evolve toward foods that taste good in your mouth. By directing your attention to other body sensations, you can guide the natural process toward preferences for low-calorie-density foods that feel good as well as taste good.

Changing preferences for food type is a slower process than changing preferences for fullness; you do not get as much help from your biological appetite regulation system. Fortunately, the two processes do support and enhance each other. Both processes depend on learning how to pay attention to internal sensations. Stomach sensations related to fullness are more obvious and show up while you are still eating. Feedback from your body about type of food is more subtle and it is often delayed, sometimes by more than an hour. That is why you have to make a deliberate effort to check in with your stomach feelings at some point after you stop eating. Write down your observations at that time. The feedback from your stomach comes too late to change what you have already eaten. You have a brief *moment of clarity* in which you know what you could have eaten that would now be feeling good. You must find a way to store that information in a form that is easily accessible the next time you are making a food decision. Hence the value of written personal guidelines.

Your food type preferences are likely to end up looking a bit different from mine or from anyone else's. Each person's body and history with food is unique, so we won't all like (or feel good about) the same foods even though we can all learn to prefer moderate fullness.

How to Know if Your Preferences Are Changing

Changing food preferences occurs gradually, so it is likely to sneak up on you. When it does happen you may notice some of the following:

- You like the way you feel when you stop at moderate fullness.

- You find yourself saying, "No thanks, I don't really want any more, and meaning it."

- You don't feel so great when you go past moderate fullness.

- You no longer like the feeling of being overfull, and certainly not getting stuffed.

- You find yourself thinking, I would have been satisfied without the chips, extra bread, second serving, additional slice, etc.

- You find yourself thinking that more of a certain food would taste good, but it wouldn't feel good.

- You find yourself saying, "It used to take a lot more food for me to feel satisfied."

- You find yourself stopping after a small amount of a treat food and giving or throwing away the rest because you have satisfied your craving and you don't want to eat the rest just because it it there.

- You find it easier to be around treat foods without always deciding to have some and without always eating until the food is gone.

Remember, a preference is just a statement about what you choose to eat, not what you think tastes better or is healthier. It is important to use words to accurately describe your inner experiences so that as your preferences change, you recognize that you don't feel as deprived as you used to. For example, if you eat too much cake and feel sick, don't say, "I don't like cake." It is more effective to say, "I like the taste of cake the moment it is in my mouth, but I don't like how I feel after eating it, especially when I eat more than one piece." Or, you might say, "I like the taste of cake for the moment it is in my mouth, but I prefer the way I feel afterward when I choose fresh fruit for dessert." Or, "I like the taste of cake, but not as much as I used to, and I like the taste of fresh fruit better than I used to." In other words, don't try to trick yourself into thinking you have changed your preferences. Be honest. You may still like the taste of a food but only in a smaller amount, or you may still like the taste of a food but not the way you feel later on.

MOVING TOWARD SELF-COACHING

In the next chapter you are going to learn how to phase out the written forms that you have been using up to this point and how to internalize the tracking you have been doing. You are going to learn how to coach yourself so you can stay on the normal eating path for the rest of your life.

9   Self-Coaching for Life

At this point in the program, your moderate fullness signal should be popping up fairly automatically as you are eating. You likely know when you have gone past moderate fullness as soon as it happens. You make a note to yourself when it does happen and get back on track at the next meal. You also have a good idea of when you need to honor cravings and eat for pure pleasure (anti-deprivation eating). You are aware of the times you choose to eat for emotional reasons, and can usually stop at moderate fullness during those episodes. Now you are ready for the final step. This chapter shows you how to phase out written self-monitoring, yet continue to stay focused on those important internal cues.

Written monitoring has been the primary tool you have used to redirect your attention from the taste of food to the feel of food in your body. Written monitoring has made you more accountable to yourself. It takes real effort initially to keep your attention on your body, especially after you finish eating. It is more natural to tune out awareness of what you have eaten in an effort to forget about episodes that made you feel badly about yourself. Unfortunately, the best way to increase your motivation to eat differently is to pay attention to the consequences while (and after) you eat, not tune them out. However, focusing on feelings of guilt or shame does not work. You feel bad, but you don't learn anything useful about the way food affects how you feel. Negative feelings don't help you store new information that you can use to make a more effective decision next time. If you don't stay aware and if you don't update your personal food guidelines, you just keep repeating the same poor food choices and feeling guilty afterward (a pattern that is probably all too familiar to you). Appetite monitoring helps you focus on physical sensations instead destructive, negative thoughts. It also helps you focus on the immediate positive consequences of wise food choices so you feel motivated to choose them more often.

Once checking in with your stomach after you eat feels fairly automatic, you can replace your written self-monitoring with mental monitoring. To do this, continue to monitor your eating, but do it in your head instead of on a worksheet. You have made many changes, but you have only been eating normally for a short period of time. Since your eating environment is still relatively unhelpful in encouraging you to eat normally, you'll need to continue to monitor in your head. Old habits will creep in if you don't maintain a reasonable level of mindfulness about your eating.

EATING MINDFULLY WITHOUT WRITTEN MONITORING

Eating mindfully means eating slowly and paying attention to the pleasure you are getting from the taste of what you eat, but also attending to all the other stomach and body sensations that occur during and after you eat. Written monitoring has been your memory aid. You eat several times a day, every day, and often you eat similar foods. Many of your eating episodes are not very memorable. After a few days, most people can't remember most of what they ate and certainly not how full they got. Particularly positive or negative episodes are the only eating episodes that stand out in your memory. If you don't have an issue with food or weight, this is not a problem. You have no reason to track what you eat. In fact, your appetite regulation system is set up so you don't have to pay attention. You can eat fairly mindlessly. However, when you do have concerns about your weight, eating mindfully is of utmost importance. Monitoring keeps you honest in this regard. When you review your written records, you can see how often you got too hungry or too full, ate for emotional reasons, or ate foods that weren't worth it.

Even when you no longer have strong urges to binge, written monitoring helps you pay attention to (and reduce) overeating. You see each time you go past moderate fullness. However, it is a positive focus (not punitive), because you see how much of the time you do eat normally (stay in the gray). Monitoring gives you balanced, self-corrective feedback. In contrast, when you aren't using written forms, you are likely to slip back into mindless eating until you have a clearly negative episode. Then you feel bad and try to forget it happened.

Most people haven't learned to track successes or to praise themselves when they are effective. Being effective is what we are expected to do. Most of us are only trained to notice when we screw up. Then we give ourselves really unbalanced punitive feedback, something like, "You idiot. You did it again. You're hopeless." Or we blame someone else (for bringing cookies to work) or simply chalk it up to a bad day. In any event, we fail to do anything constructive to prevent similar episodes. The unfortunate fact is, left to your own devices, you (and virtually all humans) are not likely to self-monitor in a balanced or constructive way. On the other hand, no one wants to keep written records forever.

At this point you probably think, "I get the idea. I don't need to write down my ratings anymore. I can just remember to stop when I first feel full." However, my experience tells me you are going to have to do a little bit more than this. You must find a way to keep monitoring, but do it in your head. I call this strategy *self-coaching*. Self-coaching includes reminding yourself to eat mindfully, but it goes further than that.

Self-coaching means you check in both before and shortly after you eat. Before you eat, you consider the likely taste and feel of what you are thinking about eating. You consult your personal food guidelines; what do they tell you?

You remember to eat mindfully. After you eat, you check in again. If you feel pretty much as you had anticipated feeling, all is well and you need do no more. If you didn't predict accurately (you feel worse or better than anticipated), you have learned something new about yourself. Make a mental note of this, and (if it seems significant), update your written personal food guidelines when you get a chance. In this way, your written guidelines always reflect your most recent and most relevant experiences with food.

Initially, self-coaching requires effort and attention. Gradually, checking in becomes so automatic you may not even realize you are doing it. Once you learn how to self-coach, I advise you to do this forever. I have been using AAT longer than anyone else and I still self-coach! Most of the time I don't realize it, but when I am writing about AAT I notice my own dialogue about my eating. I still find new foods or combinations of food I didn't realize were such good options for me. I am often surprised to notice that my preferences have changed and I need to update my personal guidelines. I'll notice that some foods that used to be quite tempting are no longer as appealing, or I'll notice that I really only want a smaller amount of a particular food that I used to want more of.

WHAT DOES IT MEAN TO BE A COACH?

Coaching has become a very popular strategy to help people develop plans to change their behavior and follow through on those plans. Among other things, personal coaching has been shown to help children and adults with attention problems, people who want to exercise more or lose weight, and people who want to be more effective or efficient in their work.

Personal coaching has become popular because many people recognize that information and instruction alone are not always enough to create behavior change. Many people need frequent corrective feedback plus accountability to another person in order to stay on track and attain their goals. Otherwise, you forget your priorities, get distracted by more immediate rewards, or get too discouraged when you aren't doing well. An effective coach corrects, remotivates, and redirects attention toward what to do next time.

The role of a coach can be most clearly seen in sports. An effective coach makes athletes face what went wrong. Videotape has become an almost universal tool for coaches because they can watch the replay with their athletes to point out exactly what did or didn't happen. Videotape is the ultimate behavior therapy. You don't get to say what you intended to do or wish you had done; you only get to see what you did do. However, the point of watching replays is obviously not to change the score of a game that has already been played. The point is to play differently next time. Once the mistakes are analyzed and the good plays celebrated, athletes are directed to put that game behind them and focus on the next game. Effective athletes take responsibility for their play, but they do not dwell on what they did wrong. Nor do they focus on their teammates' faults. An effective athlete always looks to the next game as a challenge to do better.

You may find it helpful to think about your eating in the same way. You have to eat often, so you have many opportunities to do better. In other words, you always have another game to play. In fact, with eating, the season never ends so you can always improve your standing. Every athlete has "off games." Sometimes they even have a run of several poor games. However, athletes are always encouraged to work through a slump. The coach knows that if an athlete persists and keeps practicing, she will come out of a slump and revamp her swing, or figure out whatever it is that she needs to do differently. You are going to do the same thing with your eating decisions. Each time you eat, assess how you are doing. When your eating goes well, take credit for using your skills. If you have an episode that doesn't turn out so well, revise your game plan so you are better prepared to take on the next food decision.

If you are using this book on your own, you are already serving as your own coach. Some of you may have chosen to hire a coach (that is, a counselor). In fact, if you try the program and are not successful on your own, I highly recommend that you do find someone to help you implement the program. Self-monitoring is a coaching tool, but it is not as powerful as having an actual coach. Self-monitoring directs your attention to what is important, makes you face your poor choices rather than avoid thinking about them, helps you analyze what actually went wrong so you can figure out what you need to practice more, and points out what you are doing well.

The last phase of AAT is self-coaching. You no longer need the detailed feedback you get from written monitoring, but you do need a way to maintain self-corrective feedback and positive feedback for successes. Self-coaching means you make ratings of hunger and fullness in your head instead of on paper, but it also means you talk yourself through each eating decision. You also continue to update your written list of personal food guidelines.

HOW TO PHASE OUT THE WRITTEN FORMS

Even though you are now ready to stop using written monitoring forms, I encourage you to phase them out gradually rather than stopping cold turkey. Several ways to phase down are described below. Try them and figure out what works best for you.

Stop Monitoring Routine Eating Episodes

Identify the meals or snacks that have become quite routine. For example, you may rarely have any difficulty with breakfast. You may have the same afternoon snack most of the time. You don't need to keep writing down routine episodes that go well. At first continue to use the written forms, but just write a big "NE" (for normal eating) beside episodes that go well. Only when an episode doesn't go well do you write down your ratings and indicate what happened. When you handle a difficult situation really well, put a happy face beside that episode. Continue to make notes anytime you learn something new about yourself that should be added to your personal food guidelines. Eventually, you stop needing to write down anything. At that point, do it all in your head.

Reduce the Days Monitored

Identify the times that you still find challenging. For example, if you do fine until dinnertime, only write down dinner ratings. You don't even have to use the monitoring forms for this. You can enter your ratings in your datebook or just keep an index card in your purse. If you do well during the week but find weekends a challenge, just monitor on weekends. If vacations, holidays, or final exam week are difficult for you, be proactive. Use written monitoring just during those times.

Make Your Own Monitoring Form

Identify what aspects of normal eating are still a challenge for you and find a shortcut way to monitor just those aspects of your eating. For example, if your most common problem is getting too hungry, write down your hunger level every time you eat. Put it in your datebook or on an index card. If your most common problem is overeating, write down your fullness rating every time you stop eating. You will be surprised at how helpful it is to force yourself to put a number down each time you eat. It is difficult to remember just how little it takes to get moderately full. This reduced monitoring activity helps you stay accountable (to yourself), but reduces the time and effort you have to put into monitoring.

Reduce Post-Eating Regret

Perhaps your only remaining problem is *post-eating regret*. You have become a great postgame analyst. However, you need to work on your pregame talk. You have good intentions. You know what you are supposed to do. But you fail to talk yourself through each eating episode in an effective manner. You just eat and then find yourself thinking, "I wish I hadn't eaten that. I didn't really need the chips, or the second helping" or "That dessert just wasn't worth it. I would be feeling better now if I hadn't eaten that." If you don't seem to be learning from your experiences, there are a number of things that could be happening.

Are you tuning out as soon as you feel badly about what you have eaten? If so, you probably aren't entering the new information into your long-term memory, much less writing it down in your personal guidelines. It is possible that you are brushing off a negative eating episode too quickly. There's no need to punish yourself, but if you don't figure out what the lesson is in a problematic episode, you won't be able to make a different choice the next time.

Another possibility is that you aren't taking the time to do the necessary pre-eating check in. If you tend to skip this step, go back and practice the first step of AAT; make a conscious decision to start eating. Every evening you can just review your day quickly in your mind and write down the number of times you made conscious decisions to start eating and the number of times you started to eat without checking in. Doing this will remind you to check in every time you start eating.

INSTRUCTIONS FOR SELF-COACHING

As you start phasing out the written monitoring forms, you must start using a deliberate self-coaching strategy to talk yourself through your day of eating. This self-coaching serves as a substitute for the written forms. At first, you have to pay attention to make sure you check in before and after you eat. The more you check in mentally, the more automatic the process becomes. Eventually you won't even be aware that you are monitoring yourself except for the occasional times that your post-eating check-in tells you an episode didn't end up feeling too good. That feeling is the cue that prompts you to replay what just happened. The replay allows you to act as your own coach; you analyze what went wrong and revise your personal food guidelines. Follow these self-coaching steps as you go through each day:

1. When you wake up check in. Ask yourself, how hungry am I? Decide if you are going to eat now or wait a while. It's okay to wait a while or to have a moderate to small breakfast if you don't feel very hungry first thing in the morning.

2. When you decide it's time to eat, use your wise mind to evaluate the food options available and make a decision. What will taste good and still feel good afterward? Eat mindfully to get pleasure from your food, and stay tuned in so you notice your moderate fullness signal telling you when to stop eating. When you stop eating, make a mental note about how you feel. If you don't feel so good, note what type or amount of food caused you discomfort. What do you want to remember for next time?

3. About fifteen to thirty minutes after you eat, do a final post-eating check-in. Are you still feeling good, or are you noticing that you ate too much or that the food isn't sitting well in your stomach? Make a mental note. Is it really the type of food that is feeling bad, or just the amount? What do you want to remember for next time?

4. Repeat this mental check-in process whenever it's time for a scheduled meal or snack. Always make a conscious decision about what foods you are going to eat.

5. If you notice an urge to eat at any other time, check in first to see if you are hungry or if this is an urge to eat when you are not hungry. If it is an urge not based on biological hunger, ask yourself why you want to eat. Is tempting food available? If so, will distraction or leaving the situation work, or do you need to choose anti-deprivation eating to prevent feelings of deprivation later on? If you choose anti-deprivation eating, check in with yourself after the eating episode and make a mental note. Did it work well? Were you able to stop at moderate fullness?

    If your urge to eat is not a response to some external cue in the environment, remember that the reason for your urge has got to be emotional. Emotional eating is the default. You may not always be able to figure out what emotions are involved. Ask yourself how you expect eating will change your emotional state? Depending on the answer (for example, it will help you enjoy the occasion, finish a task, or feel less bored), decide which of the strategies you've learned is likely to be most successful in getting through this situation. If you decide that you are going to eat, then decide what food you really want. Consult your personal guidelines, if necessary, to remind you what type of food is going to both taste good and feel good later.

6. Constantly remind yourself that the goal of AAT is to maximize the total pleasure you get from the food in your life and to minimize feelings of deprivation. When you can do this while maintaining your amount boundaries, you are going to be the most successful you can be in managing your weight. This point is difficult to remember. The message most of us have gotten is that the goal is to be as thin as possible and to achieve that goal you must suffer; you can't eat what you want. That is a negative approach. When you take the positive AAT approach, you work toward getting the most pleasure from the calories you do eat.

If you keep self-coaching, you'll keep self-correcting and you'll be able to maintain an eating pattern that works for you no matter what else changes in your life.

Sample Self-Coaching Script

The following is a sample self-coaching script. It provides suggestions for what you might say to yourself.

Morning: **Check in before eating:** I'm not really hungry, but I know I do better the rest of the day if I have breakfast. What would feel good? The usual—Grape-Nuts with blueberries—just a small bowl.

Check in thirty minutes after eating: Yes, I still feel good. I didn't get too full.

Midmorning: **Check in before eating:** I'm not really hungry, but I have a protein bar in case I can't make it until lunch. I know it's important for me to have the bar available; some mornings I get hungry and need it, other times I don't.

Around Noon: **Check in before eating:** I'm aware of feeling hungry, so I need to go ahead and eat. I know I should not try to wait until one o'clock. When I wait, it takes more to get satisfied. What would taste and feel good? I think a salad with tuna and those sweet little tomatoes I like. That way I get some protein, fiber, and a taste I like.

Check in thirty minutes after eating: Yes, that worked. I feel comfortable. I'm not too full and I feel good about adding in the tomatoes to give the salad more taste. With them, I didn't feel like I needed something else sweet. I decided I was moderately full and didn't even want to have the rye crisps today.

Midafternoon: **I had an urge to eat so I checked in:** I'm a little bit hungry, but I'm aware that I mostly want to take a break from working on the computer. I could just take a break and go chat with Sue, but I know that I usually do better if I have an afternoon snack, so I will go ahead and eat now. If the urge comes back later, I'll try distraction. What would taste and feel good? Cookies would taste the best, or chips (and I can get them from the machine), but I know from past experience that I don't feel like they are worth it afterward. I will feel better if I eat a sweet potato. I like the taste and it feels like a substantial amount, so I'll get over neutral and feel satisfied longer. I'll have to microwave it, but I'm not starving so I can wait the eight minutes. I will put it in and go check the mailroom while it's cooking. I need to remind myself that I feel really good afterward when I have a sweet potato for a snack.

Check in thirty minutes after eating: That was definitely a good choice. My stomach feels good, and I feel good about having a tasty low-calorie-density snack.

Late Afternoon: **Had an urge to eat so I checked in:** I'm already a little hungry, and I won't be able to have dinner for two hours or more. I need to tame the hunger a little, or I'll be too hungry by dinner. However, I will feel bad if I have a real snack this late. I remember my personal guideline: What works for me in this situation is to have a protein bar. In this situation, when I eat a bar, I don't want to eat more because it's not that good. I just want to tame my hunger a little because I want to enjoy my dinner. Eating a bar works well for me because I don't have to go into the kitchen or make a decision about food. The bars are kind of a nonfood. I eat them to manage hunger not for pleasure. I can hardly tell any difference in terms of fullness when I eat a bar, but it takes the edge off my hunger so dinner goes better.

Check in thirty minutes after eating: That worked. I can wait until dinner, and I feel good about being able to have just a bar. I didn't get into a prolonged snacking period. If I have peanut butter with crackers, it's hard to stop, and I end up eating enough calories before dinner that I don't feel like I should even eat dinner. I know what my problem is. The time I naturally get really hungry is much earlier than standard dinner time. I would do much better if I could eat dinner at 5:30 P.M. every day, but I can't have dinner ready that early and I want to eat with my family. My personal guidelines tell me that when I try to wait for dinner, I end up snacking too much while I prepare dinner. Then I eat a regular dinner and feel badly afterward, or I don't want to eat much at dinner and feel like I'm not eating in a normal and healthy way. I feel more normal when I use the bar to tide me over until dinner. Then I can eat a meal that feels normal.

Dinnertime: **Check in before eating:** I'm aware of hunger, and look forward to eating something I will like. What will feel good? Spaghetti sounds good, but I need to remember my personal guideline. I need to serve myself only one cup of the pasta. If I put more out there, I usually eat it and then I don't feel very good later. I have to remember to eat the salad even if I don't think I need it at the time. I feel better afterward when I have a salad with dinner. I feel fuller, and I feel like it is healthier. Remember to stay aware and stop at moderate fullness even if there is food left on my plate or I still want to have a little bit more. I'm pretty accurate by now. I know from my food guidelines that this is usually about the right amount to be satisfied and not too full when I check in later.

Check in thirty minutes after eating: That was a good choice. I didn't overeat. My predictions were pretty much on target. As usual, I notice that I feel slightly more full and satisfied now than I did right after I decided to stop. At that point, I was considering whether or not I wanted another quarter cup of pasta. Now, I am really glad I didn't eat any more. My stomach feels good. This experience confirms my food guidelines. One cup is enough pasta for me. I need to remember that it takes my body a little while to get the message that I have had enough. That is why it is critical to stop at moderate fullness and not keep eating until I feel clearly full. If I eat to that point, I usually feel a bit overfull when I do the thirty-minute check-in. The thirty-minute check-in really helps me update my food guidelines—it gives me much better feedback about how much I actually need to eat. I tend to overestimate how much I need to eat and end up feeling some of it wasn't worth it and that I would have been happier if I had eaten just a little less.

Evening: **I had an urge to eat, so I checked in:** I'm aware that I am not really hungry, but I really want to eat something. I know I just want the taste and feel of food in my mouth. I think this is emotional eating; I just want to distract and shift my mood. I feel bored and don't want to do my work. I could try some of my alternative strategies, but I don't feel like it. I think this situation calls for effective emotional eating. What would feel good and be effective (make it possible for me to sit down and finish my report)? Cookies or ice cream would feel good, but I wouldn't feel good afterward. However, I have strawberries, and if I have that with some low-fat frozen yogurt it will feel like a treat, but an okay treat. Remember to put it in a small bowl, put the carton away, sit down, and eat it slowly and mindfully to get the most pleasure I can.

Check in thirty minutes after eating: Yes, that did work. I felt like I had a treat so it was easier to go back to work. I was able not to go back for more even though I knew it would still taste good. I reminded myself about effective emotional eating—more doesn't work any better than one serving. Actually, every time I have more than one serving of a treat, I end up feeling worse. This doesn't mean I will necessarily have a treat every evening. Each time I will check in and make sure that effective emotional eating is called for. However, I feel good about how I handled this situation. I think that if I had tried not to eat at all, I would have resented it, found it hard to concentrate on my work, and I might have had a what the heck response later anyway, which would have resulted in me eating even more.

ESTABLISHING A RELAPSE PLAN

Self-coaching is different from a relapse plan. Self-coaching is a daily, ongoing process that helps keep you on track. Self-coaching helps prevent relapse by prompting you to self-correct after any specific eating episode that doesn't go well. Self-coaching is part of normal eating. It is a natural way to keep yourself on track.

In addiction treatment, an individual episode that doesn't go well is called a *lapse* to distinguish it from a *relapse,* a period of days or weeks in which a person goes back to using a substance in a problematic way. This is where eating difficulties are somewhat different from addictions. After treatment for addictions, a person is either abstinent (not using at all) or has stabilized at a moderate use level. Thus, in coping with addictions, a single problem episode often stands out to the person coping with the addiction or to others around them. In contrast, normal eating is a daily challenge. You will be eating at least three times a day, so one modest overeating episode is not very obvious either to yourself or to others.

Thus, I do not think it is helpful to think of any one overeating episode as constituting a lapse, even if you don't feel very good about what you ate in that one episode. Normal eating includes occasional overeating and occasional restriction. For eating behavior, single episodes that don't go well should be considered normal learning experiences, not lapses. Everyone who has learned to use AAT finds they continue to learn more about what does and doesn't end up feeling that good. You are always updating your personal food guidelines.

What Is an Eating Lapse?

As just noted, single episodes of overeating or getting too hungry do not constitute a lapse. If you have a binge, get very stuffed, or purge, consider those episodes to be lapses. And if continued over several days, such episodes would be considered a relapse. Thus, if you find that you have given in to the what the heck response and gotten stuffed, analyze the lapse so you can figure out what happened and make adjustments.

You can use the questions below to guide your lapse analysis. If you aren't willing to write it all down, just go through the steps of this analysis in your head. If you want to write out your lapse analyses, make several copies. Leave the following pages blank so you can make more copies as needed.

LAPSE ANALYSIS

How often does this kind of situation occur? _____

If this is a highly unusual situation, you don't need to analyze further; the situation isn't likely to reoccur. Just make a mental note that getting too full didn't feel good and don't compensate by skipping your next scheduled meal.

If this is a common situation, you need to be able to handle it better, so force yourself to analyze the lapse even though you would rather not think about it.

Identify your vulnerabilities. Was there anything about me that made me particularly vulnerable this time? For example, were you tired or stressed-out? Did you just get bad news or have an argument? Were you working under a deadline?

_____

_____

_____

Identify possible early intervention points. Were there points early in the sequence of what happened that seemed innocent at the time but set me up to make a poor choice later on? If so, what were they?

_____

_____

_____

Find the critical decision point. What was the specific point at which I knew I was going to binge, get stuffed, or purge?

_____

_____

_____

Identify unhelpful thinking or excuses. At that decision point, what did I think (or feel) that encouraged me to go ahead and eat more (or purge)?

_____

_____

_____

Use your wise mind to find alternatives. What could I have said to myself to challenge that unhelpful thinking or that excuse?

_____

_____

_____

Evaluate your use of skills. Did I even try to use alternative activities to cope with my urge to eat without actually eating?

_____

If no, what activity am I going to try in this situation the next time?

_____

If yes, what happened? Why didn't it work?

_____

Can I try something different next time?

_____

_____

Did I even try making a conscious decision to eat? If so, what excuse did I use to keep eating past moderate fullness?

_____

_____

Update your personal food guidelines. What did this lapse tell me about how I react to situations involving food?

_____

_____

_____

How do I need to revise my personal food guidelines to reflect this new information?

_____

Do I need to seek external help in generating new strategies to cope with my urges to eat instead of being pigheaded and trying the same old strategies that aren't working?

_____

Cultivate your willing attitude. Why am I so unwilling to try something new? Why do I insist on trying to make things work out the way I want them to instead of accepting the reality that I must be willing to do whatever will work, at least for the time being?

_____

_____

_____

Stay positive. Remember that learning to use appetite cues effectively is a process and it will get easier and feel more natural the longer I do it.

Weight Change as a Sign of Relapse

If you aren't getting stuffed or bingeing, it is more difficult to identify what constitutes a relapse of overeating. Overeating is so normalized, you may not even notice if you start eating more than you need to maintain a stable weight. Changes in weight are the most reliable sign you have. When your current goal is to maintain a stable weight, the first step of your relapse plan is to set up regular weighing with a specified range that reflects normal weight fluctuation. Weekly weighing at the same time of day, with the same clothes on, and on the same scale is necessary, because all of these factors influence weight readings.

Even then, weight is not a totally reliable indicator of changes in stored fat, because water retention (or dehydration) can cause several pounds difference. Thus, a five-pound deviation on either side of your target weight (or a ten-pound range of acceptable weight) is generally recommended. Some individuals find their weight is normally quite stable while others find their weight fluctuates a great deal, especially at certain times of the month. Keep a written graph (see sample) to help you stay tuned into your weight. Weight is so aversive to think about that your tendency may be to avoid weighing yourself. This is a problem, because if you do go outside your range, you need to label this as a lapse and take immediate action to prevent it from turning into a relapse. The first figure illustrates normal fluctuation during a period of weight maintenance. Use the blank figure to track your own weight when your goal is weight maintenance.

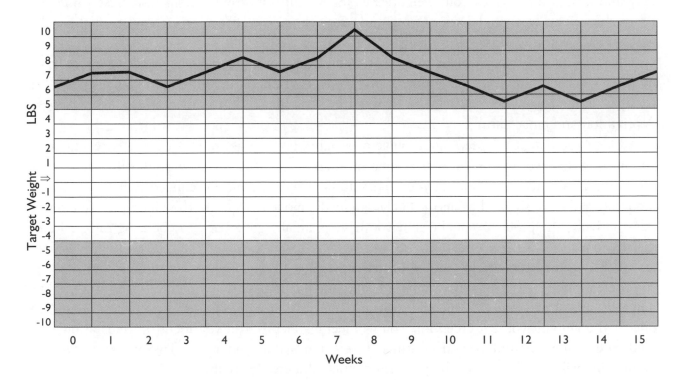

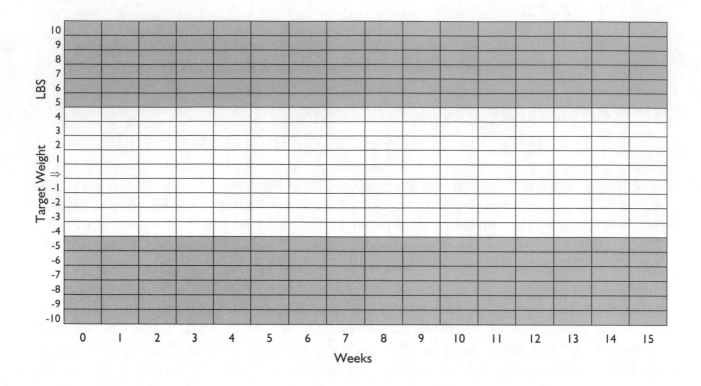

If you are very sensitive to the numbers on the scale and weighing upsets you, develop an alternative way to track your weight. You can use a specific belt or pair of jeans, whatever will give you early notice if your weight is creeping up. If you have been underweight in the past, you may find it best not to track your weight; tracking weight is mostly necessary for those who have been overweight. It is much easier to respond to weight gain early on, as such action can usually get you back within your target range within a week or two.

If you wait until your weight gain is ten pounds or more, the thought of taking a month or more to get back into your range may sound so aversive that you will be tempted to put if off until a "better" time. Or, you may be tempted to try a quick, drastic diet, which may retrigger deprivation and binge eating.

Once you detect a lapse (e.g., a binge or weight above target range) I strongly recommend committing to two weeks of written monitoring as the first step toward refocusing your attention. I call this "recalibrating your appestat." Just as a thermostat can get a little "off," your moderate fullness signal has most likely gradually moved back to the definitely full level. Alternatively, the problem may be that you have gradually gone back to choosing high-calorie-density foods.

When you notice weight gain, your first thought is likely to be to change the type of foods you are eating. This is probably what you have done in the past. You might have to do that, but don't try that strategy first. Remember, within AAT it is far more important to be sure you have not let the amount you eat creep up. You will feel less deprived if you focus on reinstating your moderate fullness boundary and continue to eat foods that you want. Two weeks of written monitoring will usually correct the problem of gradual increases in amount.

If going back to moderate fullness is not enough to get you back on track, start monitoring your "not worth it" foods. Cut back on the foods that aren't giving you much pleasure or aren't even meeting your needs for self-soothing. Mindless eating is a waste of calories.

Monitor for two to three weeks and then reevaluate your progress. If you are back in your weight range (or close to it), you don't need to take further action. However, if you have made no progress, have actually gained weight, or have started to experience even more urges to binge, it is time to implement a more intensive relapse plan. You need a plan that encourages you to reach out beyond yourself. You have tried self-coaching strategies, and they are not getting the job done. Seek some outside input to get your self-regulation system back on track.

Reaching Out for Support

An excellent strategy is to enlist a friend as a support system, preferably a person who might benefit from learning AAT. You take on the role of teacher and teach your friend the AAT principles. This will help you put them back into practice. Set up a meeting (or at least a phone call) twice a week to check in with your buddy and solve problems. If you have previously attended any type of support group, go back to it. Or, find a new one. It can be a women's group or a therapy group. You can even establish your own lunchtime support group at work or through your church. Helping someone else is one of the best ways to help yourself and reduce the feelings of isolation and discouragement that make it hard to get back on track with your eating.

Consider all possible alternatives to get the support and motivation you need. If you have previously benefited from seeing a counselor, nutritionist, trainer, or motivational coach, go back for some booster sessions. I recommend committing to at least four sessions up front. A single session usually isn't enough. Make sure you follow through. It doesn't matter if the outside help is knowledgeable about AAT, as long as it provides support to get you refocused on what you need to do. You already have all the food and eating information you need. This book tells you step-by-step what to do in terms of how to make eating decisions. If you have relapsed, then you probably need something you can't get from a book. What you need is motivation, support, and accountability (provided it is not offered in a punitive manner). If you are not getting enough of those things from within, it is your responsibility to figure out how to get more of those things from outside yourself.

Most importantly, please don't feel badly if you find that you do need outside support to maintain normal eating. Many people are not successful with pure self-help approaches (such as following a workbook on their own). Humans like to think that we are self-motivated and self-actualizing, but we really aren't very well equipped to motivate ourselves. We are built to respond to the environment and to respond to other people. We may be able to analyze problems and initiate behavior change, but we are not as well equipped to maintain those changes unless the changes are supported by their natural consequences, or by the people around us. Make sure you have identified the consequences and the people who make it worthwhile for you to eat normally.

Don't be too proud to ask for the help you need to create the life you want and deserve. Getting there is the only thing that counts. You won't get any special points for being able to do it all by yourself. In fact, you may be surprised to find that asking for support can be a very positive experience. Providing support is one way that humans feel connected to each other. Allowing someone to know your vulnerabilities and to provide support to you usually deepens the relationship and makes it more meaningful.

# Leaving the Maze of Disordered Eating

Jill was in college when she first decided to seek professional help for her concerns about eating. She didn't think she had an eating disorder. She had several friends who did, and her problems seemed different from theirs even though she thought she was just as upset by her weight as they were. She had tried to change how she felt about herself, but it wasn't working. She didn't know what direction to take, but a friend suggested she go talk to the counselor at student health who had helped her roommate overcome bulimia.

When she went in to talk to Dr. Shanks, Jill had a slightly higher BMI than the average college woman, but she was well within the normal weight range. She was attractive and sociable. Nonetheless, she reported she felt like "the fattest person in the world." She thought that other people also thought she was too heavy and that she should be able to do something about it. She said her family was all "big-boned," and her mother had always complained about her own body in addition to encouraging Jill to lose weight. Her older sister had similar issues. In high school Jill dieted so much that occasional binges were triggered. She had tried purging, but said she couldn't really do it very well and gave it up. However, she exercised fairly intensively in her effort to keep from gaining weight. She developed many rigid food rules. She was always thinking about what she should and shouldn't eat. She restricted most of the time, except for the several times a week when she would give up control and eat whatever she wanted. She managed to maintain a fairly stable weight but could never lose much. If she lost a little, she would gain it right back. By the time she came for help in early November of her sophomore year, she was bingeing three or four times a week, restricting the rest of the time, and feeling miserable about her weight all the time. When her therapist introduced the AAT model, Jill began to hope that there might be a way out of her obsession with eating and weight. The model made a lot of sense to her and she could see that, at least theoretically, normal eating was a better option than alternating between restricting and bingeing. She was also surprised to find that there was a name for her problem—she met all the criteria for a diagnosis of binge eating disorder.

After two weeks of appetite monitoring, Jill could identify her moderate fullness and moderate hunger signals and had set up a regular eating schedule. She took the self-monitoring forms home during Thanksgiving break and was surprised that she handled the week much better than usual and ate much less on Thanksgiving, though she still ate more than she intended. She had only three binges during the final three weeks of the semester. She again took forms home to continue working on eating normally during semester break. When she came back to school, she felt that her eating was pretty well regulated. She was now convinced that it did more harm than good to restrict to the point that she would get too hungry; she decided she wasn't going to do that anymore. She no longer had strong urges to binge, although she still felt badly about her weight and shape.

At this point, Jill felt she was ready to try phasing out the written forms. She had two sessions with her therapist during the following month to make sure she could maintain her new eating pattern without the written monitoring. She reported one slip, a binge that occurred after a romantic encounter in which she felt taken advantage of. However, she was able to get back on track. In their final session, Jill and her therapist agreed that she still needed to work on the long-term issues they had identified: negative body image and being more assertive with others (especially men). The student center had a group called "Women, Relationships, and Food" that would help her address these issues. Her therapist explained that many women found it more effective to address these issues with a group of their peers. Jill participated in the weekly group until the end of spring semester. At that point she checked in with her initial therapist, reporting that she had only one lapse in the past three months. She said the group helped her realize that her weight concerns were very normal, and she was not alone in having difficulty rejecting the ultrathin ideal that seemed to be quite strongly endorsed on her college campus. She gained the strength to set realistic standards that better fit her body type and her priorities in life. She now felt well prepared to continue eating from within on her own. She brought her therapist the following essay and gave her permission to share it with you, hoping to inspire others to leave the maze of disordered eating.

My memories about obsessing over the appearance of my body are easier for me to retrieve than my earliest memories of daily life. The association between fatness and myself encompasses all my memories past and present. Disheartening comments from family members and peers became ingrained into my mind, resulting in a constant comparison of my body to the bodies of anyone around me. Starting at eight years old I restricted the food entering my body and binged at times until I was numb. During this time I was unaware of the damage I was causing myself so early in life. The differences that set me apart seemed unchangeable, and the body parts that allowed me to be a mobile and breathing human being caused me an infinite amount of self-consciousness. Instead, I should have been grateful for this body that enabled me to exist and experience life.

The tug-of-war between restriction and overindulging engulfed my everyday existence. Each morning as I dissected myself in the mirror, I made a promise to change my life and live differently. "Today will be the first day of the rest of my life," became words I hoped to abide by. I promised to eat normally, exercise, and, above all, be skinny. Each dimple and bulge was scrutinized as I gazed at my distorted reflection. My mind raced through methods I might use to reconstruct my appearance. I prayed to God to have the strength to restrict so that next week my thighs would be dimple free, and the week after that my stomach would no longer hang over my jeans. My disgust with my body typically resulted in skipping breakfast and eating carrots for lunch. Often, later in the day, I would find myself digging through my entire pantry, searching for something to eat that would never fill the emptiness inside. Victory in the daily battle was determined by my level of hunger. When I was extremely hungry I became very happy. I felt I had triumphed over my body. If I ate more than my allotted food or, even worse, binged, I felt I had failed. Another 5,000 calories ingested in one sitting was one more step away from my ideal body.

This fixation on my imperfect body controlled my preteen and teen years, and, despite my hatred of my negative thoughts, these unshakable notions followed me to college. I was trapped in a darkness that in retrospect resembles a maze. The dizzying suffocation of living in the shadows of an unfriendly maze, lacking an obvious escape route, was physically and emotionally exhausting. Eventually the angst inside me made me fear for my sanity. At this point I knew that seeking help was crucial for my well-being. After twenty years, I finally realized that attempting this journey alone would not likely generate the results I was hoping for.

I had grown tired of turning the same corner I had previously encountered a thousand times. One day, just an ordinary day, I found myself running down the path I had been on my entire life, realizing it was taking me nowhere. At that moment, clarity filled my mind and body as I gazed up at the unconstrained blue sky that poured over the walls of the maze. I realized there was freedom outside my distorted mind. I was intimidated by the magnitude of the walls surrounding me, as they engulfed all hope of escape. They were too high to jump, but I knew that beyond them a life waited for me, a life free from obsession and self-hate. The silence that had built up over a lifetime was shattered with my screams. As I screamed for what seemed like an eternity, all of the anguish and pain that built upon itself for years managed to escape this cage of my body, releasing itself into the open air. As tears streamed down my cheeks, I realized I did not deserve the harsh criticism that I had tortured myself with for so long. I wanted to rid my mind of the chaos and confusion that controlled my perceptions. I wanted out, because I knew there was a better life beyond my experiences. How would I escape? I wanted out, I wanted love, and I wanted to love me. I fell to my knees, realizing that though I was in the maze alone, I did not have to attempt my escape single-handedly.

Countless women in this society have experienced this maze and its deceitfulness. For a long time I was oblivious to all those who were willing to guide me through the maze. These guides had once been lost too, and these wise veterans had worked their way through the dead ends of their own repeated mistakes. They knew each trick and roadblock in the maze. Patiently taking my hand, they would lead me out of the maze, into the free world. A world without walls or constraints. One filled with freedom and love.

Those who guided me were there to lead the way, but by no means were they capable of curing me themselves. There was no guarantee that we would reach the end if I did not do my part. They would provide insight and suggestions, but nothing more. If I was deficient in my efforts, further down the road I could get reeled back into the maze, with the possibility of being trapped there indefinitely.

My guides took turns leading me through the narrow paths of the maze, offering me their words of wisdom. Each woman had a unique story, a way she figured out how to navigate the maze. And each shared stories about what finally aided her escape. My personal journey would be slightly different from that of those who taught me, but my path would inevitably lead to the same place: freedom from disordered eating and undeserved self-hatred. Wandering down the damp paths, I approached forks in the road representing my decisions. At each corner, I stopped and contemplated which choice would have the most positive effect on my life. Decisions did not come easily. Not knowing the outcome of my choices often caused hesitation. Frequently, anxiety clouded my vision, as I was fearful I would take the wrong turn. In many instances I did. But these mistakes only made me stronger, these learning experiences led me closer to healing. Eventually, when I found myself retracing steps and encountering the same turns again, my new knowledge helped me make the right decisions.

During times of extreme frustration, my guides would explain to me why I had naturally turned left when I should have gone right. My life up to this point finally began to make sense. Turning left felt comfortable, because it was all I had ever known. In order to succeed in facing the obstacles presented each day, I would have to venture off my familiar path and embark into the unknown. In my heart, I knew that taking a right turn would eventually lead to the end, so I gritted my teeth and traversed the unbeaten path. On several occasions I made mistakes and took wrong turns, not heeding the advice I had been given. In these instances, I panicked, fearing that I would never fully be free, but my mentors assured me that each of us makes mistakes on our way to recovery, and I should not become discouraged. They did not intervene. By witnessing my progress they let me know I would be okay. By learning to make my own decisions I would save myself.

Time and patience with my mind and body was crucial in conquering the maze. After understanding I had an eating disorder that I was certain did not exist, I was able to work toward recovery. Now I am running on the straight and narrow. Yes, I am still inside the maze, but I can see the light of the outside world in the distance. The faster I run, the happier I become, knowing that there are no more turns to learn, just the constant practice of what I have already learned. Any day now I will reach the end. As I stumble out of the darkness, I will embrace the freedom that awaits me. The beautiful new world will greet me with fresh air and green grass. Knowing I have learned, through trial and error, hatred and acceptance, I will continue to nurture myself with a self-love previously unknown to me.

I will no longer deprive myself of the life and happiness I deserve, that every human being is worthy of. With this one chance at life, I will not waste my opportunity. I cannot go back. I am me, all of me: body, mind, and soul.

CONCLUSION

I end this workbook with Jill's essay because her metaphor of the maze so perfectly describes the way you need to apply the AAT principles you have just learned. I have given you some new tools and heightened your awareness of the internal cues that can successfully guide your eating, but only you can put these principles into practice as you face the many decisions about eating that are going to arise each day. Only you can run your maze.

Like finding your way out of a maze, overcoming disordered eating consists of many small decisions to take this path or that one. No one decision is catastrophic. When you hit a dead end, you just turn around and get back on track. No one runs this maze perfectly; there is no reason to panic when you take a turn that doesn't work out. Every wrong turn helps you learn what doesn't work, nothing more.

Changing disordered eating patterns is rarely accomplished by uncovering profound insights related to your difficult emotions, though such insights may help motivate you to do the work you must do. Successful change is more about having the determination and persistence to hang in there every day, refusing to tune out your awareness of your body or your unhelpful thought processes, and instead, choosing to stay aware and make conscious decisions each time you want to eat (or you want to refuse to eat).

Fortunately, like most behaviors that you repeat multiple times, eating decisions do become more automatic over time. At first, you will need to coach yourself intensely throughout the day as you face your urges and your negative thoughts about your weight. Another client put it this way: "I know in my heart of hearts that if I just pay attention to hunger and fullness, my weight will take care of itself. But I have to remind myself of that frequently." I wish you well as you find a new path in your maze of disordered eating. May your internal signals guide you to a more satisfying and meaningful life beyond eating.

If you would like to share your experiences using AAt, I invite you to post them on my Web site (http://psych.colorado.edu/~clinical/lcraighead/) or write me at Campus Box 345, University of Colorado, Boulder, CO 80309.

Appendix A

The Purging Trap

This appendix expands the basic AAT model presented in chapter 2 to include a path that describes some of the unhealthy ways people attempt to compensate when they perceive that they have eaten too much or have eaten "forbidden" foods. The most common way people react to these so-called "transgressions" is to simply return to the restriction path, often with a vengeance. In other words, they cut intake even more. They skip meals, or even fast for an entire day. The basic AAT program already addresses the many forms of excessive restriction. Restriction, either of total caloric intake or of specific foods, is problematic because feeling deprived or being too hungry when you start to eat makes it harder to stop at moderate fullness. In addition, breaking food rules can trigger the what the heck response. Thus, in AAT avoiding restriction is an essential element of normal eating. However, the basic AAT model does not address the other two ways that you may attempt to compensate for food once you have eaten it. Exercise works off calories ingested while purging gets rid of some of the calories before your body absorbs them.

Exercise can be effective and may be harmless if not taken to extremes, but it is pretty time-consuming and effortful. In addition, exercise may lead some individuals back to overeating. When you believe you have burned off (or can burn off) extra calories, you have less motivation to stop at moderate fullness. The AAT program focuses on eating behaviors, so I will not address the issue of excessive exercise directly but be aware of the way you may use unhelpful thinking to justify excessive exercise.

This appendix addresses issues associated with using vomiting and laxatives. The health risks associated with various purging strategies are well documented (see Fairburn 1995).

However, you may not find these reasons compelling enough to stop purging. You may think you won't be affected or that you have plenty of time to stop purging before you develop health problems. Or, you may just believe that the health risks are worth it.

This expanded AAT program is designed to help you stop using unhealthy purging behaviors. I want to give you a very compelling reason to stop purging. The most important reason to stop purging is that it actually gives you permission to binge. Purging is the trap that keeps you stuck in the binge-purge pattern of bulimia. Bulimia is a difficult pattern to change because you are, quite understandably, in a real dilemma. You are afraid to stop compensating until you stop binge eating, yet compensating undermines the very motivation you need to stop binge eating. Why stop at moderate fullness as long as you know you can compensate? How do you get out of this vicious cycle?

THE AAT MODEL FOR BULIMIA

AAT has been used effectively to eliminate compensatory behaviors. However, the model for intervention is modified slightly as it requires an additional point of intervention (see figure A.1). That is, you have one more place to make a decision. What are you going to do after you think you have overeaten or broken a rule, or when you have binged? While you may not always choose to compensate, you know it is an option. When you choose the purging option, there are very potent consequences. You feel great relief. You have taken care of your problem. You may even feel better physically if you did eat a very large amount and have now relieved the pressure in your stomach. Regardless, you definitely feel better psychologically. Compensating reduces your guilt and your fear of weight gain.

You may overeat because you like the taste of food going down. Compensating may initially seem like a reasonable compromise, until you start suffering consequences to your health. However, future health consequences don't seem very important in the moment when you feel badly about what you have eaten. It is easy to rationalize purging. Health is a good reason to stop purging, but you really need a stronger, more immediate reason to stop.

Fortunately, there two other really good reasons you need to stop purging as soon as possible. The first reason is psychological. At best, compensating is a shortcut. You have no motivation to do things the hard way when you know a shortcut. Shortcuts are not necessarily a bad thing. People who find shortcuts that work are applauded, and they often make a lot of money. However, purging is not one of those great discoveries; it only works in the short run. It is better to consider it a form of cheating. When cheating works, you get hooked on it. As long as you are getting away with it, it's hard to stop. The problem with cheating is that you start cheating more often or taking bigger chances until you get caught, or eventually someone figures out a way to close whatever loophole you found.

Purging after overeating follows a similar pattern. Most people start small. They only purge when they really have eaten a lot or have eaten very high-fat foods. It seems like a reasonable thing to do. You get away with it, so you get hooked. It gets easier to do. It doesn't feel so bad. Eventually you start to rely on purging instead of relying on moderating your intake. Once you

Figure A.1: The AAT Model for Bulimia

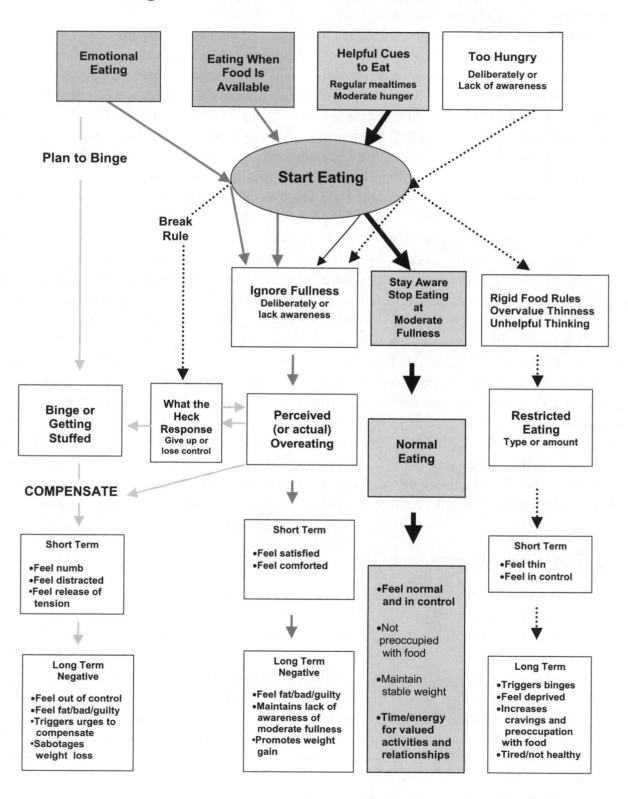

have given yourself permission to purge, you automatically have given yourself permission to binge. Purging is no longer as effective because you start bingeing more often. Unfortunately, as you escalate the number of times you purge, you increase the health risks.

The second reason to stop purging is physiological. Every single time you compensate this way, you are training your body to ask for more food! You are doing nothing to train your body to prefer moderate fullness. Remember, you can't talk to your body directly and explain why you need to purge. Your appetite and fat storage systems have their own feedback loops and these systems only learn through actual experience, not through verbal instruction. What does your body learn when you purge? Your body learns that it can't trust its internal feedback system to regulate eating. You have thrown a monkey wrench into its system and made the system malfunction. Fullness signals no longer match up to the nutrients your body actually receives. Fat storage signals are confused. The relationship between what you eat and how much is available for use by your body is distorted. What does your body do? Your body is designed for survival; it responds by trying to get you to eat more. Your body's motto is, "When in doubt about how much I'm going to get to keep, try to get as much in here as possible!"

As long as you purge, you will have difficulty with cravings and hunger. Your biology is not going to help you learn to prefer moderate fullness when you don't let it keep whatever food you eat. Also, recent research suggests that repeated vomiting may result in delayed gastric emptying. This means that when you eat, your stomach does not act as quickly to pass the food on to your small intestines. This is a problem because you do not start to feel the effects of food (the feeling that your hunger is being satisfied) until nutrients begin to be absorbed—which occurs primarily in the small intestine. When this process slows down, your signals to stop eating are distorted. You find it very hard to get satisfied. It seems like it takes a lot of food to feel full. While feeling unsatisfied may also reflect psychological issues such as feeling deprived in other areas of your life, it may reflect the fact that your body knows it doesn't get to keep all of what you eat, so your biological signals for satiation are malfunctioning. In the long run, purging turns on you, making it harder for you to achieve either your weight goal or your other life goals.

The Bad News

The bad news is that scientists have not found any legitimate shortcuts to weight loss. You have to do it the hard way by moderating intake (or, of course, increasing activity). AAT offers you a way to moderate intake that feels pretty natural and doesn't feel too depriving. However, AAT needs your help in order for normal eating to change your preference for fullness. You must withdraw the permission you have given yourself to compensate for overeating. You must learn to sit with the feeling of overfullness so your body can learn that this is not what it wants. All types of purging strategies undermine the effectiveness of AAT by disrupting your internal signals. Purging makes it more difficult for you to identify internal signals like hunger and fullness, which can be your best allies in learning to limit your intake in an effective yet healthy manner.

It is all right to exercise, because exercise (within limits) is healthy and is not a shortcut for weight loss. It is, in fact, another hard way to get or stay slim. However, even with exercise you need to be careful about your mind-set. Exercise done within a compensatory mind-set is just like purging; it lets you believe you can get away with overeating. If you exercise in order to compensate for a specific episode, you are undermining your motivation to learn to stop at moderate fullness, just as if you had purged. The only difference is that exercise does not disrupt your biological system the same way purging does.

The Good News

I understand that it is very scary to consider giving up purging. While you might not like how purging feels or its effects on your health, you probably believe that purging is the only reason you have been able to lose weight or the only reason you are able to prevent weight gain. The good news is that you are almost certainly wrong. Even if purging was the way you initially lost weight, it is probably not the reason you are maintaining your current weight. Your body has most likely adapted to your strategies (your body has become more efficient). Your metabolism will normalize once you eat more normally, so you will probably not gain weight if you stop compensating. Treatment studies support the conclusion that few women gain weight when they stop purging.

If you are willing to stop trying to lose weight, AAT offers you a more effective way to prevent weight gain. Thus, I am not asking you to give up purging without providing you the skills you need to prevent weight gain. I encourage you to stop purging immediately, as soon as you start your appetite awareness training. If you are able to give it up cold turkey, you will benefit more quickly from AAT. However, most women I treat cut down more gradually, because that feels safer. As you learn the AAT skills to stop binges and overeating, you need to practice the skills described in this chapter to also resist urges to compensate. The two processes support each other. As your overeating decreases, you will have less motivation to purge, and as you resist purging, you will have more motivation to stop at moderate fullness.

RESISTING THE URGE TO COMPENSATE

The strategies you are going to use to resist the urge to compensate are similar to the strategies to resist urges to binge (described in chapter 6). The first step is awareness. Acknowledge that you have the urge to compensate. Remind yourself that an urge is just a feeling and you have a choice about how you want to respond to that feeling. It is possible to have an urge and not act on it. Remind yourself that you do this all the time. If you acted on every urge you experience, you would have worse problems than eating too much.

It is not helpful to pretend you don't have an urge when you do. You are just tricking yourself, and you may end up impulsively acting on the urge before you have time to make a plan. Some people notice the urge to compensate developing while they are still eating. If you do, take action immediately to get away from any further opportunity to eat. When you have the idea of purging in the back of your mind, it is much harder to resist eating more. You think, "It doesn't really matter if I eat more, because I'm going to purge anyway." This kind of thinking (what the heck) is really unhelpful. Even if you are going to purge, it is better for you to have kept the amount you eat small. This is because you are trying to become aware of your moderate fullness signal. Every single time you get stuffed, you are teaching your body to require large amounts of food to feel satisfied. This is the opposite of your goal. You want to learn to feel satisfied at moderate fullness. If eating triggers a weak urge to compensate and you are debating whether or not to purge, you will certainly feel even more like purging if you eat more. To get out of this trap, you have to resist two urges at once. Resist the urge to give in to the what the heck response and eat more (binge), and also resist the urge to compensate (no matter what you have eaten).

After you ensure that food is no longer available, your next goal is to ride out the urge to compensate. Distraction is the most helpful strategy, because in this situation you do not want to focus on how uncomfortable your stomach feels. Make yourself a list of distraction strategies ahead of time. Put the list on an index card and carry it with you. This may sound ridiculous, but many people find it very helpful. In the moment, when the urge is strong, you may be so anxious that your mind goes blank. Put yourself into a situation where it would be difficult to purge. If at all possible, go where there are other people. Other people provide distraction and make reduce the opportunities to purge.

Remember, urges follow a predictable path. Urges increase, plateau, and diminish like a wave. If you can just ride it out, the urge will subside. Sometimes, an urge will subside and return again (and again), but each time it crests and flattens out. This is the only time that I do not encourage you to focus on your uncomfortable stomach sensations. Doing so will make your urge to compensate stronger. Women who binge but who do not have permission to compensate benefit from focusing on the aversive sensations in their overfull stomach. For them, paying attention increases their motivation to stop at moderate fullness in the future. However, when you have permission to purge, it is more important to resist the urge to compensate in the moment than it is to pay attention to your stomach sensations.

MONITORING URGES AND RESISTED URGES

When you finish reading this chapter, go back to chapter 4 and start following the basic AAT program. You might prefer to wait until after you stop having binges to work on purging, but continuing to purge will make it much harder for you to stop bingeing. You will be more successful more quickly if you agree to work on stopping binges and purges at the same time.

Follow the general instructions given in chapters 4 to 7 on how to complete the monitoring forms. The form provided in this appendix adds two elements that address purging and more deliberate restriction. You need to be very aware when you deliberately refuse to eat even though you are hungry.

Try to resist the urge to purge. Remind yourself that compensating does not undo all the damage of binge eating. In fact, compensating makes you more likely to binge next time, because you still have permission to purge. When you have overeaten (or binged), the best thing you can do for yourself is to refuse to compensate. Sure, you will retain a few extra calories, but you will be reducing the permission you give yourself to binge, so you will be taking in far fewer calories in the long run. This trade-off is worthwhile. You will be more successful in attaining your real objective (minimizing calorie intake) when you refuse to compensate. Compensating is a short-term strategy that backfires!

Always mark the times you notice an urge to purge, even if you are able to refrain from purging. Over time, you will see that your urges become less and less frequent. At some point, you will find that you no longer even consider purging as an option. You know it isn't doing anything for you and that purging isn't necessary to maintain your weight. Once you have made a commitment not to purge, the thought will pop into your mind less frequently. When you have withdrawn permission to purge, you know that the hardest part of your recovery is over.

Most women are able to stop purging before they are able to completely eliminate binges. Stopping binges takes a little more time because binges are often triggered by emotional eating. It is hard for you to refrain from bingeing once you think you've eaten even a little too much or have eaten forbidden foods.

Once you rarely have urges to purge, you no longer need to use the forms in this chapter. You can continue the program and use the other forms that are presented throughout the book. Let's look at an example of the way AAT works for bulimia.

Susie's Story
(as told by her therapist, Dr. Shanks, Psy.D.)

Susie was a twenty-year-old junior when she came to the student health service for treatment for bulimia. She had come in with her roommate the year before for one session, but she did not make a second appointment. When she came in this time, she said she had realized she couldn't stop purging on her own and needed help. She was very motivated to change. She was sick of hiding her problem and felt that it had taken over her life. She had been purging (by vomiting) for two years at least every other day and sometimes daily. Her weight was in the middle of the normal range. Since she had decided to get help, she had already been able to reduce purging to every other day, but she felt stuck at that point.

At her first session, her therapist introduced the AAT model and showed her how to complete the monitoring forms. During the next week, she reported five binges and five additional times she had an urge to binge but was able to stop before getting stuffed. After four of the binges she purged, but she was able to resist the urge one time. By the second week she realized most of her binges were triggered by restricting (getting too hungry) and skipping meals (ignoring hunger). She only binged twice, but had urges to binge three more times. However, she purged after both binges. The third week she had the urge to binge four times but was often able to make conscious decisions to eat instead (anti-deprivation eating or effective emotional eating). She binged only once. She had the urge to purge three times and was able to refrain one time. The next week was finals, so it was not too surprising that she had a little more difficulty. She had four planned binges and two unplanned binges but reported an additional twelve times she felt the urge to binge and refrained. She purged after three of the planned binges.

At this point, Susie was going to be home for five weeks over semester break. During those five weeks, she kept monitoring on her forms. She had many urges to binge (thirty-two) but only binged ten times, and eight of these episodes occurred during a difficult visit at her father's house when she felt overwhelmed and not very supported. Still, she only purged after five of the binges. She wanted to purge six additional times but resisted. She was getting much better at using distraction or just sitting with the aversive fullness sensations.

Once she was back at school, she had a great week—one binge-purge episode and no additional urges to binge or purge. She reported that using the forms had been very helpful to her. She realized that she did eat moderately (in the gray) most of the time and that she did not "blow up", i.e. gain weight, as she had feared would happen if she stopped purging. Now she was convinced the purging wasn't making much of a difference in her weight and she noticed how much less she wanted to binge when she knew she was going to keep the food down. She also noticed how much better she felt in general and how much more energy she had. In particular, she was shocked to find out how much more time she had to do other things. Several of her friends commented on how much happier she seemed and how much more fun she was to be with.

At this point, Susie reduced her sessions to every other week. She was doing well, but wanted to make sure to keep on track. She was encouraged to join a support group at the center so she would have a safe place to work on developing a more positive body image as well as developing more self-respect and self-efficacy about taking charge of her life. A year later, Susie remains purge-free. She taught her best friend the principles of AAT and they support each other in maintaining normal eating.

INSTRUCTIONS FOR MONITORING COMPENSATORY ACTIONS

1. For the first two weeks, use the monitoring forms in chapters 4 and 5 to increase your awareness of internal appetite and external environmental cues. Then, start the monitoring as described in chapter 6 but use the form below instead (since you need to monitor purging as well as bingeing). Make copies and use this form until you have essentially eliminated binges due to what the heck. Then go to chapter 7. At that point start circling EmEat when you identify emotional eating. Continue to use this form until you have essentially eliminated purging. Then go on to chapter 8 and start using those forms as you increase your comfort with eating a wider range of types of food.

2. When you knew that you were going to binge and purge before you started eating, circle the "PL-B/P" (Planned Binge/Purge). All planned episodes are also EmEat, so circle that and describe the emotions. When you don't plan to binge but do what the heck, circle Heck and B (Binge). When you don't plan to purge but feel bad about what you ate and purge, circle Heck and P (Purge).

3. Each time you are successful in resisting an urge to binge, star U-NB (Urge- NoBinge). Each time you are successful in resisting an urge to purge, star U-NP (Urge-NoPurge).

4. Write down how many meals and snacks you plan to eat. Whenever you skip a planned episode or when you know you are hungry but you refuse to eat, circle IgnoredHunger. This indicates deliberate restriction (when you should have eaten). You can only rate hunger and fullness when you actually choose to start eating.

5. Complete the daily summary to remind you of the priority of your goals. Check NoP if no purges. Check NoB if no binges. Check all Normal Eating if you are able to stay in the gray all day. Try to keep your deprivation rating from getting high by choosing anti-deprivation eating as needed. Note ADE and EEE in your Notes to Self when you use these strategies. Note unhelpful thoughts/ excuses that encourage you to purge and use your wise mind to challenge those.

PURGING AFTER SMALL AMOUNTS OF FOOD

Some women continue to have urges to purge after eating even small amounts of forbidden foods. I call these *residual purges*. If you continue to purge when you are no longer bingeing, then you are using purges for a different reason. Recently, some researchers have labeled this problem "purging disorder" because this kind of purging is not compensation for excessive eating. It is a deliberate strategy to maintain a low weight. If you have come to this point, you are probably caught in the fear of weight gain trap. You are just not willing to take the risk to see that you can maintain your weight simply by eating normally. Try reading appendix B to see if you can convince yourself to take this scary leap of faith.

To help you overcome your fear of weight gain, commit to not purging for four weeks without allowing yourself to weigh. Give your body a chance to show you that purging is doing nothing for you. You need to allow your body this much time so your weight can restabilize. You may initially get some water retention if your system has been disrupted by your methods of purging. Water retention will disappear unless you panic and go back to purging. My experience with many young women has shown me that those in the normal weight range rarely gain weight when they stop purging.

If you are not willing to accept weight maintenance as your goal, you may need professional help. You need to reevaluate your weight goal in light of the health risks you are taking by continuing to purge. Once you stop purging and learn how to eat normally, you will be able to maintain a stable weight. At that point, you are in a better position to reevaluate your weight-loss goal. If you are over normal weight, appendix C shows you how to use AAT guide-lines to lose weight in a safe, moderate way that will not retrigger binges (and thus urges to purge).

Monitoring Compensation

Notes to Self:
Write down unhelpful thoughts or excuses. Use your wise mind to challenge them. When you mark EmEat, describe your emotions or the food you wanted to eat.

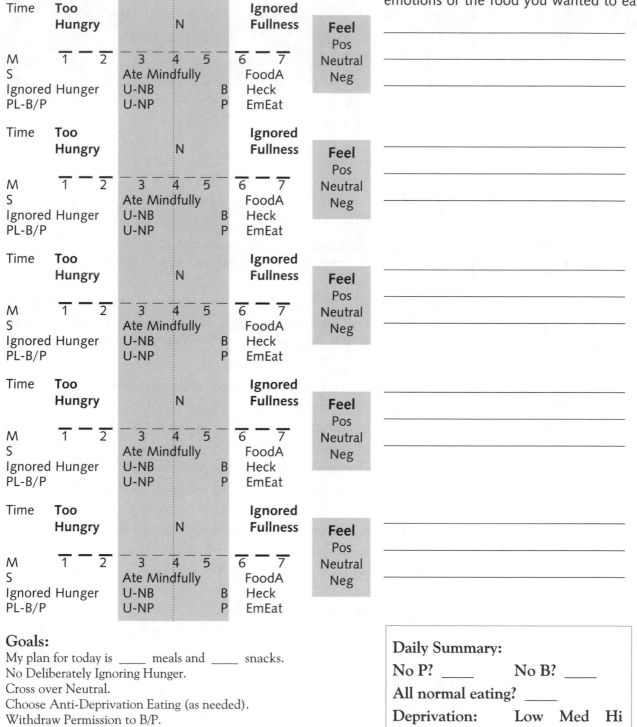

Day: M T W Th F S Sun

Time	**Too Hungry**	N	**Ignored Fullness**	**Feel** Pos Neutral Neg
M S	1 2	3 4 5	6 7	
S		Ate Mindfully	FoodA	
Ignored Hunger		U-NB	B Heck	
PL-B/P		U-NP	P EmEat	

Time	**Too Hungry**	N	**Ignored Fullness**	**Feel** Pos Neutral Neg
M	1 2	3 4 5	6 7	
S		Ate Mindfully	FoodA	
Ignored Hunger		U-NB	B Heck	
PL-B/P		U-NP	P EmEat	

Time	**Too Hungry**	N	**Ignored Fullness**	**Feel** Pos Neutral Neg
M	1 2	3 4 5	6 7	
S		Ate Mindfully	FoodA	
Ignored Hunger		U-NB	B Heck	
PL-B/P		U-NP	P EmEat	

Time	**Too Hungry**	N	**Ignored Fullness**	**Feel** Pos Neutral Neg
M	1 2	3 4 5	6 7	
S		Ate Mindfully	FoodA	
Ignored Hunger		U-NB	B Heck	
PL-B/P		U-NP	P EmEat	

Time	**Too Hungry**	N	**Ignored Fullness**	**Feel** Pos Neutral Neg
M	1 2	3 4 5	6 7	
S		Ate Mindfully	FoodA	
Ignored Hunger		U-NB	B Heck	
PL-B/P		U-NP	P EmEat	

Goals:
My plan for today is _____ meals and _____ snacks.
No Deliberately Ignoring Hunger.
Cross over Neutral.
Choose Anti-Deprivation Eating (as needed).
Withdraw Permission to B/P.
Note Urges to Overexercise.

Daily Summary:
No P? _____   No B? _____
All normal eating? _____
Deprivation: Low   Med   Hi

WITHDRAWING PERMISSION TO PURGE

You will be less prone to relapse if you can get to a point where you completely withdraw permission to purge. At this point, you say to yourself, "Purging is simply no longer an option. No matter what, I will just sit with my uncomfortable feelings. Even though I feel like purging, I know intellectually that no single episode of eating has that much effect on my weight. I can't use weight as an excuse to purge. All I need to do is get back on track the next time I eat. I know that allowing even one episode of purging will put me back in the mind-set that makes me think I can get away with overeating. That mind-set is much more likely to undermine my ability to manage my weight than whatever calories I retain by not purging." Research supports the conclusion that it is important to completely stop purging. In treatment studies, women who stop purging are more likely to remain recovered a year following the end of treatment than women who cut back but still occasionally purge.

PLANNED BINGE-PURGE EPISODES

When you first started binge eating, you most likely did not intend to purge. You just got so upset when you ate too much that you had to do something to feel less anxious. However, once you started purging, you got hooked. You started planning to purge whenever you binged. You tried hard not to binge, but you knew if you did end up bingeing, you were going to purge. Once this pattern gets established, people usually binge more often. They may not plan to binge, but since they have an out, they've lost the natural incentive to limit what they eat. Some women find it much easier to purge after eating large amounts, so once they decide they are going to purge, they eat more on purpose. Their binges become larger and larger. Some women also experience a what the heck response after purging. They feel that they have already purged, so they may as well binge and purge some more. In this way, a pattern develops in which some women binge until they can't eat more, purge, then binge and purge, often several times in sequence. Once a pattern such as that gets established, you may have to plan the whole episode, because it may take several hours. In this type of episode, you have planned both the binge and the purging ahead of time.

A planned binge-purge episode feels quite different from an unplanned episode and requires some different strategies to counteract it. There are two types of planned binge-purge episodes. In one case, you are trying very hard not to binge. You have strong urges to binge but you keep putting them off. However, you are preoccupied with thoughts about eating and you get very frustrated trying to get these thoughts out of your mind. Since you have permission to purge, it starts to seem sort of reasonable to just get it over with. You plan a binge-purge episode in the hope that you will get some relief. You usually do get relief for a period of time before the urge to binge returns. You may establish a regular pattern of planned binge-purge episodes that works pretty well for you. For example, you might restrict very well all week, knowing that on Saturday night you will eat (or drink) whatever you want and purge. Planning this release actually helps you restrict prior to that time. The way to reduce these planned episodes is to practice more regular anti-deprivation eating (described in chapter 5). You must honor strong cravings to eat certain foods so your urge to binge does not build up to the point that you feel such intense pressure to give in.

The other type of planned binge is a learned coping strategy. If you have learned to use bingeing as a way to numb or change negative feelings and you also have permission to purge, you may plan a binge-purge episode when you feel very stressed or upset. You know a binge-purge episode will change your emotional state. This type of episode is a form of emotional eating. Whereas some women just plan to binge when they feel upset, you plan to binge plus purge. If this strategy works for you, you start to rely on this strategy and plan binge-purge episodes more often.

You will have to find alternative ways to manage your negative emotions before you will be able to give up this type of planned binge-purge episode. Planned episodes will be the most difficult to eliminate. Don't even try to stop them first. Start with the unplanned episodes that are triggered by excessive restriction or ignoring fullness. Once you have eliminated most of those episodes, you will be able to see more clearly when bingeing and purging is triggered by negative emotions. As discussed in chapter 7, if you have trouble figuring out what your emotions are or have difficulty developing more effective alternatives to regulate the intensity of your emotions, you should seek professional help. Self-help is generally not sufficient to address this level of problem eating.

If you find that you need additional help to stop bingeing and purging, I recommend that you look for a therapist who uses cognitive behavioral therapy (CBT). You may also benefit from reading self-help material by Fairburn (1995) and by McCabe, McFarlane and Olmstead (2003). This kind of therapy has been studied the most extensively for bulimia and has been shown to be highly effective. However, at the present time most cognitive behavioral therapists have been trained to use food monitoring as the basis for treatment. If you prefer to use the AAT appetite monitoring forms, just take this book to your therapist. Any cognitive behavioral therapist will be able to adapt their approach to use this appetite monitoring system instead of food monitoring. One specific CBT approach that is particularly compatible with AAT is dialectical behavior therapy (DBT). DBT is based on self-monitoring your emotions and developing skills to regulate those emotions. It does not require food monitoring (Safer, Telch, and Agras 2001). I have found the skills training from DBT and appetite monitoring to be an effective combination that clients find highly acceptable (see description of our intensive outpatient program using AAT at lalunacenter.com).

You can read about DBT skills yourself (Linehan 1993), but you may find you need a therapist to provide the coaching necessary to help you master those skills. Please consider consulting a therapist if you have severe or long-term problems with bulimia or if you have tried AAT in this self-help format and find you need more help. Planned binge-purge episodes and extremely negative body image are the aspects of disordered eating that are the hardest to change on your own. However, many women have recovered fully from eating disorders with adequate professional assistance.

Appendix B

The Fear of Weight Gain Trap

This appendix is devoted to enhancing your sense of control over your eating and your comfort with eating those foods you consider forbidden that are (in reality) perfectly healthy. These are usually high-fat or high-calorie foods. As you know, AAT was originally developed to stop binge eating, but AAT can be used by anyone who wants to feel better about how they eat and enjoy eating a wider range of foods. If you do not binge or purge and rarely overeat, you may worry excessively about possible weight gain. You are probably afraid that if you start eating more high-fat or high-calorie foods you will gain more weight than you are willing to accept. Hence, this appendix will show you how to eat a wider range of foods (including high-fat, high-calorie foods), and how to reduce your preoccupation with food and eating. If you do need to gain some weight in a safe, controlled way, I will give you some additional guidelines to accomplish that objective. If you have been told by a medical professional that your weight is unhealthy but you do not consider it a problem, you will first need to consult a trained professional to help you decide if you are even willing to work toward a healthier weight. You may find *The Anorexia Workbook* (Heffner and Eifert 2004) and *Change Your Mind Change Your Body* (Kearney-Cooke and Isaacs 2004) helpful in evaluating your weight goals. Once you decide to make health your first priority, AAT can help you feel as safe as possible eating a wider range of foods or maintaining your sense of control over the process of weight gain.

PATTERNS OF RESTRICTED EATING

Fear of weight gain can lead to several different patterns of restricted eating. These patterns differ in terms of how low a weight you maintain, your feelings of control, and your feelings of deprivation. You may be distressed about many aspects of your eating or you may only be distressed by the level of preoccupation with food and eating that you experience. If you have not already done the self-assessments in chapter 3, please go back and complete those before proceeding with the work in this appendix. These assessments will help you determine which pattern is closest to your personal experience. After describing these patterns, I will show you how AAT can be adapted to address these common forms of excessive restriction.

Seemingly Successful Restriction

If you are a seemingly successful restrictor, you probably don't think you have a problem with your eating. You may be quite thin, but you are close enough to the normal range that you aren't compromising your health. Other women envy your ability to maintain a thin, minimally healthy weight. However, you may not feel good about the way you eat. You may have a rigid, atypical eating pattern that creates stress in social situations involving eating or upsets your significant others. You have probably learned how to ignore hunger unusually successfully. Or, perhaps you have been smart enough to figure out that getting too hungry doesn't work, so you eat just enough to avoid triggering significant hunger alarms. Unlike less successful restrictors, you respect your biological limits. Nonetheless, you are not able to relax and enjoy what you do eat. You may have to organize your life around controlling your eating, but you may feel like the effort is worth it.

Barely Successful Restriction

If you are a barely successful restrictor, you may be thin but you feel like you are just barely hanging in there. Unlike the seemingly successful restrictor, you often feel on the verge of losing control even though you rarely do so. You have to work so hard to stay in control that you know it isn't normal. You see that other women don't have to work this hard to control their eating. They don't think about food as much as you do, and they don't worry obsessively that they might gain a pound if they have a regular meal or enjoy a treat. You may also exercise a great deal and wonder if it is excessive. You feel okay about your weight, but you resent the effort you have to put in and fear you won't be able to maintain this level of effort. You know there has got to be a better way, but you don't know how to get there. You know you are paying too high a price for maintaining your weight. Significant others may resent that your weight concerns dictate your life and often come before their needs.

You have a lot of rigid food rules, but unlike the seemingly successful restrictor, you don't have a set of rules that work well. Chances are you have not been respecting your biological limits. At a minimum, you have not been respecting your psychological limits. If you were, you wouldn't feel that your control might give way any minute. You may believe that hunger is your worst enemy. Ironically, hunger is not your main problem. Deprivation, not hunger, is your enemy. However, you are probably out of touch with your feelings of deprivation and hunger because you have been trying to ignore both of these feelings in order to restrict successfully.

Too Successful Restriction

If you are clearly below a healthy weight, you have been restricting too successfully. Cognitively, you may already be in recovery, meaning you no longer want to lose more weight. But you still have work to do. You have to retrain your body to accept and process food normally. This will take a while to accomplish. When you try to follow a reasonable food plan, you may get so anxious or upset that you are not always able to eat everything on your plan. If you do manage to eat it, you may feel uncomfortable, perhaps even slightly nauseous. You need help to eat what you must eat to be healthy and learn to enjoy food once again.

You may be recovering from a clear episode of anorexia (in which you may have lost significant weight) or you may have slid below a healthy weight in a less obvious way. The negative effects on health due to low weight can take a long time to become obvious to you (or to others for that matter). The culture's ultrathin ideal means that unhealthy weights are what many women strive to maintain. You may not acknowledge that your weight has dropped too low until you stop having your periods or tests show that you have early signs of bone loss.

THE FEAR OF WEIGHT GAIN TRAP

Regardless of your specific pattern of restriction, you are caught in what I call the "fear of weight gain trap." You are operating based on fear, not facts. You believe your strategies are the only way to keep from gaining more weight than you can accept, but the truth is that this level of restriction may no longer be necessary. The only way to find out if this is true is to confront your fears and check out your beliefs. But you are too afraid to take the chance. If there is a better way, you are not going to find out about it unless you take a little risk.

A very old story illustrates this fear trap. An old woman is doing a strange dance in the street. A young woman comes up and asks, "Why are you dancing in the street?" The old woman replies, "I am keeping away the elephants." The young woman says, "You don't have to do that. There are no elephants around here." In reply, the old woman says, "Of course not. See how well it works?" What kind of dance are you doing because you think it is necessary to maintain an acceptable weight?

AAT offers you an alternative to rigidly controlled restriction. You can replace the cognitive rules you have developed to control your eating with internal appetite signals. Eating from within is easier than using purely cognitive rules about how to eat. In AAT, the eating signals come from within. When you learn to trust your natural signals, you can relax and enjoy eating again. Your body is doing most of the work for you. Of course, you do have to stay mindful of what you are doing. You can't just check out and expect your natural signals to do all the work. But, you don't have to serve as the eating-disorder policewoman, watching every second to make sure you don't break a rule.

UNDERSTANDING THE PROBLEM OF EXCESSIVE RESTRICTION AND UNDERWEIGHT

AAT contends that your psychological self is the only part of you that wants to restrict or to maintain an ultrathin or below-normal weight. Your biological self likes the taste of food and wants to be healthy. It doesn't particularly want to be over a healthy weight, although your biological self doesn't believe that is as terrible as does your psychological self. The problem is that your psychological self can't talk to your physical self and convince it to go along with its plan. Your physical self doesn't listen to words; it only responds to what it experiences. Therefore, you must find a way to work with your physical self and establish a goal that both parts of you find acceptable.

Marsha Linehan (1993 p. 89) uses the analogy of the horse and rider to illustrate the relationship between what she calls the mental self (the rider) and one's emotions (the horse). She points out that your mental self must be somewhat separate from your emotional self in order to achieve some control over emotional experiences, but you must also accept your emotions as part of yourself and not as something outside of you. Linehan says, "to the extent that the rider is 'one' with her horse she can control the horse. If the rider is separate and attempts to impose her will on the horse, the horse will fight back and she will not be able to control it smoothly. On the other hand, if the rider is mindless, so to speak, and has no identity separate from her horse, she can only cling to the horse for dear life and the horse will assume all direction.

I like to extend this analogy to illustrate the relationship between your psychological (mental) self and your biological self (your body). Imagine that your body is your horse. Your psychological self is the rider; it determines the kind of relationship it has with your body. If you understand your body's biological needs (for food) and fears (of starvation) and work with it in a loving and positive way, your body will respond well and will do its best (within your genetic limits) to please you. You won't have to work very hard to maintain reasonable control over your body.

If you don't understand your body and treat it in a harsh and punitive way, your body will fight back. Then you will not have a mutually rewarding relationship. You will have to work hard to maintain your control. Your body may stop losing weight or may develop strong urges to overeat or binge. Right now, your body may be trying to throw you off. It doesn't want to accept your direction. You may wish you had a different horse (i.e., body), but I assure you, your body wishes it had a different rider, a rider who listened to its needs and treated it well. Regardless, you can't swap out the body you came with; you and your body are stuck with each other.

Your psychological self is the only part that has any power to change the current adversarial relationship that has developed into a positive, cooperative one. Your body doesn't have the capacity to initiate this change, but your body will respond to the psychological self if you change your tactics. You must become a "horse whisperer." You must tune into your body, acknowledge the trauma it has been through (in this case, at your own hand), and slowly gain its trust. You can again become one with your body and ride it gracefully through life, or you can continue trying to whip it into shape and have a very rough ride; you may even get thrown off.

How do get your body to accept your direction? You can't use words; it doesn't understand your words. Your body doesn't want to make you unhappy, but its drive to eat is stronger than its allegiance to your psychological self. Your physical self doesn't know about the ultrathin ideal. Your psychological self may choose to stay vigilant and refuse to eat, but its control will always be perilous. Your body doesn't have a strong drive to be overweight, it just wants to not feel hungry or be underweight. Your psychological self must become a humane yet conscientious caretaker. As caretaker, you provide mostly healthy food, allow occasional treats and require adequate (but not excessive) exercise. If you can do this, your body will be quite happy and cooperative.

Since you have been starving your physical self, it is understandable that right now you have significant fears about maintaining control over the process of reintroducing more foods or gaining weight. If you suddenly allow a starving animal free access to food, it is likely to overeat for a while unless it remains too scared that it will be punished for doing so. You probably wouldn't become overweight even if you did that, but if you want to be sure, it makes sense for you to set the pace at which you allow weight gain. Make no mistake, an underweight body always wants food. However, it may need a lot of reassurance that it is now all right for it to eat formerly "forbidden" food. Your goal is to redevelop a peaceful relationship with your body. By listening to its wisdom and respecting its needs, you will find your balance and be able to ride more smoothly through life.

USING APPETITE MONITORING TO REDUCE RESTRICTION

Although appetite monitoring was developed to reduce binge and overeating, it also targets restriction. The goal is to listen to your body so you maintain the smooth ride just mentioned. If your problem is restriction, you need to put your attention more on identifying hunger and your response (or lack thereof) to it. Your daily goals will be different from those identified for people with other problem paths, but the end point is the same. The end point is normal eating, a pattern in which your eating decisions are guided by your awareness of internal appetite signals (hunger and fullness).

Eliminate Hunger Violations

The first step in AAT is always to tune into your natural stomach signals. However, you rarely overeat and don't binge so your first goal is to avoid getting too hungry. It may be difficult for you to recognize moderate hunger since you have been trying to ignore hunger in order to restrict. On the other hand, you may find that you are quite aware of being hungry, but you deliberately ignore that signal (skip a meal or refuse to eat). The appetite monitoring form in this appendix is designed specifically to call more attention to how often you do that. You have two tasks. You need to eat anytime you detect moderate hunger. Anytime you detect moderate hunger but choose not to eat at all, circle Ignored Hunger on your form. Anytime you decide to eat, rate your level of hunger before you start. If it is lower than 2.5 on the scale, circle the words "Too hungry." I call this a "hunger violation" to remind you that excessive restriction is not helpful. Excessive restriction increases food obsessions and makes it harder to maintain control when you eat. You will be able to moderate your intake more effectively when you don't set off hunger alarms.

You are going to use your wise mind to challenge the unhelpful thinking and the excuses you give yourself for not eating when you are hungry. Read chapter 6 to learn about using your wise mind. Practice challenging your thoughts by talking back to that part of you that still wants to restrict. Give that part of you that is still trying to restrict a name. Some people call this part their eating-disorder voice, their inner critic, the negative mind, the gestapo, or the eating-disorder police. Schafer's (2004) account of her recovery from an eating disorder gives very useful examples of how to separate from (and start ignoring) your eating disorder's voice. This is the part of you that is scared of losing control. Talk to this part as you would to a beloved child who is terrified of an imaginary monster in the dark. The monster you are scared of is your appetite. Do not punish this scared part of you. Instead, reassure it that you are going to proceed slowly and carefully. For now, eat whatever type of food you feel comfortable eating, even if it is mostly "diet" food. You will work on expanding your food choices later on. The first step is just to eliminate hunger violations so you will feel more in control as you start eating other foods.

Establish a Regular Schedule and Cross Over Neutral

Set up a regular schedule of at least three meals and two planned snacks. Your goal is to eat normally, which means eating five times a day and crossing over the neutral point (the midpoint on your monitoring scale) each time you eat. If you can't start out with five scheduled times, start with two or three, whatever you can manage, and gradually increase.

Start paying attention to how food feels in your stomach. I encourage you to try getting up to moderate fullness (5.5) each time you eat, but this may be hard so in the beginning just try to cross over neutral as often as you can. Some women who have been severely restricting have so much trouble with the sensation of food in their stomach that they only feel comfortable eating very small amounts. If so, it is okay if you need to eat more than five times a day in order to avoid hunger violations. As you get more comfortable eating slightly larger amounts of food, you will be able to consolidate your eating into five or six episodes a day, which is likely to feel more normal to you.

For you, the most important part of AAT is the reassurance that you are not going to start overeating. Thus, while I encourage you to get as full as feels comfortable, you don't have to try to get stuffed. You may notice that on your monitoring forms, the gray (desirable) area goes up to 6 (comfortably full). This is because you do not have a problem with bingeing or being above normal weight. Thus, anytime you actually do want to get comfortably full, you are encouraged to do so. You do not need to stop at moderate fullness (5.5). Make copies of the monitoring form in this appendix and use it as long as you need to. Once you are eating normally most of the time, you can go to chapter 8, where you will practice getting comfortable eating a wider range of foods.

INSTRUCTIONS FOR MONITORING RESTRICTION

1. Follow the general instructions for appetite monitoring in chapter 4.

2. Establish a daily goal (the number of times you agree to eat). Work up gradually (if necessary) to three meals and at least two snacks. Notice whenever it is time for a scheduled meal (or snack) or when you feel hungry but you have the urge to restrict (not eat). When you are able to challenge your thoughts and feelings, and go ahead and eat, star U-NR (Urge-NoRestrict) and indicate M or S. When you don't allow yourself to eat, circle IgnoredHunger.

3. Rate hunger with an X each time you do start eating. Anytime you are at a 2 or below when you start to eat, circle Too Hungry (indicating a hunger violation).

4. Each time you successfully cross over neutral, circle the N and put a star beside it. You are encouraged to eat up to a 6 (comfortably full), particularly if you are trying to gain weight. If it is helpful to you, mark an X to indicate level of fullness after you finish eating, but if doing so bothers you, the circled N will be adequate to indicate that you triggered some sensation of fullness.

5. Write down the unhelpful thoughts and excuses that encourage you to restrict or to feel badly even though you are eating normally. Use your wise mind to challenge those thoughts.

6. Complete the daily summary as a reminder of your goals. Indicate how many times you circled IgnoredHunger (deliberate restriction) and got Too Hungry (hunger violations). Indicate how many times you crossed over neutral. Indicate how many times you felt positive about an eating episode (circled Pos). If you need to gradually gain weight, indicate how many times you enriched (included a higher density food that you would not typically have eaten). Rate your overall level of preoccupation for the day.

GAINING WEIGHT IN A HEALTHY FASHION

If you agree that you need to gain some weight to be healthy, you can use AAT to figure out how much and what types of foods you need to add in order to gain at a rate that is not too scary for

Monitoring Restriction

Day: M T W Th F S (Sun)

	Too Hungry							Ignored Fullness	**Feel**
Time 10:00	Hungry			N				Fullness	Pos Neutral Neg
M	1	2	3	4	5	6	7		
S			Ate Mindfully						

U-NRes
(Ignored Hunger)

	Too Hungry							Ignored Fullness	**Feel**
Time 1:00	**Hungry**			(N)				Fullness	Pos* Neutral Neg
		X			X				
(M)	1	2	3	4	5	6	7		
S			Ate Mindfully*						

U-NRes
Ignored Hunger

	Too Hungry							Ignored Fullness	**Feel**
Time 5:00	Hungry			N				Fullness	Pos Neutral Neg
M	1	2	3	4	5	6	7		
S			Ate Mindfully						

U-NRes
(Ignored Hunger)

	Too Hungry							Ignored Fullness	**Feel**
Time 6:30	**Hungry**			(N)				Fullness	Pos Neutral (Neg)
		X			X				
(M)	1	2	3	4	5	6	7		
S			Ate Mindfully						

U-NRes*
Ignored Hunger

	Too Hungry							Ignored Fullness	**Feel**
Time 10:30	Hungry			N				Fullness	Pos Neutral Neg
M	1	2	3	4	5	6	7		
S			Ate Mindfully						

U-NRes
(Ignored Hunger)

Write down unhelpful thoughts/excuses that encourage you to restrict. Use your wise mind to challenge those thoughts.

Excuse--had plans to go out to lunch _____

_____

Able to cross over N _____

_____

Excuse--trying to wait for dinner even though hungry _____

Neg tht--you already had lunch today. WM says--staying with meal pattern is only way to stop obsessing

Excuse--my rule is no eating after dinner. Wise mind said--you feel tired and irratble but I ignored it

Goals:

My plan for today is __3__ meals and __0__ snacks.
Resist urges to skip meals or ignore hunger.
Cross over Neutral.
Eat what I want (reduces preoccupation).
Challenge negative feelings/fears.

Daily Summary:
ignored hunger __3__
hunger violations __2__
times you ate __2__
times you crossed over N __2__
times you felt positive __1__
Preoccupation: Low   Med (Hi)

Monitoring Restriction

Day: M   T   W   Th   F   S   Sun

Write down unhelpful thoughts/excuses that encourage you to restrict. Use your wise mind to challenge those thoughts.

_____
_____
_____

Time	**Too Hungry**	N	**Ignored Fullness**	**Feel** Pos Neutral Neg

M — 1 — 2 — 3 — 4 — 5 — 6 — 7
S   Ate Mindfully
U-NRes
Ignored Hunger

_____
_____
_____

Time	**Too Hungry**	N	**Ignored Fullness**	**Feel** Pos Neutral Neg

M — 1 — 2 — 3 — 4 — 5 — 6 — 7
S   Ate Mindfully
U-NRes
Ignored Hunger

_____
_____
_____

Time	**Too Hungry**	N	**Ignored Fullness**	**Feel** Pos Neutral Neg

M — 1 — 2 — 3 — 4 — 5 — 6 — 7
S   Ate Mindfully
U-NRes
Ignored Hunger

_____
_____

Time	**Too Hungry**	N	**Ignored Fullness**	**Feel** Pos Neutral Neg

M — 1 — 2 — 3 — 4 — 5 — 6 — 7
S   Ate Mindfully
U-NRes
Ignored Hunger

_____
_____

Time	**Too Hungry**	N	**Ignored Fullness**	**Feel** Pos Neutral Neg

M — 1 — 2 — 3 — 4 — 5 — 6 — 7
S   Ate Mindfully
U-NRes
Ignored Hunger

Goals:
My plan for today is ____ meals and ____ snacks.
Resist urges to skip meals or ignore hunger.
Cross over Neutral.
Eat what I want (reduces preoccupation).
Challenge negative feelings/fears.

Daily Summary:
ignored hunger ____
hunger violations ____
times you ate ____
times you crossed over N ____
times you felt positive ____
Preoccupation: Low   Med   Hi

you. You don't really know how your body is going to react when you start increasing your intake. Thus, you should take it slowly and gradually increase the foods you are eating until you find your weight gain window, the level of intake at which you gain a moderate amount of weight each week. You don't need to gain weight quickly. In fact, you could create problems trying to do so. If you eat in a very unnatural way to gain weight, you are likely to stop what you are doing once you get to your goal weight and go back to your old way of eating. If you do, you will start losing weight again. That is how you became underweight to begin with. This is a problem for many women after they leave inpatient treatment programs for anorexia. Unless there is an excellent transition program to help them make the transition to a level of normal eating which will maintain a stable weight, they revert back to their old patterns of restriction. They are afraid to keep eating like they did in the hospital, but they haven't learned how to eat normally.

If you need to gain weight, follow the steps above to gradually introduce a normal pattern of eating. Try to eat to the comfortable level of fullness each time you eat, and eat the types of food that feel okay to you. If this is not adequate to achieve your goal weight, go on to the following step (enriching types of food).

Enrich the Types of Food You Eat

Many women find they gain a modest amount of weight when they first start eating normally, but most find their weight gain hits a plateau well before they achieve their goal weight. I do not recommend trying to eat larger amounts than are comfortable. This doesn't feel good and may scare you. Instead, you need to find a comfortable way to increase your calorie intake. Enrich your menus with different types of food.

Start by making a list of high-calorie-density foods that you would be willing to eat. Rank these foods in terms of how distressing they are and set goals to gradually incorporate the least distressing ones into your meals and snacks. Each week add several of these foods to your menus. You will be monitoring your progress in gaining weight, so continue to enrich until you find that you can maintain a slow but steady weight gain. Each time you are able to enrich what you choose to eat, write an "E" (for enrichment) on your form. Many women start by stepping up to low-fat or regular foods from the nonfat foods they have been eating (you might try this method with foods like milk, cheese, cottage cheese, salad dressings, or ice cream). These are the least painful ways to increase calories. You don't feel like you are eating that much more. In fact, you aren't eating larger amounts; you are just eating the normal versions of foods that are already on your menus. Other alternatives are to add good fats, like olive oil, to your cooking preparations and to add condiments such as olives and nuts to various dishes. You can also make healthy additions to your salads. Foods such as hard-boiled eggs, garbanzo (or any other) beans, chicken, salmon, hamburger, or avocado can be tasty and enriching additions to salads.

The idea is to increase caloric intake while avoiding uncomfortable fullness sensations that may make it harder for you to eat your meal. If you need more suggestions for healthy, high-calorie-density foods, consult a nutritionist. You may also find it helpful to watch how a friend whom you consider healthy eats. The goal is to find the amounts and types of foods that feel pretty normal, yet allow you to slowly gain the weight you need.

List the high-calorie-density foods that you are willing to start using to enrich your intake. Start with the least difficult ones.

_____

_____

_____

_____

Monitor Your Weight

Monitoring your weight is a very challenging aspect of weight gain. On the one hand, you need to monitor your progress so that you know if you need to enrich more to gain weight. It is also useful in order to reassure yourself that your weight gain is in fact gradual and under your control (half a pound to a pound a week is the recommended rate). When you feel ambivalent about gaining weight, it is easy to fool yourself. You often think you are gaining when you are not. You may even think you are gaining when you are still losing weight. It is difficult to monitor small but meaningful increases in weight without a scale. On the other hand, seeing the numbers on a scale increase is terrifying for many women. The numbers have all sorts of negative associations, and certain numbers may be very upsetting.

If you are sensitive to numbers, the best option is to have someone else look at the scale for you and just give you directional feedback (for example, "You are going in the right direction, just keep it up" or "You still need to enrich your intake a little more this week"). If you don't have someone to help you with this, you may find it helpful to pick a pair of jeans that represents your goal weight and use them to determine whether or not you're moving toward your goal weight. However, clothes do not readily detect if you lose a little weight, so this method is not as good at alerting you when you are not eating enough. Nonetheless, they will remind you that you are not yet at your goal and thus need to enrich a bit more.

Regardless of how you track weight changes, make sure that you wear slightly loose clothing all of the time. While tight clothes would let you know if you are successfully gaining weight, you are likely to have trouble interpreting tight clothes as a sign of progress. It is more likely to upset you. Instead, eliminate any clothing that becomes even slightly tight as you start to gain the weight you need to become healthy. Throw it out or give it away. Do not keep anything in the back of your closet that will remind you of your unhealthy thin weight. It's too seductive! You will be tempted to go back to it. Wear clothing that is loose enough to remind you that you need to gain weight, but not so loose that you can fool yourself into thinking you're gaining weight when you're not.

Coach Your Loved Ones

Your loved ones are likely to be so thrilled that you are gaining weight that they may inadvertently say the worst possible things at the worst possible times—comments that will just fuel your fears about weight gain. Thus, you need to prepare them by assertively letting them know that no comments about your weight are helpful. Most women trying to gain weight do not want any comments about their appearance. Even a comment like, "You are looking so good" or "You look so healthy," may not be helpful. Let your significant others know if there are some encouraging statements that you like, but coach them when they make comments that are not helpful. It is hard enough for you to accept the need for weight gain without other people rubbing your nose in it.

What to Do When You Reach Your Weight Goal

You are probably worried that you will gain too much and go past your goal weight. You may fear that you will want to eat too much once you get to your goal. Interestingly, very few women who have been too thin have that problem as long as they have regained their weight in a gradual way. For reasons that are not totally clear to anyone, deliberate weight gain seems to plateau just as does deliberate weight loss. Part of the answer may be that as your body comes out of starvation mode and starts to process food more normally, it is no longer hoarding nutrients. Most women are shocked to realize that they are eating substantially more calories a day than they had previously, yet they can maintain a stable weight.

Appetite monitoring encourages you to reach your goal weight gradually without encouraging overeating that triggers excessive fears that you may lose control of the process. Once you reach your goal and feel comfortable maintaining your weight, you can phase out the written monitoring process. Chapter 9 shows you how to do this. You will need to continue to coach yourself to keep eating normal foods and getting comfortably full. You will also need a relapse plan. In your case, that means a plan for detecting small weight losses and preventing them from spiraling into a major weight loss.

Restriction is something you had been doing for a long time, so you are likely to start restricting without even realizing it if you get stressed-out about other things in your life. It's a good idea to establish some way to regularly monitor your weight. The best option is to make yourself stay accountable to a physician or nutritionist who is willing to monitor your weight at least once a month and keep you informed if you start to slip. In addition, it is helpful to designate a certain piece of clothing as a marker. If the designated skirt gets too loose in the waistband, you need to take action. What has changed? Are you skipping meals, cutting out snacks, or going back to nonfat foods? Give yourself two weeks to get back into your goal weight range. If you are not back in the range by then, implement your relapse plan. Your plan may involve telling a trusted friend, consulting your nutritionist or counselor, or joining a recovery support group.

Appendix C

The Weight Loss Window

In the world of AAT, a deliberate weight-loss program is the last resort. You are encouraged to see if you can trigger gradual weight loss first by eating normally and second by paying attention to how food feels in your stomach. However, if you already are using both those strategies and you have still not been able to create an adequate calorie deficit to lose weight, you may choose to experiment with a specific weight-loss diet or food plan that appeals to you. Just be sure to adapt the plan so it respects the most basic AAT principle: You must not get too hungry or feel highly deprived no matter what specific food plan you are using.

I am cautious about deliberate efforts to reduce calories for several reasons. When your primary goal is to reduce calories, it is very tempting to ignore your biological limits. People are able tolerate more than moderate hunger, but when you try to do that you are quite hungry when you do allow yourself to eat. When you are that hungry, it is harder to stop at moderate fullness, so you don't save as many calories as you would think. You are also more vulnerable to the what the heck response, which is likely to undermine your calorie savings even further. If you don't lose weight quickly, you get angry and upset because you are trying very hard and getting little payoff. Then you become even more vulnerable to emotional eating.

However, I acknowledge that for many people eating normally is not quite enough of a reduction from their typical caloric intake to produce a satisfactory rate of weight loss. If you want to take the next step toward weight loss, AAT suggests you stop just slightly earlier than moderate fullness, a level I call *low-normal eating*. This is the lowest amount you can eat on a regular basis without feeling hungry or deprived. Anytime you eat at below-normal levels, you are at risk of retriggering eating problems. If you have ever had a problem with binge eating, you must approach deliberate calorie reduction even more cautiously than a person who has no history of failed dieting or disordered eating.

NORMAL AND LOW-NORMAL EATING PATTERNS

What is the difference between normal and low-normal eating? Normal eating (as defined in AAT) means eating regularly scheduled meals/snacks and eating what you want as long as you stop at moderate fullness. You can also eat at other times as needed to prevent getting too hungry or feeling deprived. Your goal is to maximize the pleasure you get from food and minimize feelings of deprivation while respecting your moderate fullness boundary. You may or may not lose weight while eating normally, but I have not seen anyone gain weight who was honestly following these guidelines.

Low-normal eating means that you deliberately work to reduce your total daily caloric intake in order to trigger weight loss. However, you do not ignore all the things you have learned about how your body and your feelings work. When people diet, they often try to eat as few calories as possible in order to lose weight as fast as possible. They try to ignore hunger and feelings of deprivation and "just do it." Most people can't do it, at least not for very long. However, even if you can "just do it," severe restriction is not a smart strategy. Your body starts to fight back as soon as its famine alarm gets triggered. Severe restriction becomes less and less effective the longer you do it. Low-normal eating is a better goal. It is both less effortful and a more efficient way to lose weight than severe restriction.

AAT recommends two strategies to achieve low-normal eating. First, lower your fullness boundary slightly. Stop by 5 (just full) instead of going to 5.5 (moderately full) on the monitoring scale you have been using. You must still choose anti-deprivation eating occasionally to avoid feeling highly deprived. Second, learn to make wise (low-calorie-density) food substitutions that balance calories with pleasure. You can create calorie savings, but do so in the least aversive ways possible. I call this "be good to yourself dieting."

THE WEIGHT LOSS WINDOW

How much of a calorie savings do you really need? Enough to trigger weight loss, but not enough to trigger deprivation or your body's famine alarms. Considerable evidence suggests that calorie deficits should be designed to produce no more than a one to one and a half pound loss per week. Each individual seems to have a unique weight loss window. Your window tells you the degree of calorie savings you need to sustain this recommended rate of loss but no more. If you cut back more, your body thinks that a famine has ensued. Your body goes into starvation mode and hoards all possible calories to help you make it through the perceived famine. Unfortunately, it is not possible to talk to your body and explain that you are trying to lose weight on purpose. Your physiological systems simply do not respond to self-instruction. Your only option is to work within the limits of your physiology. Your physiology is designed to help you maintain a stable weight, so you must figure out a way to stay below your body's radar system for detecting famine.

Your radar system has two levels. The first level, the hunger alarm system, is designed to keep you eating on a daily basis. Some people learn to ignore hunger, but it's not a great strategy because you still can't fool the next level. The second level takes slightly longer to kick in. If you eat at significantly below-normal calorie levels for more than a day or two, your famine alarm gets turned on. In an attempt to conserve whatever calories you ingest, your metabolism slows down. When you set off either alarm system, it becomes harder to lose weight. You get diminishing returns for your dieting efforts.

If you are going to diet, at least diet strategically. You will pay a very high price for cutting back any more than absolutely necessary to trigger slow weight loss. You will feel hungry and miserable. After all, you are not built for dieting. When your body is operating in starvation mode, it does not process food normally.

To avoid triggering your famine alarm, reduce your intake only slightly at first. Then make adjustments until you find your weight loss window. It doesn't pay off to restrict any more than that, even if you can tolerate feeling hungry. In addition to the physiological adaptations, excessive restriction creates subtle feelings of deprivation and resentment that sneak up on you, triggering periodic cravings or binges. If you are working way too hard at dieting, you will not be able to sustain that level of effort. Avoid the famine trap!

THE FIVE AAT WEIGHT LOSS GUIDELINES

Hundreds of books have been written by nutritionists, physicians, counselors, and psychologists telling people how to lose weight. I have taken everything I have read and distilled it down to five basic guidelines that are compatible with basic AAT guidelines. I believe these guidelines represent the cumulative wisdom that can be taken from all that is currently known about the most effective ways to lose weight. My personal and clinical experience has taught me that people differ in terms of how much they need to emphasize any particular guideline. Whatever calorie reduction plan you devise must respect not only the basic biological realities of weight loss, but also your own learned preferences for foods and for fullness. These five principles will steer you in the right direction. Using the self-coaching strategy you have already learned, you can experiment with different diets or food plans and revise them until you find one that works for you. Do not rely on anyone else to tell you how your body will react, or to give you a magic plan that will make you lose weight.

Hundreds of popular diets have come and gone over the years. Each year there is a new, trendy diet plan. Usually the same basic ideas cycle back within a few years in a slightly different format. Every single diet has worked for many people, but no specific food plan has worked for everyone who has tried it. The plan that worked for your neighbor, your daughter, or your hairdresser may or may not work for you. However, you can tailor any diet plan to meet your individual needs as long as it does not contradict the basic principles of AAT, which ensure that you respect your body's basic biological functioning.

Portion Control

The most fundamental principle of dieting is simple: Eat less. AAT is designed specifically to help you do this, but not by telling you how much to eat. Diets establish portion control from the outside. They specify serving sizes. You weigh, measure, or count fat grams. AAT establishes portion control from the inside. Your stomach tells you when to stop.

To lose weight, lower your fullness boundary just slightly, going from the moderate fullness level (5.5) to the *just full* level (5). The monitoring form below is marked to encourage you to do that. This area is marked with diagonals to look like a windowpane, which reminds you that stopping before this point helps you get into your weight loss window. You don't have to stop at 5 every single time you eat. But the more often you can, the more calories you save. You may find that stopping at this level is enough to trigger weight loss. If so, you will not even need to try to change the types of foods you eat.

The weight loss window reminds you not to lower your boundary for hunger. Do not even think about reducing your calories by skipping meals or eating so little that you are below a 2.5 before you next eat. Avoid setting off your hunger alarms at all costs when you are trying to lose weight. It is just too easy to overeat when you are quite hungry. You have to expend a lot more effort to stop at the just full level when you start out hungry. All your calorie savings need to come from the upper end, the fullness end of the scale. You have to pay more attention in order to stop at low-normal fullness than you did when you were stopping at moderate fullness. It's not "normal" to stop there. You have to get even better at predicting how you are going to feel twenty to thirty minutes after you stop eating, because you will tend to overshoot the low-normal level and find that you are, in fact, more than just full when you do your post-eating check-in.

Remember the analogy of the nursing baby all the way back in chapter 1. If the baby is interrupted before the just full point, she wants more and will protest. It is difficult to soothe or distract her; she really wants more food. If she is interrupted at the just full point, she would eat more if allowed, but it isn't too difficult to distract her attention to something else. This is the strategy you should use when you are trying to lose weight. Stop as soon as you are just full and distract yourself, or get away from the food so it isn't that effortful to refrain from eating more. You may need to reduce your exposure to food more than you would when you are just eating normally. You will not be able to rely on normal serving sizes. You will mostly be eating less than you have come to expect is a normal serving size.

The key to deliberate weight loss is to change your expectations. You are not eating normally, so you cannot expect to be able to eat as much as others or to eat a normal portion size. However, you are not required to feel hungry and you can still have treat foods when you need them. When you decide to have treats, you may choose to stop at moderately or even definitely full. In those situations you are eating to prevent deprivation, not to save calories, so make sure you eat enough to feel satisfied; just avoid getting stuffed. Create your calorie savings during routine eating when you are not struggling with particularly tempting foods or uncomfortable emotions. Make dieting as easy as possible for yourself.

Substitute Lower-Calorie Foods

The second dieting strategy is to substitute lower-calorie alternatives for foods you would otherwise choose to eat. Kirshenbaum (2006) makes a strong case for adopting a very low-fat diet rather than a low-carb plan; his comprehensive, no-nonsense approach is an excellent guide for those willing to make that commitment. Recent work by Dansinger et al. (2005) supports the widespread clinical wisdom that *adherence* is the key to weight loss success; average weight loss did not differ among the various diet programs they studied. Learned personal food preferences most likely determine how well and how long a given individual will stick to any specific diet plan. You must figure out what you can tolerate, whether it is lowering fat or carbs or just calories in general. However, simple substitutions are often ineffective because they may not feel as satisfying.

As mentioned earlier, satisfaction is primarily psychological. A lower calorie food may work fine to reduce biological hunger but it may not reduce urges to eat that come from psychological hungers. When you really want cheesecake, celery (even with nonfat cream cheese) will not satisfy you. In that situation, you tend to increase the amount you eat trying to get more of a sense of satisfaction. When you eat more, you lose much of the potential calorie savings, plus you still end up feeling you didn't get to eat what you really wanted. When you don't have specific cravings, low-calorie substitutes may work fine.

A more sophisticated substitution strategy is to identify the taste or texture of the food you want and look for a lower-calorie substitution that gives you a similar taste or feel (Shapiro 2001). When you do this, you are less likely to feel unsatisfied. However, you must still be careful not to eat more of the lower-calorie substitution than you would of the food you really wanted. For example, if you want a chocolate shake, choose a fudgesicle. If you feel satisfied with only one, you save considerable calories. If you need to eat two of them to feel satisfied you still save some calories. But if you end up eating the whole box because you aren't satisfied, you don't save very many calories. You certainly don't save enough to justify your feelings of deprivation. However, you may find you can keep deprivation low by having fudgesicles most of the time, and by making a conscious choice to have a small shake occasionally.

Use Volumetrics

The third dieting strategy is similar to substituting lower-calorie foods, but it specifically promotes the use of alternatives that are lower in calories primarily because they are higher in water content. This approach, called "volumetrics," is a specific way to lower calorie density. As mentioned earlier in this book, foods that have fewer calories for a given volume (or weight) are called low-calorie-density foods. Most people know that fudge, cheese, and meat are considered calorie dense. You get a lot of calories in a small amount. You feel more stomach fullness with lower-density foods, like vegetables.

However, many people are not aware of the enormous value of using stews, soups, and casseroles as a strategy to reduce calorie density. Eating these low-calorie-density foods is very compatible with AAT as long as you remember to maintain your fullness boundary. Research reported by Barbara Rolls (2005) clearly demonstrates that people eat less when they eat high-volume foods. This is presumably because you feel full more quickly. When you are committed to AAT and stop at moderate fullness, low-density foods are particularly helpful. When you eat calorie-dense foods, you undermine the effectiveness of AAT. You will not feel as full as quickly and you may consume more calories than you would otherwise.

Use the Glycemic Index

The fourth basic strategy of dieting is to minimize hunger by carefully regulating one's blood sugar level. This strategy is helpful for almost everyone, but it is absolutely essential for people who have more unstable blood sugar levels. The premise is that certain foods, identified as high glycemic index foods, increase blood sugar rapidly, but then allow blood sugar to drop precipitously (Brand-Miller et al. 1999). A rising blood sugar level feels quite good. You have energy and can pay attention. However, rapidly falling levels feel quite bad. You feel tired, shaky, sleepy, and you may find it hard to concentrate. Thus, high glycemic index foods make you feel better more quickly, but the effect doesn't last long. You usually want to eat again fairly soon either because you feel hungry or because you need another energy boost (the so-called carbohydrate craving). Foods identified as low on the glycemic index raise blood sugar more slowly and let it drop more slowly. Low glycemic index foods tend to be high in fiber, which increase the sense of fullness and take longer to digest. People usually describe these foods as "staying with you longer."

Low glycemic index foods are very compatible with AAT. These foods tend to feel good in your stomach; they still feel good thirty minutes after eating. You will likely find that you can eat less and feel more satisfied when you incorporate as many of these foods as possible into your menus. It is particularly important to consider these foods for snacks. Traditional snack foods are designed for quick energy, so they are usually high glycemic index foods, not to mention high in calorie density—the worst possible foods to promote weight loss. A recent study suggests that a low-glycemic index diet may reduce cardiovascular risk indicators even more than a low-fat diet (Ebbeling et al. 2005).

Set Time Limits for Deliberate Dieting

Many weight-loss experts now recommend that you limit any period of deliberate weight loss to not more than four to six months. You may even need to stop a bit earlier if you find that you have hit a plateau and are no longer losing weight. There are two reasons for this recommendation. First, it is easier to commit to a specific period of time of extra effort, knowing that you will not have to keep up quite the same level of effort forever. Second, most people have difficulty losing more than 10 to 15 percent of their body weight at one time.

Scientists do not know exactly why weight-loss plateaus are so common and so difficult to overcome. One hypothesis is that your famine signals may have been turned on by the weight loss even if you have lost the weight slowly and have not restricted your calories excessively. If so, returning to a more normal level of eating for a period of time is the only way to turn off those signals. Once your body has adjusted to your new weight and no longer thinks there is a famine, you may be able to cut back again and lose additional weight before your body again concludes there is a famine. Another hypothesis is that you get tired of maintaining the lower intake and gradually start eating just slightly larger amounts or having a few more treats—not enough to gain weight, but enough to erase the moderate calorie deficit that is needed to sustain gradual weight loss. In other words, you drift back to a level of normal eating without realizing it.

Regardless of the reason, the solution for weight plateaus is the same: You need to deliberately stop dieting and commit to a period of normal eating and maintaining a stable weight. When your intention is to eat normally, you will not feel discouraged when you fail to lose weight. Give your motivation and your physiology time to recover. When you feel confident you can maintain your newly lowered weight, you may again be able to nudge your body into losing a bit more weight.

INSTRUCTIONS FOR MONITORING FOR WEIGHT LOSS

1. Continue to rate your appetite as before. You will be most successful when you reduce mindless eating (not doing much for you) while maximizing the pleasure you get from what you consciously choose to eat (keep deprivation low). Each time you remember to eat mindfully (and enjoy your food), put a star by Ate Mindfully. Each time you eat when not hungry, circle that? Ask yourself, was this ADE or EEE, so it was worth it? Or, was this mindless eating (Food A)? Each time you eat past 5 (just full), explain; was this mindless eating (not aware) or deliberately ignoring fullness cues because of enjoying taste?

2. Before you eat, take a moment to consult your personal food guidelines to decide on food type. Use your wise mind to balance calorie density and your need for pleasure from food. Ask yourself, what will taste good now and still feel good thirty minutes after you finish? After you eat, extend mindfulness of stomach and body sensations twenty to thirty minutes and then rate food type (to see if you predicted accurately how you would feel). Anytime you discover new information about how you respond to a particular food (for example, when you find a low-calorie-density food that you like or notice you feel satisfied with a smaller amount), make a note to add this information to your personal food guidelines. Noting amounts and types of foods that end up feeling good helps you remember to choose those foods more often in the future. Initially, write down each type of food and evaluate it as Worth It or Not Worth It. However, since you may need to use this form for quite a while, at some point you may choose to write down only the foods that didn't end up feeling worth it. That will take less time yet still focus your awareness on eating that isn't doing much for you.

3. Stop eating at the just full point (5.0) as often as you can; this is another way to minimize calories without triggering deprivation. However, monitor your feelings of deprivation. At times, you may need to make a conscious choice to eat a bit more of special treat foods (ADE). In the long run, you will be more effective when you keep deprivation low. Weight loss is a marathon not a sprint.

4. Complete the daily summary to remind yourself that your first priority is to maintain normal eating (don't get too hungry or get stuffed). The second priority is to work on lowering your fullness boundary to just full. Notice that being too hungry when you start makes it too hard to stop at the just full point. The third priority is to reduce eating when not hungry. The fourth priority is to work on altering your preference for lower calorie density foods by trying more of them, but you must be careful as you do this to insure that deprivation remains relatively low. Challenge the unhelpful thoughts that suggest severe dieting is a viable long-term strategy. You are living proof that it isn't. Excessive restriction of type or amount leads to deprivation and preoccupation that sabotage your goals.

BE GOOD TO YOURSELF WHILE DIETING

Deliberate calorie reduction is very effortful. Thus, when you have committed to a period of effortful reduction, it is important that you do everything you can to make it as pleasant as possible. I make the following recommendations to help you stick with your resolve during periods of deliberate weight loss, when you need to devote a lot of effort and attention to reducing your intake.

Pick a Reasonable Time to Start

Try to pick a time when dieting can be a priority, and when you have strong social support. Do not start a diet when you have just had a baby, just started a new job, are moving, and so forth. You can begin AAT (normal eating) anytime. Do not put that off. When you feel comfortable with normal eating, then decide if and when you will commit to weight loss. Remain ready to return to normal eating when you hit a plateau or encounter a high-stress time that is not conducive to weight loss. Many people find it effective to take short time-outs from dieting and set maintenance as their goal during holidays and vacations. However, they do not take time-outs from normal eating and just eat what they want. If you have substantial weight to lose, you are likely to require several periods of weight loss and restabilization at lower weights.

Do One Thing at a Time

Consider your priorities, and start one self-improvement project at a time. Otherwise you will dilute your resources and attention and will be less likely to succeed at any one of them.

Monitoring for Weight Loss

Day: M T (W) Th F S Sun

Balance need for pleasure from food with knowledge of calorie density of options

Worth It	Not Worth It

Time 8:00

Too Hungry				N		Ignored Fullness
		X			X	

(M) — 1 2 3 4 5 6 7
S
Ate Mindfully*
Ate When Not Hungry

pineapple
cottage cheese
toast

Time 11:00

Too Hungry				N		Ignored Fullness
		X		X		

(M) — 1 2 3 4 5 6 7
S
Ate Mindfully
Ate When Not Hungry

turkey
sandwich
orange

chips (mindless/ not that good tasting)

Time 3:00

Too Hungry				N		Ignored Fullness
		X		X		

M — 1 2 3 4 5 6 7
(S)
Ate Mindfully*
Ate When Not Hungry

smoothie

Time 5:00

Too Hungry				N		Ignored Fullness
		X	X			

M — 1 2 3 4 5 6 7
(S)
Ate Mindfully
(Ate When Not Hungry)

cookies (FoodA!)
kids had in car

Time 6:30

Too Hungry				N		Ignored Fullness
		X		X		

(M) — 1 2 3 4 5 6 7
S
Ate Mindfully*
Ate When Not Hungry

BBQ & half bun
salad
vegetables

chips
second helping
of BBQ
(tasting good)

Extra snack at 10 PM -- (Not Hungry)

ice cream
(ADE)

Note effective use of food (ADE & EEE): _ice cream--if I refused to have with husband I would have felt deprived--could have cut out the chips earlier as that wouldn't bother me._
Note new information for personal food guidelines: _one serving at dinner is "just full" --second serving is too much_
Note Exercise: _aerobics class_

Daily Summary:
All normal eating? ✓
 # times just full _3_
 # times ate when not hungry _2_

Deprivation:
(Low) Med Hi

Monitoring for Weight Loss

Balance need for pleasure from food with knowledge of calorie density of options

Day: M T W Th F S Sun

	Worth It	Not Worth It

Time   **Too Hungry**   N   **Ignored Fullness**

M   1   2   3   4   5   6   7
S
Ate Mindfully
Ate When Not Hungry

Time   **Too Hungry**   N   **Ignored Fullness**

M   1   2   3   4   5   6   7
S
Ate Mindfully
Ate When Not Hungry

Time   **Too Hungry**   N   **Ignored Fullness**

M   1   2   3   4   5   6   7
S
Ate Mindfully
Ate When Not Hungry

Time   **Too Hungry**   N   **Ignored Fullness**

M   1   2   3   4   5   6   7
S
Ate Mindfully
Ate When Not Hungry

Time   **Too Hungry**   N   **Ignored Fullness**

M   1   2   3   4   5   6   7
S
Ate Mindfully
Ate When Not Hungry

Note effective use of food (ADE & EEE): _____

_____

Note any new information for personal food guidelines:

_____

Note Exercise: _____

_____

Daily Summary:

All normal eating? ___

times just full ___

times ate when not hungry ___

Deprivation:
Low   Med   Hi

Many people make the mistake of going on an all-out self-improvement program. This approach usually starts off great, but it runs out of steam fast. I encourage you to focus only on your eating while you are deliberately reducing intake. Resist the urge to stop smoking or biting your nails at the same time. Why? Because every effort to modify your behavior takes attention. You only have a limited amount of attention. The further you try to spread your attention, the less any one project gets. Weight loss is effortful; it requires a lot of attention and planning. The only exception to the one-at-a-time principle is exercise. Many people find that starting an exercise program enhances rather than detracts from their motivation to change how they eat.

Make Weight Loss a Priority

Consider your priorities and prepare to devote adequate resources to weight loss. Otherwise, don't bother. You will end up frustrated and angry. Sometimes when people go on diets, they also try to save money. It is similar to the self-improvement idea. If you are going to stop eating junk food, you think you might as well become more frugal as well. Wrong! When you are losing weight, you need to pamper yourself in every other way possible. As I explained earlier, eating at low-normal levels is not awful, but you are clearly cutting out some of the pleasure you have been getting from food. It is imperative that you keep your feelings of deprivation low to avoid triggering a what the heck response. Therefore, look for ways to make up for the loss of pleasure as much as possible. Do not scrimp on the cost of really high-quality foods. Spend more to get good fruits and vegetables. Avoid cheap food. The higher the quality of the food you eat, the less deprived you will feel when you forgo the fried foods, desserts, cream sauces, and large amounts. Choose fresh berries in champagne not frozen berries in cool whip.

When you are eating out, order the type of food you predict will taste and feel best regardless of cost or serving size. Be prepared to give away or throw away the rest if you get served more than you need to reach moderate fullness. Unfortunately, needy people cannot benefit from the food you don't eat, so don't try to justify eating more by refusing to waste food. When you start balking at the cost of eating well, ask yourself this question: "Do I want to go ahead and pay more now to get exactly the food that works for me, or do I want to end up spending at least that much money later to have someone try to help me lose the weight?" Eating well will increase your success at weight loss so it will save you money (if only in medical expenses).

Increase Nonfood Pleasure

Pamper yourself in nonfood ways. It is helpful if you set up small rewards for reasonable changes. It is even better if you can enlist someone else to provide rewards for you. This reduces your tendency to give yourself the reward regardless of what you do. For example, every week that you have five days of low-normal eating, you could get your nails done or get your husband to agree to take the kids for an afternoon. After two weeks, perhaps you get a massage. You can get very creative, especially if you have a cooperative partner. Even if you aren't willing to set up specific rewards for making behavior changes, do not get more strict with yourself or try to save money in other ways while you are deliberately dieting. Deprivation in any area of your life can spill over into the food arena and sabotage your efforts. Be really good to yourself and you will be more successful in losing weight.

HELP OTHERS GIVE YOU SUPPORT

Weight loss is hard for you, but it is probably also hard on your significant others. It is important that you let them know exactly what you are doing, how long you are committed to doing it, and what you do and do not need from them. Go back and reread the section on assertion in chapter 5 so you will be prepared to handle their responses, both positive and negative. Remember, the changes you are making are likely to have some impact on them. Be sure you have talked to them about the changes you plan to make and how these will, or will not, affect them. If you are changing the way you cook or the type of food you have available in the house, let them know and work out compromises they can live with.

Let people know if you want encouragement or if you prefer they not draw any attention to your eating. Let them know how to approach you if they are having a problem with your changes. The point is to acknowledge that your family and friends will have feelings about what you are doing. Don't act like this is none of their business. If you can make them constructive partners in your weight-loss program, you will be more successful and feel better about the changes you need to make. Many women are the primary caregivers in their family. It is hard for them to be "takers." You may feel guilty about making weight loss a priority or having to inconvenience other family members even a little. Many family members are quite willing to be helpful when they feel their own concerns are acknowledged and when they know exactly what you want them to do (or not do).

DON'T PUT YOUR LIFE ON HOLD WHILE DIETING

While it is critical to make weight loss a priority, and even though you need to limit yourself to one self-improvement project at a time, don't put anything else in your life on hold. You may be tempted to wait to start some new activity until you lose twenty pounds or feel better about how you look. Wrong! You can both lose weight and carry on with life. It is important to carry on for many reasons. For one, eating can be a response to boredom or an unfulfilling life. Thus, the more active and full your life, the less of a problem you will have with certain kinds of emotional eating. In addition, many people feel anxious about starting new activities. They use their weight as an excuse to avoid activities that could be really positive. If being overweight allows you to avoid activities that make you anxious, you will have little incentive to lose weight. You know if you lose weight, you may lose your excuse for not doing certain things, as well. So, you have got to face those fears so you no longer have a reason to fail at losing weight.

Accept Your Current Weight, Whatever It Is

The main reason people end up putting off their life until they reach their ideal weight is that they are overly concerned about the way they believe that other people are evaluating their weight. People also have magical beliefs that if they can just reach their goal weight, everything else will fall into place. Then they won't have to work so hard to fix all the other things they don't like about their life. A client once brought me a wonderful cartoon showing a young woman stepping on a scale. It said, "Please, please, please say 110 so I can meet Prince Charming and live happily ever after." Sorry, it's just not that easy.

Accepting your weight is clearly a challenge, especially if you are objectively overweight. However, the paradox is that the more you accept the weight you are, the easier it becomes to change it. When you are extremely distressed about your current weight, you are less successful in changing your weight because emotional eating is a big part of your problem. When you overvalue weight (whether you are normal weight or overweight), you are very vulnerable to the what the heck response anytime you break a rule or overeat.

Many women are afraid to give up their distress about their appearance. They believe this distress is the only reason they don't weigh even more than they already do. They believe that if they accept their weight, they will reduce their motivation to lose weight. This is not accurate because fear-based motivation is notoriously ineffective. Fear is more likely to lead to avoidance than to constructive action. Feeling bad about your weight makes it really aversive for you to take a good look at your eating patterns, yet awareness of yourself is the most effective tool you have. When you tune out, you can't learn how your body works or figure out what to do next time. Accepting your weight (for the time being) allows you to stay tuned in and learn from observing your responses to food. Hutchinson (1999) is a useful resource to encourage body acceptance.

What I really mean by accepting your weight is sticking to the facts. Accepting your weight does not mean you have to be happy with it, just that you recognize what it means and what it does not mean. You don't have to be a Pollyanna, but you must not exaggerate whatever negative effect it has on your life. All your other problems are not due to your weight. Accepting your weight also means that you do not base your own sense of worth primarily on your weight. You consider weight in balance with all the other aspects of your life. You can still affirm that weight is an aspect that you want to change, but don't exaggerate its importance to the point that you are too upset to make changes effectively.

The same principle applies to whether (or not) other people accept your weight. Do not assume everyone else is focused on your weight. Acknowledge that there may be some people with whom your weight is a liability. However, don't exaggerate its importance to other people just because it is so important to you. Don't refuse to recognize when people like you just the way you are. Give people a chance to get to know you. Don't assume they are unwilling to love you as you are. Other people may be pleased if you lose weight, but this is not the most effective reason to lose weight. Accepting your weight means you want to lose weight to please yourself, not to cater to anyone else's needs or prejudices.

Examine Your Values

Filling in a pie chart is a very popular exercise to help you evaluate the importance you are putting on your weight. Just draw a circle and make slices to represent the major areas that make you feel good or bad about yourself as a whole human being at this moment. Be sure to include special attributes, skills, personality traits, and significant life roles. Be sure to make one slice be weight. Write down what percent of your self-worth depends upon how much you weigh. On a second circle, draw the same slices, but size them according to how important you would like each area to be in determining your self-worth. See if you assign more or less importance to weight than you initially did. Ideally, the percentages should be fairly similar. Subtract the percentage of your desired importance from that of its current importance to determine the extent to which you are overly concerned about your weight. Perhaps you have made weight more important than you really want it to be. List the roles and personal traits you want to affirm as being more important than your weight. When you find yourself dwelling on your weight, review this list. You can still value weight, but you can pay more attention to the attributes that you actually value more highly than your weight. Keep your weight concern in its proper place in your hierarchy of values.

Do You Have a Problem with Values or Priorities?

Being overly concerned with weight tells you how important you think weight is, how much you value it. It does not tell you how skillful you are at translating this value into a priority in real life. Herein lies the problem for many people. Many women with disordered eating do have a problem with values. They value weight so highly that they are willing to sacrifice other values (like friendships, intimacy, health, or performance at work or school) in order to achieve (or maintain) a low weight. However, many women who are overweight just have a problem with priorities. They do not overvalue weight. They just want to be a healthy weight. However, they don't have the skills to translate this reasonable value into the appropriate priority in their daily life. When you eat mindlessly, you don't realize that you are making a values choice in that moment. You minimize the significance of the moment, and, all too often, excuse your unhealthy eating choices. You do believe that other things are more important than your weight. On the other hand, when you stop and think about your weight, you feel miserable because you are not doing what you need to do to manage your weight more effectively.

This is a no-win situation. You are miserable about being overweight, yet you are not able to take effective action. Your values and your priorities aren't matching up. Some things should be more important than weight, but you are letting too many things take priority over getting yourself healthy. Accepting your weight and becoming more fit is a much more positive solution than being miserable about it. Once you have learned to use AAT to maintain a stable weight (not keep gaining), you are in a better position to evaluate the degree to which weight loss is truly a priority for you. Some of you will decide to work toward increasing the priority given to dieting efforts. Others will decide to eat normally and accept a weight they can maintain while eating normally.

You have two options if you need to find a better balance between your values and your priorities. You can reexamine your values and decide that you have exaggerated the importance of weight. You may still work on losing weight, but the excessive pressure will be off. You may *prefer* to lose weight but you don't *have* to lose weight to feel okay about yourself. You take the "over" out of your weight concern.

If, on the other hand, you decide that you have not made getting healthy as high a priority as you would like, you can use priority awareness training to bring your attention to the discrepancy between your stated values and your choices in the moment.

To increase your priority awareness, add the following steps as you monitor your appetite. Each time you end up with a fullness rating over 5 (go into the window pane area), write down what took priority over stopping at just full. Sometimes you will need to choose anti-deprivation eating or effective emotional eating. When you eat for those reasons and are able to stop by 5.5, you are still making a wise choice. Write "ADE" (anti-deprivation eating) or "EEE" (effective emotional eating) to indicate if that is why you went past 5 (just full). Those decisions pay off. You end up eating less than you would if you start feeling deprived and trigger a binge. However, when you go past just full for other reasons, write down what you allowed to take priority over making a healthier eating decision.

You might write, "The kids were really hungry, so I had to stop for fast food" or "My husband wanted to take me out, so I went." At the end of the week, sit down with your daily forms and make a list. You will be able to see how many times you put other people's needs first, put work needs first, or whatever. Then evaluate each situation. Sometimes you may agree that your decision was reasonable and it was appropriate to put the other person's needs first. Many times, you can see (in retrospect) that you could have put a higher priority on your health/weight.

For example, if you have to stop at a fast-food place, stop at one you know has a salad you like, and use only half the dressing provided. Or, if you stop for fast food because of the kids, don't try to save money by planning to just eat the kids' leftovers. Buy the salad. If you accept your husband's invitation to go out, request the fish restaurant instead of the Mexican place where it is harder to stop at just full.

Many people, especially women, are able to maintain somewhat lower weights (within the normal range) while they are young and single; they can give their weight a higher priority than most other aspects of their life. However, as other life responsibilities accumulate, this gets harder and harder to do. Use priority awareness to find a weight that honors your stage of life and reflects your true values. AAT (normal eating) allows you to maintain a stable weight while living a rich, full life. Use AAT to lose weight only when you can make it enough of a priority that the effort doesn't reduce the quality of your life. Otherwise, use AAT to eat normally and prevent weight gain. Live a rich, full life free from obsessing about eating and unrealistic weight goals. Take a stand. Refuse to be miserable about a reasonable weight that takes into account your specific characteristics (your age, weight history, genetics, and values).

Challenge your priorities for a few weeks and you will get a good sense of what you need to do. Do you need help making yourself a priority, or do you just need to put more effort into creative solutions to both meet your needs and meet your obligations to others? If you need to lose a substantial amount of weight, you will have to make substantial changes in your lifestyle. You will benefit from monitoring your priorities to make food choices that are truly congruent with your values. And you will need the encouragement and support of those around you. Take the time to explain yourself to your loved ones so they understand why you are changing. Above all, if you decide to diet remember to maintain the basic principles of AAT. You must always come back to normal eating to maintain a stable weight. Otherwise, you will continue to swing between the restriction and the overeating paths, and you will remain stuck in the maze of disordered eating.

References

Allen, H. N., and L. W. Craighead. 1999. Appetite monitoring in the treatment of binge eating disorder. *Behavior Therapy* 30:253-272.

American Psychiatric Association. *Diagnostic and Statistical Manual of Mental Disorders IV.* 1994. Washington, DC: American Psychiatric Association.

Brand-Miller, J., T. Wolever, S. Coagiuri, and K. Foster-Powell. 1999. *The Glucose Revolution: The Authoritative Guide to the Glycemic Index.* New York: Marlowe & Company.

Brownell, K. D., and K. Horgen. 2004. *Food Fight: The Inside Story of the Food Industry, America's Obesity Crisis, and What We Can Do About It.* New York: McGraw-Hill.

Campos, P. 2004. *The Obesity Myth: Why America's Obsession with Weight Is Hazardous to Your Health.* New York: Gotham.

Cash, T. 1997. *The Body Image Workbook.* Oakland, CA: New Harbinger Publications.

Cooper, Z., C. Fairburn, and D. Hawker. 2004. *Cognitive-Behavioral Treatment of Obesity: A Clinician's Guide.* New York: Guilford Press.

Craighead, L. W., and H. N. Allen. 1995. Appetite awareness training: A cognitive behavioral intervention for binge eating. *Cognitive and Behavioral Practice* 2:249-270.

Craighead, L. W., K. A. Elder, H. M. Niemeier, and M. A. Pung. 2002. Food versus appetite monitoring in CBWL for binge eating disorder. Paper presented at the meetings of the Association for Advancement of Behavior Therapy. Reno, NV.

Dansinger, M. L., J. A. Gleason, J. L. Griffith, H. P. Selker, and E. J. Schaefer. 2005. Comparison of the Atkins, Ornish, Weight Watchers, and Zone diets for Weight Loss and Heart Disease Risk Reduction. *Journal of the American Medical Association* 293(1):43-53.

Dicker, S., and L. W. Craighead. 2004. Appetite-focused cognitive behavioral therapy in the treatment of binge eating with purging. *Cognitive and Behavioral Practice* 11(2):213-221.

————. 2003. Appetite monitoring in CBT for bulimia nervosa. Paper presented at the International Conference on Eating Disorders, Academy for Eating Disorders. Denver, CO.

Ebbeling, C. B., M. M. Leidig, K. B. Sinclair, L. G. Seger-Shippee, H. A. Feldman, and D. S. Ludwig. 2005. Effects of an ad linitum low-glycemic load diet on cardiovascular disease risk factors in obese young adults. *American Journal of Clinical Nutrition* 81:976-982.

Elder, K. A., L. W. Craighead, H. N. Niemeier, and P. Pung. 2002. Appetite awareness in the early intervention of binge eating. Paper presented at the International Conference on Eating Disorders, Academy for Eating Disorders. Boston, MA.

Fairburn, C. 1995. *Overcoming Binge Eating.* New York: Guilford Press.

Gaesser, G. 2002. *Big Fat Lies: The Truth About Your Weight and Health.* Carlsbad, CA: Gurze Books.

Heffner, M., and G. H. Eifert. 2004. *The Anorexia Workbook: How to Accept Yourself, Heal Your Suffering, and Reclaim Your Life.* Oakland, CA: New Harbinger Publications.

Hollingsworth, A. B. 2001. *Flatbellies.* Chelsea, MI: Sleeping Bear Press.

Hutchinson, M. 1999. *200 Ways to Love the Body You Have.* Freedom, CA: Crossing Press.

Johnston, A. 1996. *Eating in the Light of the Moon: How Women Can Transform Their Relationships with Food Through Myths, Metaphors, and Storytelling.* Carlsbad, CA: Gurze Books.

Jonas, S., and L. Konner. 1997. *Just the Weight You Are: How to Be fit and healthy whatever your size.* Shelburne, VT: Chapters Publishing, Ltd.

Kearney-Cooke, A., and F. Isaacs. 2004. *Change Your Mind, Change Your Body: Feeling Good About Your Body and Self After 40.* New York: Atria Publications.

Kirschenbaum, D. S. 2006. *The Healthy Obsession Program: Smart Weight Loss Instead of Low Carb Lunacy.* Dallas, TA: Ben Bella Books.

Linehan, M. M. 1993. *Skills Training Manual for Treating Borderline Personality Disorder.* New York: Guilford Press.

McCabe, R., T. McFarlane, and M. Olmstead. 2003. *The Overcoming Bulimia Workbook: Your Comprehensive Step-by-Step Guide to Recovery.* Oakland, CA: New Harbinger Publications.

Niemeier, H. M., L. W. Craighead, M. A. Pung, and K. A. Elder. 2002. Reliability, validity, and sensitivity to change of the preoccupation with eating, weight, and shape scale. Paper presented at the annual meetings of the Association of Behavior Therapy. Reno, NV.

Rolls, B. 2005. *The Volumetrics Eating Plan: Techniques and Recipes for Feeling Full on Fewer Calories.* New York: Harper Collins.

Safer D. L., C. F. Telch, and W. S. Agras. 2001. Dialectical behavior therapy for bulimia nervosa. *American Journal of Psychiatry* 158:632-634.

Schaeffer, J., and T. Rutledge. 2004. *Life Without Ed.* New York: McGraw-Hill.

Shapiro, H. M. 2001. *Dr. Shapiro's Picture Perfect Weight Loss Shopper's Guide.* Emmaus, PA: Rodale.

Wheeler, L. A. 2003. *Ain't Life a Beach?* Island Heritage Publishing: Waipahu, HI.

Winget, L. 2004. *Shut Up, Stop Whining, and Get a Life.* John Wiley & Sons, Inc.: Hoboken, NJ.

Linda W. Craighead, Ph.D., is associate director of research at Raimy Psychological Clinic and professor of psychology at the University of Colorado in Boulder, CO. She received her Ph.D. from Pennsylvania State University in clinical psychology. She has written many articles and presented many papers to other professionals on behavior modification and its applications to conditions such as depression, chronic obesity, and weight management. In recent years she has concentrated on appetite awareness training for people with disordered eating habits who are at risk of developing full-fledged eating disorders.

Some Other
New Harbinger Titles

The Cyclothymia Workbook, Item 383X, $18.95

The Matrix Repatterning Program for Pain Relief, Item 3910, $18.95

Transforming Stress, Item 397X, $10.95

Eating Mindfully, Item 3503, $13.95

Living with RSDS, Item 3554 $16.95

The Ten Hidden Barriers to Weight Loss, Item 3244 $11.95

The Sjogren's Syndrome Survival Guide, Item 3562 $15.95

Stop Feeling Tired, Item 3139 $14.95

Responsible Drinking, Item 2949 $18.95

The Mitral Valve Prolapse/Dysautonomia Survival Guide, Item 3031 $14.95

Stop Worrying Abour Your Health, Item 285X $14.95

The Vulvodynia Survival Guide, Item 2914 $15.95

The Multifidus Back Pain Solution, Item 2787 $12.95

Move Your Body, Tone Your Mood, Item 2752 $17.95

The Chronic Illness Workbook, Item 2647 $16.95

Coping with Crohn's Disease, Item 2655 $15.95

The Woman's Book of Sleep, Item 2493 $14.95

The Trigger Point Therapy Workbook, Item 2507 $19.95

Fibromyalgia and Chronic Myofascial Pain Syndrome, second edition, Item 2388 $19.95

Kill the Craving, Item 237X $18.95

Rosacea, Item 2248 $13.95

Thinking Pregnant, Item 2302 $13.95

Shy Bladder Syndrome, Item 2272 $13.95

Help for Hairpullers, Item 2329 $13.95

Coping with Chronic Fatigue Syndrome, Item 0199 $13.95

The Stop Smoking Workbook, Item 0377 $17.95

Multiple Chemical Sensitivity, Item 173X $16.95

Breaking the Bonds of Irritable Bowel Syndrome, Item 1888 $14.95

Parkinson's Disease and the Art of Moving, Item 1837 $16.95

The Addiction Workbook, Item 0431 $18.95

The Interstitial Cystitis Survival Guide, Item 2108 $15.95

Call **toll free, 1-800-748-6273,** or log on to our online bookstore at **www.newharbinger.com** to order. Have your Visa or Mastercard number ready. Or send a check for the titles you want to New Harbinger Publications, Inc., 5674 Shattuck Ave., Oakland, CA 94609. Include $4.50 for the first book and 75¢ for each additional book, to cover shipping and handling. (California residents please include appropriate sales tax.) Allow two to five weeks for delivery.

Prices subject to change without notice.